PROOF OF AUTHENTICITY
FACTS ABOUT
BLOCKCHAIN

A LOOK INSIDE THE
DECENTRALISED ECONOMY
– IS BLOCKCHAIN
ADVANCING OR AT THE
BRINK OF DESTRUCTION?

FARABI SHAYOR *BSc, MSc, MIScT*

Proof of Authenticity: Facts About Blockchain
Looking Inside the Decentralised Economy - Is Blockchain Advancing or at the Brink of Destruction?

Second Edition

Copyright © 2018-2020, Farabi Shayor, some rights reserved.

Copyright © 2018-2020, research and design by
Research Intelligence Systems Ltd.

Publisher: Indepedently Published
Location: London, United Kingdom

ISBN: 9-7986-4003-6350.

intelxsys.com

This book is licensed under Creative Commons Attribution-NoDerivatives 4.0 International (CC BY-ND 4.0). You are free to share, copy and redistribute the material in any medium or format for any purpose, under the following terms: 1) you must give appropriate credit, provide a link to the license, and indicate if changes were made. You may do so in any reasonable manner, but not in any way that suggests the licensor endorses you or your use; and 2) if you remix, transform, or build upon the material, you may not distribute the modified material.

Limitations of LIABILITY/DISCLAIMER: Startups working in the field disruptive industries take a significant time to be established as their product is mostly untested and unscalable. No warranty can be provided regarding the existence of any company mentioned in this book, as it is highly likely that some of the companies may be dissolved, go into administration or file for bankruptcy between the time the book was written, and it is read. All the examples are based on the field of blockchain observed between February 2016 to December 2018.

THIS BOOK HAS BEEN WRITTEN FOR EDUCATIONAL AND RESEARCH PURPOSES ONLY. HENCE, THE BOOK DOES NOT INCLUDE ANY PAID PRODUCT PLACEMENT. The author of this book has no interest in any commercial gains by promoting any application or platform. Therefore, any contents reused from this book should strictly be used for informational and educational purposes. It should be used as a form of general guidance to understand blockchain and its function. The author also has no intention to endorse any blockchain network, startup or its software.

The author makes no representation with respect to an absolute accuracy of details because most of the information is based on secondary data. The reader should be aware that this product does not intend to provide any form of professional investment advice to the investors, either new or experienced in the world of blockchain or cryptocurrency. The author may decide to change and update information in future editions, based on factors including but not limited to the discovery of further use cases, cryptocurrency financial market dynamics, scalability of blockchain networks and sustainability of the technology.

The Ethereum-based "Smart Contract" system discussed in this book, the underlying protocols and decentralised software platform (the Ethereum blockchain), is still in an early development stage and yet to scale. There is no warranty or assurance that the process for trading or interacting with smart-contracts on blockchain platform will be uninterrupted or error-free, and there is an inherent risk that the software could contain defects, weaknesses, vulnerabilities, viruses or bugs causing complete loss of ETH contributions and/or other cryptocurrencies. Anyone willing to learn about blockchain application development, trading and so on, will therefore, have to understand the risks and implications.

All the brand names, logos and identities are the trademarks or copyright properties of the respective owners. IntelXSys and the author hold the license to use some of the photos used in this publication. Any other images are published with accurate attributions, and republished under the Creative Commons (CC BY) license, which allows copying and redistributing the material in any medium or format, as well as remix, transform, and build upon the material commercially.

Foreword

Distributed technologies work without the necessity of a middleman. Until blockchain technology was invented, users were forced to exchanged value and trade employing a third-party intermediary. What started of as a means to solve the barriers around global transaction of currencies, is now being evolved into a technological paradigm shift that could potentially impact and improve many forms of industries.

A lot of people around the world confuses the market dynamics and conditions of cryptocurrencies with the underlying technology. Every time the market goes bullish, it is branded as a bubble. When it corrects by over 80%, it is branded as a scam. But how many of us looked at the US stock market charts and compared it with performance of the cryptocurrencies? Many of us believe that bitcoin, altcoins and other cryptocurrencies are a form of investment, controlled by the cryptocurrency market, but how many of us realise that it was aimed towards billions of unbanked people around the world?

There are lots of questions around the technology itself. Bitcoin has paved the way for a new technological evolution, but is the technology maturing or is it at the brink of destruction? What are the real-life use cases? How is Ethereum being used to create real life tradable commodities? Are there any successful startups creating disruptive products? What are the governments doing to adopt blockchain technology to facilitate global trade?

The progresses are overshadowed by the unconstructive promotion of the impact of cryptocurrencies. This book is an attempt to look into the world of decentralisation and why they are beneficial for the society. It is divided into different blocks, which focuses on various topics - starting from the explanation of how blockchain technology works, Ethereum as a case study of blockchain technology, a closer look into the tokenised ecosystem, to which companies have already built products that can disrupt our day-to-day lives. As scalability is an important factor for the existence of blockchain, this book sheds light on the current advancement on solving imminent scalability problems and how it could revolutionise the financial and economic sector.

This is not an attempt to explain speculative use cases – it is an attempt to highlight the existing companies that have successfully built a product, the startups working around the world to solve the scalability issues around blockchain technology.

The readers are not required to have any technical knowledge to understand the contents of this book. Although, a very basic understanding about business development and basic economics are appreciated. In order to visibly separate the signal from the noise, this book is a must read for the technology enthusiasts.

Acknowledgement

This book would just not have been possible without the never-ending love from my sisters and their children. I want to state the names of the little ones, Tiana, Dante and the newborn Konen - they left the UK to relocate to New Zealand in 2018. Tiana and Dante grew up right before my eyes; they are very close to my heart, and I miss them every day.

A lot of research-based work has been put into this small book, as most of the information was based on secondary data analysis. Being a technology entrepreneur, honestly, I would say that it was a training on "how to sustain phases of sufferings". I am very grateful to all my coworkers for inspiring me to do this research. A special thanks to Mr Shyeem Rahman, EEE-graduate who assisted me with the citations as well as contributed in a couple of chapters. Also thanks to my team members including Shama for helping me. Furthermore, I am also thankful to my few of my closest friends here in the UK and abroad, including Nazib, who have been extremely supportive throughout my entrepreneurship journey.

I want to acknowledge my parents for supporting me throughout this entire process. My parents have been a source of expert guidance. Lastly, I am grateful to my loving and supportive friends who provided some amazing feedback.

This book is dedicated to the hardworking people in the blockchain industry who are continuously working to make other people's lives better, and to you, reading this, if you stick to the book until the end.

TABLE OF CONTENTS

BLOCK 01	HISTORY OF PEOPLE VS TECHNOLOGY	08
02	THE FAITH WE HAVE IN MONEY	20
03	A DEEP DIVE INTO BLOCKCHAIN	34
04	CRYPTOCURRENCY MECHANICS	58
05	BLOCKCHAIN BEYOND THE SEPCULATION OF CRYPTOS	76
06	ETHEREUM STANDARDS & DAPPS	98
07	DISCOVERING A NEW CHAPTER IN ECONOMICS	112
08	USE CASES OF BLOCKCHAIN	134
09	FUTURE OF ETHEREUM & SCALABILITY	152
10	TIME TO GET INVOLVED	178
11	*NOTES & BIBLIOGRAPHY*	197

BLOCK 1

HISTORY OF PEOPLE VS TECHNOLOGY

BLOCK INFORMATION

TX# 0x101	A BRIEF HISTORY OF RESISTING NEW TECHNOLOGIES	11
TX# 0x102	RESISTANCE REDEFINED	13
TX# 0x103	HOW BLOCKCHAIN AFFECTS US	14
TX# 0x104	UNDERVALUING A TECHNOLOGICAL SHIFT	16
TX# 0x105	TALK ABOUT PROMISES	17

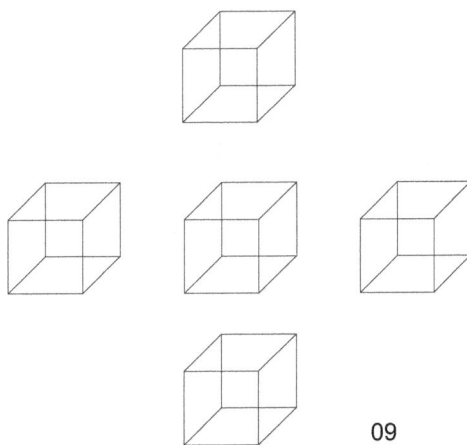

ECONOMICS BLOCK

BLOCK 1

HISTORY OF PEOPLE VS TECHNOLOGY

A Brief History of Resisting New Technologies
Human beings have a long history of resisting technological innovation. The resistance from people of the society came during the early years of industrialisation. The past thousand years of the history explains a pattern that has continued until today. There are a few important reasons why people oppose innovations. Many researchers have conducted their study into why people have been resisting technological changes over the years. Harvard professor Calestos Juma believes that innovations are bound to be opposed, and this resistance to any new technological innovations come from several factors.[1] Consider the music industry – even a decade ago, we couldn't have thought about listening to music without having a cassette or CD player.[2] Over the past five years, the industry has radically shifted towards online streaming, and now companies like Google and Spotify are leading the race towards digitalisation of music. People simply go online and either watch YouTube, or stream on Spotify, or other streaming service providers. When the change started to happen, many key players in the music industry resisted this change, as they thought that Spotify would cease to exist.[3] They are the first group who oppose to new technologies. The leaders in the industry feel frightened that they will lose control over the market because of a technological shift. Besides, modernisation does not only bring change to political or economic power but also affects us enormously on a global scale. A significant part of the population resists an innovation because people are habituated with a process or a product, and fast pace of technology creates a sense of heightened anxiety. Professor Juma, in his book *"Innovation and Its Enemies: Why People Resist New Technologies"*, explains:

"...the pace of technological innovation is discernably fast. This creates intense anxiety leading to efforts to slow down the adoption of technology."

Furthermore, scientists and innovators often make decisions and think about creating a new product without being able to understand the impact that invention might have on society.[4] Although the technologists and innovators focus a lot on the positive side of any new tech, the general public would resist by stressing on the disadvantages of that new technology. Most of the claims made are due to fear of its impact, than the actual possibility of their claims turning into reality. There was a time when the society battled the invention of cars.[5] However, cars and aeroplanes have become an integral part of our life, although it replaced and disrupted some industries. There was also a time when the society resisted coffee and the possibility of the addiction to coffee-based products. When the internet was invented, it received a significant amount of resistance from the society because of the potential change or the fear of changes dreaded by thousands of people around the world. The question is, why is it hard for people to accept change? Behavioural psychologists have studied human beings for many years to understand why people resist. According to psychologists, modification or alteration requires a few steps and backtracking. Often, humans are unaware of stepping into unknown territory, therefore perceived risk or the fear associated with the change is one of the biggest reasons why people resist change.[6]

However, the confrontations against all these technologies did not stop the innovators from digitalising almost everything that we used to do – from writing documents in a typewriter to signing contracts and sending emails. When Facebook, Google and Amazon led the race to create web 2.0, the society again resisted changes. Many people think that news bias isn't possible. However, media manipulation isn't new, and the dominant ideology reflects the *avoidance of distress* to those who hold more political and economic power.[7]

While media bias still exists to possess more control, many experts do not hold back from being pessimistic about disruptions.[8] In the history of civilisation, our society has a good track record of being pessimistic about scientific progresses. Here's how experts resisted some of the major technological breakthroughs:
1873 - Renowned British doctor with the title of Surgeon-Extraordinary to Queen Victoria predicted that brain and heart surgery would never happen.[9] The rest is history.

1966 - Time Magazine published an article called the 'The Futurists' to highlight how the world would look like in the new millennium. The author explicitly predicted that online shopping would fail. However, later in 2011, they admitted that their prediction was wrong.[10]

1995 - On a Newsweek column, renowned astronomer Clifford Stoll claimed that online databases and the world wide web would never replace the daily newspaper.

2006 - New York Times columnist David Pogue said that apple would not expand towards the cellphone market and release a cell phone.[11]

2007 - Microsoft CEO Ballmer predicted that iPhone would never have the highest market share.[12]

Resistance Redefined

The ongoing hostility against the growth of cryptocurrencies and blockchain technology isn't something new. Evidently, because of how disruptive a new technology is, people are likely to resist as they aren't sure about the influence of this technology on their future lives. On the other hand, banks and traditional financial institutions are aware of the fact that this technology might completely disrupt their industry. Others are in distress as blockchain and cryptocurrencies might be used in evil ways, rather than being utilised to make people's lives better. People often forget the fact that even the internet was, and is still used to conduct criminal activities. If we scroll back a little earlier in history, the currency was invented as a means for the governments to stop criminals from laundering money globally. Unfortunately, that did not prevent the offenders from conducting money-laundering activities around the world.[13] Every new kind of technology comes with its benefits and disadvantages. Compare it to a weapon – how an item can be used by a member of the law enforcement to save people's lives, and on the other hand used by criminals to end it. It's a matter of perspective and an intention of how people want to use a specific product, a service, or a technology.

It would also be misleading to say that criminals don't use social media for illegal activities. At the end of the day, if you look at the positive side, web 2.0 has drastically transformed the way we communicate, made our lives much more accessible, comfortable and convenient. As citizens of the 21st century, and particularly at this point in our lives, we can't even imagine living or spending time without social media or the mobile phone. However, none of them would have been possible without the disruption of the internet in our lives. The technology has provided cheaper access to knowledge to the people living under the poverty line, created millions of jobs and helped us to bring our friends, families closer than ever.

Banks, financial institutions, the world wide web, the internet, social media and online marketplaces – all these institutions were created to bring the people around the world onto one hub to ease the method of exchange. Exchanging value is a fundamental process that we go through almost every day, whether it's an exchange of a cup of coffee for money or trading high-value assets between two people. For nearly 300 years, banks have been the safest place to store high-value assets, including cash, gold and other commodities.[14] Banks are the place where you will visit and trust them as a third-party intermediary to complete a transaction with a person sitting on the other side of the world. As people, we are hard-wired not trust a random person. We believe in a bank because it verifies that unknown person for us.

Similarly, online marketplaces have enabled easier means of trading. To check the authenticity of information, we would conduct our research into reviews posted by other buyers, carefully observe the photos to make sure that the seller is selling the correct product on the marketplace. However, there are multiple third parties involved in this process. On a typical scenario, you would be using PayPal for those type of transactions. PayPal would then ask you to add bank information. The bank will send the money to PayPal. As a buyer, you aren't paying anything except probably delivery fees. However, as a seller, you are required to pay fees to both, eBay, PayPal and the bank.[15] What if we could remove all of these middlemen and replace it with a piece of code? People often don't realise how banks and these financial institutions are monopolistically controlling the world of global finance.

How Blockchain Affects Us
By explaining the core values and the fundamentals of why the blockchain was invented, it can be easily related to the three constituents mentioned above – why the society and its people resist this technology. Firstly, blockchain technology enables trade facility without having to rely on a bank to verify a transaction, and therefore it removes

the necessity of using a bank.[16] This process fundamentally changes how we send or receive money. Will it replace banks? Probably not. Nevertheless, the growth of blockchain would reduce the power of the most dominant financial institutions. Apparently, they are afraid of it.

Secondly, a habit or a certain way people conduct day-to-day activities. We were taught that money should be stored in a bank and not in our wardrobes. We have created the habit of using banks to enable exchange and to conduct trades around the world. As blockchain technology requires shifting habits, people are not necessarily prepared to accept this change. Since we are familiar with a process, why bother going through all the hassle to learn something different? In most of the cases, some people fail to comprehend that this new type of service would return more benefits compared to the existing process they're using. When Nokia was a critical player in the telecom industry, the brick phone was on trend.[17] Many adults I know entirely resisted the shift and said that they would 'never' actually own a cell phone, because firstly, we already had *landlines*, so we did not need a mobile phone to carry around everywhere, and secondly, it might damage our brains using constant emission of radio waves.

Thirdly, the emergence of blockchain will create new ways of how we send or receive money, store and track objects, create and register assets, and claim ownership of those assets on the internet. This is precisely how the technological shift relates to another crucial constituent – *shifting power*. The internet brought a significant change in the world of communication. People mostly communicate by sending emails and social media compared to written posts.[18] The dependency has shifted from letters to *Yahoo! or MSN chat rooms*, then to *SMS* and now *WhatsApp*. Although it took time for people to understand and adopt new ways of communication, eventually everybody understood that significant technological change delivers *enhanced efficiency*. Social media not only shifted power of free comunication to the public, but it has also brought a fundamental change by giving people a *voice to speak* to millions without the need to leave their homes. Blockchain decentralises the process of governance and helps to create organisations, communities and institutions that truly revolves around their members.

Undervaluing a Technological Shift

A significant problem lies in the uncertainty and the fear of the unknown. The global media thrives on creating content that is interesting to read. The uncertainty of the society is a critical leverage for the media run by the billionaires who are resisting this technological shift. That's why there are more articles on the negative side of a new technology, every time a new wave arrives; although the ideal solution would be to spread real knowledge to reduce that fear. In this course of action, people are more inclined to fall for a piece of negative news, resist themselves from going deep into conversation about the new technology and the potential benefits it can bring to the society and our lives.

The road to technological shift is full of blockades. Experts believe that we have entered the world of *exponential* technology.[19] At the early stages of the smartphone revolution, Nokia tried to create many different forms of mobile phones, starting from the folding gadgets and ending in a war with Apple to create touchscreen phones. Samsung, Huawei and Apple have won that war, and the battle to build a device with virtually everything inside it.[20] Once the technologist and innovators have been able to accomplish the products that they dreamt about thirty years earlier, we entered into the world of *accelerated adoption*, where the path to innovation is not linear. A similar story can be observed with the adoption of personal computers, as the user base is growing continuously for the past decade.[21] Is blockchain technology moving to a similar path?

The negativity remarkably overshadows the current success stories within the blockchain industry. While many experts are busy destroying blockchain because of the prices of cryptocurrencies, how many articles have you read on a startup trying to solve a real-world problem? There is so much unwanted and unnecessary chatter about the prices of bitcoin and other cryptocurrencies that the new developments along with the ongoing improvements going on in the background are being ignored. There is not enough focus or emphasis on what the innovators are trying to achieve, and what problems they are trying to solve. Cryptocurrencies and other products are built using blockchain; it does not correlate with the prices or the dynamics of the cryptocurrency market. This book is aimed at dissecting this issue. It is about discussing the real-world use cases, existing and upcoming, as well as conversing various necessary technical details, which creates the foundation of these use cases. The book focuses on the existing ideas, as well as the new signs of progress, and how it could change and impact on our daily lives - in a better way.

Talk About Promises

I must admit that some ideas that are already profitable may cease to exist in the long run. However, these companies are building the road towards the betterment of the society. To be fair and honest, any new disruptive technology is susceptible to become obsolete, which affects the success rate of the startups working to scale it. There are many factors behind the unsustainability of new technology – it could be that the technology isn't ready for mass adoption, or the products are light-years ahead from when it's invented. Another reason could be that the technology is not growing enough due to lack of involvement. In this book, we will discuss various aspects of blockchain technology and understand what's happening beneath the scepticism. This book aims to logically explain the technology, analyse different characteristics and who are in the process of solving the final barriers to better adoption. Various blocks on this book are aimed towards readers who are interested in understanding what's going on in the background. Experts believe public education and a better understanding can lead to reduced fear of change that a technology might bring.[22] It is recommended that everyone reads from the beginning till the end, in order to gain a better understanding of the overall technology.

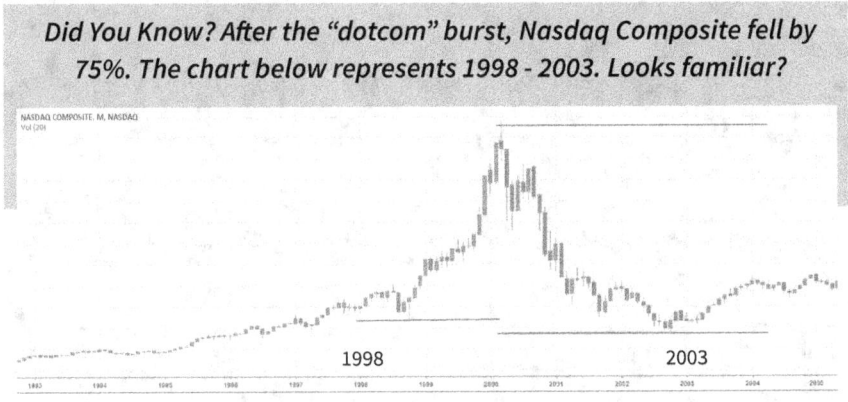

Chart 1.1: Nasdaq composite. Source: Tradingview.com

1996 - The founder of Ethernet, Robert Metcalfe predicted that the internet will go "spectacularly supernova" and collapse the same year.

Source: Gordon Goble, Digital Trends[23]

Photo: mimagephotography/envato

2019 – Here we are…

BLOCK 2

THE FAITH WE HAVE IN MONEY

BLOCK INFORMATION

TX# 0x201	WHAT IS A CURRENCY?	24
TX# 0x202	WHY DO WE TRUST BANKS?	27
TX# 0x203	CONTROL OF FORMALISED THIRD-PARTY INSTITUTIONS	28
TX# 0x204	WHY DID BLOCKCHAIN COME INTO EXISTENCE?	31

ECONOMICS BLOCK

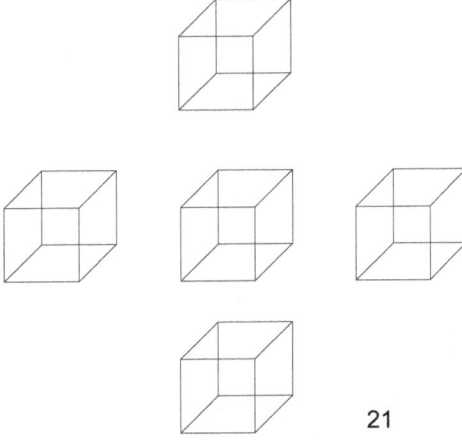

BLOCK 2

THE FAITH WE HAVE IN MONEY

To fully grasp the understanding around bitcoin, it is essential to go through some of the critical factors we learn in business economics – what money actually is, and how it works in the world of finance.

Researchers have studied us for many years to understand our behaviour pattern, such as, reason to buy a product from a market, or how we trade and exchange value.[1] Consumer behaviour research data is still one of the most valuable businesses in the world – the reason why companies like Facebook and Google are at the top of their game.[2] Academics have also studied various other institutions to enable improved trading conditions. As we are literally hard-wired to trust a bank to conduct trade – these financial institutions have controlled the world economy for a while.

The formation of various types of institutions aided in the process of increasing trust among people trading globally. Before the establishment of banks, people used to trade with commodities such as gold and silver.[3] When banks were established, people around the world started to trust banks as a means to facilitate national and international trade. With the technological advancements, banks and other business organisations moved online. Eventually, after the dot-com bubble, a significant change occurred to ensure a better use of the technology. A lot of formal methods we used to conduct before the 90s, such as writing checks, turned to 'pay using mobile banking app'. Amazon and eBay changed the game of trading when the companies broke international barriers by establishing online marketplaces.

As technology progressed, innovators realised that too much in the hands of institutions resulted in a social imbalance. With an aim to change this framework, blockchain technology was invented. The goal of creating blockchain was to reduce dependency on third-party intermediary, and instead create automation to make current trading processes faster. It is a relatively new technology that came into a real-world application using the deployment of the bitcoin network.[4] The evolution of blockchain and the birth of bitcoin is a mere continuation of the research conducted into space, and the outcome of an improved way to conduct trade.

What is a Currency?

Currencies were invented thousands of years ago as a medium of exchanging value. The early form of trading was the barter system, where people used to transfer *like-for-like products*. For instance, farmers would trade their cows in return for vegetables and other produce. As the method of trade evolved, gold and silver became a form of exchange around the world 6000 years ago.[5] Researchers in the early 20th century believed that commodity-backed reserve currency had multiple benefits, including existence of an *international currency* and predictable monetary policies.[6] In 1869, printing process of dollar bill became centralised and controlled by the government.[7] The scholars, however, had different opinion regarding the 'actual value' of the paper money. In 1892, researcher Karl Menger explained in his paper that commodity should be exchanged in return for products that are more useful, and exchange of such expensive commodities for coin and papers are 'mysterious'.[8] Around the time World War II ended, the United Nations brought the best finance experts and economists to conduct research on what could be the next significant change in the world of trade. In a conference held in 1944, a treaty was signed among the nations to choose US dollar as a *reserve currency* for the world as a whole. This treaty was known as Bretton Woods system, which eventually became a foundation of how foreign exchange markets would work.[9] The government decided to make US dollar the central reserve; therefore, all other currencies would be pegged against it. During the time the treaty was signed, it was agreed that the US dollar will be backed by gold to dollar rate of USD 35 per ounce.[10]

Eventually, around 1971, former US President Nixon in a surprise move, decided to stop traders around the world to convert their dollar into gold.[11] As the next evolution of paper money was imminent, countries globally concluded to create a new type of currency known as "FIAT", which was inaugurated in 1973.[12] The Latin for FIAT is 'let it be done'. Historically, all the currencies were backed by the gold, but with this single move in the financial market, fiat currencies became a standard. The governments retained the exclusive rights to control the supply circulation of fiat currencies. After that decision, only coins and bank-notes were deemed legal tender. It was the first time a currency or a means of trading and exchanging value was created without an intrinsic value. The value was set to be derived from the means of supply and demand. Since fiat currencies aren't linked or backed by any physical commodity, it became a risky medium for exchange. However, we are bound to use fiat currencies that are 'backed by the faith of the government' of the country we live in.

From the 20th century, the political climate became one of the significant factors to influence the value of legal tenders around the globe. Money eventually turned into a medium of exchange that is backed by nothing but the faith of the politicians. This gave rise to the novel system of repetitively inflating the value of the currency by printing an unlimited number of US dollar, whenever the Federal Reserve required it. What's the result of printing unlimited money? Actual value of the currency has been going down for the past 40 years since fiat came into place.[13] As the digital era in the 21st century gave birth to the digital banking system, the concept of legal tender or money ultimately didn't evolve.

Murray Rothbard from the Ludwig von Mises Institute explained how money was converted into a political instrument. With unprecedented *hyperinflation* stirring along with the chances of *hyper-volatility*, Rothbard in his book explained why it was important to emphasise on an international form of payment that can be used globally for a 'free-market price system'. While the World Reserve Bank aimed to create "bancor", he explained how a centralised global currency would facilitate an incredible amount of power to a worldwide organisation as they would eventually be in control of how many currencies are to be supplied to a country, resulting in being in control of the entire financial market.[14]

In 1988, The Economist predicted the rise of 'Phoenix', a cover story predicted that in a matter of 30 years from then, there would be a digital form of a global currency that could be traded around the world, sent in

Photo: grafvision/envato

a matter of minutes without the hurdles of global transactional barriers.[15] A global currency that was predicted by the analysts in the 80s has eventually come to known as 'cryptocurrency' in the 21st century.

Why do we Trust Banks?

We have been taught by our predecessors to think linearly – banks are the only trustworthy place to store money. However, banks do not leave your money in their vault. When you sign up for a bank account and deposit your £1000 in the bank, your online banking software or mobile app will show that £1000 has been deposited to the account. In reality, that money does not sit in a small safe box or vault.

Banks earn profit by lending out the money you give them on a daily basis. There are other sources of revenue too – monthly or yearly subscription to their services, charging for missing payments, asking for fees on overdrafts and so on. Nevertheless, one of the most significant sources of income for banks is the interest received on those loans provided to its user. Where do we get a personal, car or home loan? Banks. The interest rates vary depending on the income status of a person – banks are more likely to charge higher interest if the person has low income and more likely to be a risky lender.[16] Therefore, the money you give to the bank doesn't even belong to you. Does it matter? It doesn't, as long as the bank is not going into administration or stealing money by unwantedly charging you. Countries like the UK provide financial services protection for up to £85,000 cash deposited against one person in his or her account.[17] However, it is a severe problem for billions living in third-world and developing countries. Political tension between a third-world country with nations in the west can cause severe damage to the value of its currency. The problem isn't the fact that banks have evolved and found ways to control the financial system. The issue is with the centralisation of the system and how banks alongside political regimes are in full control of everything.

Due to the nature of how politics directly controlled the value of a currency, it became incredibly unstable and susceptible to political unrest. Some countries in fact have gone *bankrupt* in the past 20 years. If we analyse the background of these stories, we will realise that they are correlated to one of the following factors – either the government of a particular country was not being able to control the financial system of their country, or there was severe political unrest. This is why millions of people lost their life savings overnight in Venezuela and Greece.

Control of Formalised Third-party Institutions

US economy is one of the largest economies in the world. US dollar is a strong foundation for the world economy. As the world reserve currency, dollar directly poses a significant influence on any market. So much so that the downfall of the US dollar could have catastrophic consequences on the global economy. How? The answer lies underneath how the banking system works – what you are about to learn will change your perception towards what you considered to be irreplaceable.

The current banking system in the US, known as 'Fractional Reserve Banking' is based on the idea that all the money deposited by a person will not be likely to be withdrawn all at once.[18] Therefore, the system would allow a bank to reserve 10% of the deposits of one customer and then lend out 90% of that money as a loan or credit to another customer.[19] Now, if customer B deposits that loan into his or her bank account, that bank can again reserve 10% and lend 90% of the rest of the money to customer C. In this way, a bank holds power to create non-existent money out of thin air just by lending out to the people. A lot of the economists argue that since the loans have to be repaid, it does not have any effect on the supply of money.[20] When cash reserve runs low, the Federal Reserve decides to print more money into circulation, resulting in the devaluation of the currency. During the last financial crisis, uncontrollable lending in the form of mortgages was one of the biggest reasons for a full-blown financial banking crisis.[21] As most of the countries directly trade with the US, the domino effect of the downturn of the financial market had a powerful impact on the other global market such as the European Economic Area.

Every time the government prints money, the value becomes weaker. It is known as *monetary inflation*. Almost every country suffers from monetary inflation. It's a process of adequately controlling the economy, and print however much money required to balance the global debts. Most of the governments in the world have this control over their central reserve, due to which political tension affects the monetary value. The United States have been printing money which resulted in this following chart between 1980 - 2019.

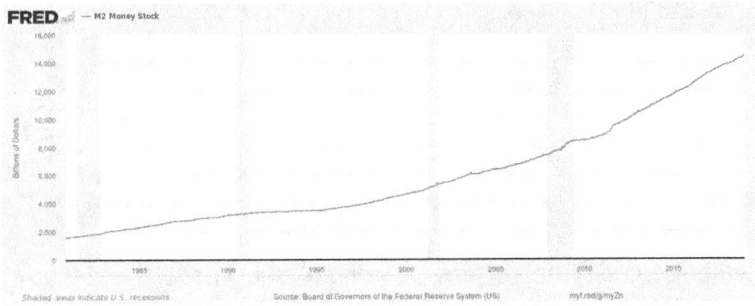

2.1: FRED, Federal Reserve Bank of St. Louis[22]

DID YOU KNOW?

US National Debt is over $20,000,000,000,000. And counting.[23]

This process is fundamentally wrong – controlling the supply to balance the financial needs of a political system. As the fiat currency isn't backed by anything, the value is dependent on the political system and relations with other countries.[24] In the current economy we live, when the people of a country completely lose faith over its government and the currency, hyperinflation may occur at any given point. Greece debt crisis was piling up when the state decided to lend more money from investors to pay back old debt. In a series of disastrous events, the Greek government had to write off a debt owed to the International Monetary Fund. Once the government and the local banks started to run out of money, it imposed currency restrictions and resulted in a national financial crisis. The European Union offered the country with more debt to increase cash flow in return for selling some assets, otherwise known as the *austerity package*, however, the citizens revolted against that decision, leading to more instability.[25] It is a bright example of a national economic crisis when the government has no control over expenditure and hence, no control over their currency.

Furthermore, Venezuela suffered one of the most significant episodes of hyperinflation. When the supply spirals out of control with respect to demand of good and services of the economy, it results in hyperinflation.[26] With an aim to control the crisis, the government started printing a significant amount of money in circulation, which resulted in hyperinflation. This sort of disaster affects almost every working-class citizen, as analysts predict that over 90% of the population now lives below the poverty line.[27]

That means if you were a citizen of Venezuela and suffered from overnight hyperinflation, it would affect your life savings. You might have been saving bolivar in a Venezuelan bank account for 20 years. When the country went bankrupt, the value of the currency significantly fell, resulting in all your money being is wiped out. Think, one day if you woke up and 20 years of your savings, gone, overnight. Amid the inflation, the volume of cryptocurrency trading was skyrocketing in the country. As the people lost faith in their currency, they quickly started to shift towards bitcoin trading to stop losing more money.

Weekly Bolivar Trading Volume in Bitcoin

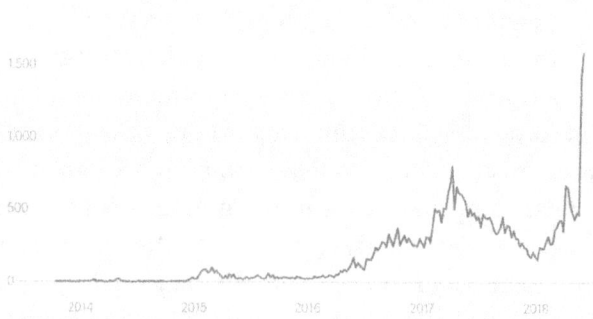

Chart 2.2: Coindance, Localbitcoins. Source: TheAtlas.com[28]

In 2018, chicken worth USD 2 was equivalent to 14,600,000 bolivars, while a kilogram of tomato was 5,000,000 bolivars.[29]

Image: felipecaparros/envato

Why did Blockchain Come into Existence?

In one sentence, to alter the way financial markets work. It was invented to challenge the current centralised and monopolistic financial world controlled by a handful of organisations. To shift the power of printing unlimited fiat currencies, cryptocurrencies came into existence with an aim to create a digital institution with no office, no centralised governance and no way to alter or tamper transactional data. Therefore, the idea was to provide an opportunity to virtually anyone in the world to be able to participate in a *decentralised governance network*, be able to invest and receive rewards as a form of electronic cash by providing a small amount of computational power to the virtual system.[30] The result was incredible – a cryptographically secured ledger, stored in a decentralised server, and a currency powered by a complex, decentralised network that is governed by its members. The fascinating result of this invention is the term 'truly unstoppable' – due to the nature of decentralised computing, it is nearly impossible to stop a typical decentralised network.[31]

Cryptocurrencies are similar to fiat currencies because it is a digital form of *cash equivalent*, which can be sent or received as a form of payment. A significant number of people believe that a bitcoin is precisely the same as fiat currency. However, there are a few differences between US dollar as currency and bitcoin as a currency.[32]

> 1. Bitcoin is a payment network.
> 2. Bitcoin is rewarded for decentralised governance – to the members of the bitcoin network who provide computational power and validate data.
> 3. It requires a lot of effort to earn one bitcoin – an incredibly complex mathematical formula processes every single transaction on the network.
> 4. Fiat can be printed as much as the governments want, bitcoin cannot be printed as it is stored and accessed digitally, and it has a fixed supply.
> 5. The political system does not control Bitcoin, neither a single institution. Instead, it is run by a decentralised network, a type of network powered by millions of people around the world. Therefore, no single entity has control over the decision-making process around bitcoin.
> 6. It is impossible to tamper the data or transaction stored on a blockchain network.

But that's not the only positive side of bitcoin. It gave birth to a new *"technological institution"* that allows data to be stored in a decentralised way.[33] Hence, instead of all the transaction being centrally stored in a server, cryptocurrencies similar to bitcoin store the data distributed across millions of computers. Therefore, no other institutions can control the process of tampering transactions, as the verification process happens automatically using a complex mathematical formula. An invention that was aimed at solving a specific use case, became what's known as the next disruption in the history of computer science.

Photo 2.3: 6 November 2017; Tim Draper, DFJ, at Venture Summit Content during Web Summit 2017 at Convento De Beato in Lisbon. Tim Draper has invested in many blockchain startups and made successful predictions about the price of bitcoin.[34]

Photo: Tim Draper, DFJ, at Venture Summit Content/by Diarmuid Greene/Web Summit via Sportsfile/licensed under CC by 2.0
© 2017 WebSummit, some rights reserved.

DID YOU KNOW?

Analyst from Barclays predict that Facebook's cryptocurrency could bring an additional USD 19 billion in revenue.[35]

BLOCK 3

A DEEP DIVE INTO BLOCKCHAIN

BLOCK INFORMATION

TX# 0x301	DEFINING BLOCKCHAIN	37
TX# 0x302	CRYPTOCURRENCY AS A STORE OF VALUE	40
TX# 0x303	BEYOND THE BITCOIN HORIZON	43
TX# 0x304	SYSTEMISATION OF THE BLOCKCHAIN BACKBONE	43
TX# 0x305	CAN BLOCKCHAIN BE TAKEN DOWN?	47
TX# 0x306	UNDERSTANDING THE COMPONENTS OF BLOCKCHAIN	48
TX# 0x307	BLOCKCHAIN VS DLT	52
TX# 0x308	BUSINESS CHALLENGES	54

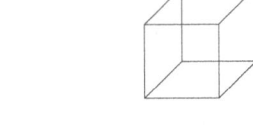
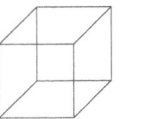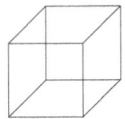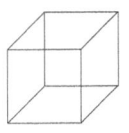
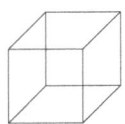

TECHNOLOGY BLOCK

BLOCK 3

A DEEP DIVE INTO BLOCKCHAIN

Defining Blockchain

Blockchain can be defined as a decentralised, replicated, transparent ledger, and a data storage network that allow users to store untampered data.[1] Unlike centralised databases, where most of the websites and applications on the internet are stored, blockchain allow users to store data on a 'decentralised' database, permitting data to be distributed to millions of computers across the network. The data is continually verified and reconciled; therefore, it is incredibly difficult to change or tamper any previously stored data or transaction on the blockchain.

The blockchain is a decentralised network where every transaction is open to the computers connected to the system and depends on peer to peer (p2p) connectivity. A distributed ledger records all the transactions that take place in the system. The ledger is replicated across all the network participants. A blockchain uses smart contracts to control the access to the ledger. This 'visibility' is the heart of this blockchain technology ethos.[2]

Because of how the monopolistic and centralised the system was, *Satoshi Nakamoto* came up with the concept of electronic peer-to-peer cash that will allow users to send money from one person to another, in a matter of seconds, from one part to the other part of the world, without having banks being involved in the middle.[3] He proposed that the transaction will be stamped with date and time, and stored in a decentralised database to avoid abuse of cash by third parties, such as financial institutions which supports the traditional financial system. Once a user intends to send the digital money to the receiver, the timestamp server generates the transaction ID or known as 'Transaction Hash'.[4] This *hash* is proof of money transfer, similar to the receipt we send to others. The timestamp is powered by a method of *consensus* – an algorithm using which the nodes in the chain validate the information on the block. For instance, the users of the bitcoin blockchain providing the computational power to the network receive rewards for verifying that transaction or the 'proof of work'. This would be the simplest way to explain the underlying technology of bitcoin, the blockchain, which is yet to be fully explored. One of the fascinating parts of the paper published by Nakamoto was how he decided to limit the supply of bitcoin, and how it would assist in creating a better economic value for the currency as the demand grows in the future.

Blockchain has been in existence for a while now. However, a significant number of people find it hard to segregate the differences between blockchain, cryptocurrencies and blockchain-based applications. This book emphasises on the importance of all of the above, analyses the shortcomings and focuses on how different factors around the technology works.

The bitcoin transactions are not stored in a centralised database in one location – the data is replicated, stored in a distributed but 'continually reconciled' ledger; which means the records are public and immutable.[5] In this process, data tampering becomes impossible because if any one of the computers attempts to corrupt the data, it will be alerted to all other databases stored in millions of computers around the world. The bitcoin blockchain was designed in a way so that anyone around the world can join the network, provided that they own the appropriate hardware. This peer-to-peer function on a user-to-user basis allowed flexibility to millions of people to earn their living from this network.

AMY INITIATES MONEY TRANSFER TO TIANA

MULTIPLE SIMILAR TRANSACTIONS (TX) ARE COMPILED IN ONE BLOCK

THE BLOCK WAITS TO BE MINED OR VALIDATED

A NODE ACCEPTS THE JOB

THE NODE SOLVES A CRYPTOGRAPHIC PUZZLE TO VERIFY THE TRANSACTION (TX)

THE TX IS PROCESSED, TIMESTAMPED AND RECORDED ON THE CHAIN

THE MINER OR VALIDATOR RECEIVES REWARD FOR PROCESSING THE BLOCK

TIANA RECEIVES THE PAYMENT

There is no intermediary to verify the transaction or the user. Between a sender and a receiver, are sitting a bunch of computers, which powers an intelligent network that removes the middleman. Blockchain can not only process a p2p transaction but also an asset, such as ownership, certificate, title, registry, a contract or personally identifiable information such as the passport. To unleash the hidden power of the blockchain, Vitalik Buterin developed a much more advanced version of the digital ledger, which would allow the blockchain to host decentralised mobile and web applications, and allow building 'unstoppable applications' using a function called *smart contracts*.[6] It was the beginning of yet another extraordinary dimension that has the changed the game in the evolution of how humans exchange value on the internet.

Smart contracts can be explained by comparing it to the process of the traditional way of sharing contracts. For instance, if you as a customer would like to sign a contract with a freelancer, you would typically email a document over to that person. Once approved, the freelancer would send the document back to you. Later, you receive an invoice, and once that's completed, or partially completed, the payments are either made based on milestones or at once, after handing over the project. Now, combine all of that work into one piece of code. All you need is a code that keeps a record of what was agreed between two parties. After electronically signed, the contract sends the payments based on either milestones or in full, after the freelancer delivers the job. The blockchain holds both users to the highest degree of accountability, as the agreement or the consent cannot be altered.[7] Since blockchain is automatable, it makes the process of exchanging value much faster. Payments made in a retail shop looks practically instantaneous, but the actual process of receiving and clearing the funds from your bank, to their merchant, and ultimately the retailer takes approximately five to seven days. Similarly, when consumer requests for a refund, the retailer would also inform you that the process would take from seven days to a month. Blockchain eliminates the verification process conducted by the banks – it shortens this timeframe by using *automatable mathematics* to validate the authenticity of these type of transactions. This is not the only 'automatable' part of blockchain – there are many other use cases with potential benefits in which blockchain technology can be used. Throughout this book, there are multiple examples of various use cases of blockchain across multiple sectors and discussion about people who are becoming the key players.

Cryptocurrency as a Store of Value

Sceptics claim that bitcoin or any other similar product has no intrinsic value.[8] While this book emphasises on different types of blockchain and distributed networks in order fully comprehend the intrinsic value, let's look at why bitcoin also has some layers underneath the technology that makes it valuable.

In the *gold-silver trading era*, commodities started to become incredibly valuable, because it took a substantial amount of effort to create gold. A gold miner is required to mine and find gold from the ground, process and finally give it a shape of coins, bars, or jewelleries to be sold and traded in the market.[9][10] Bitcoin is similar to gold, because of the network, blockchain requires the 'crypto miners' to set up appropriate hardware, maintain the mining computers which provide computing power to the network. A significant amount of work, investment and time are needed to show the proof of work, which results in the miner digitally receiving the bitcoins. Besides, the network is fully open sourced. Hence some incredibly talented people are working towards developing the underlying infrastructure. As a result of this community-driven public network, blockchain evolved from a ledger to the next version of the internet. The work that's put into mining, developing and maintaining the system makes it incredibly valuable. The only difference here is that the gold miners physically mine using construction equipment, while bitcoin miners use computational power to mine electronic cash. Once this form of digital money is mined, the ownership is automatically validated by the *network-dependent algorithm*. After the information is processed, it can be stored in a digital wallet, which can be sent to anyone around the world without the need of an intermediary third party or a bank account.

Bitcoin, the first cryptocurrency, is independent of any third party. There is no server where bitcoin is stored, and there is no centralised institution that controls the fund. Since its decentralised, there is no central authority or organisation in control of the network. The engineers and entrepreneurs together have created a foundation, where the network is run by the consensus of the members of the bitcoin community, as well as the miners who power the entire network. There is no office for bitcoin or no central server that controls the flow of circulation. It is a definition of a genuinely decentralised organisation, empowered by the members of the public. It's not a form of money controlled by a few people in a central institution. Instead, it changes the dynamics of traditional economy – the power shifts to the people. As the third-party intermediary is wholly removed from the process of sending or receiving this new form of money, there is no financial intervention, or a middleman deciding or validating a specific transaction. This is the first time the need of a third party can be eliminated, thus reducing the dependability on the financial institutions to conduct and validate a transaction. As a user, you trust the network, and the network does its job to verify the transaction for you.

This wave of change can be compared to how the mailing process has changed. The internet has become a medium of connectivity without having to incur any costs globally. Even two decades ago people around the world were entirely dependent on postal services to send and receive a written form of communication. Gone are the days of writing letters to a friend living on the other side of the planet. Now, instead of posts, all we need is a free email address or a social media account to send a message in a fraction of a second, eliminating the need to be dependent on a third-party monopolistically controlling the process of communication. Internet did not wipe out the Royal Mail or US Postal Service – we still send official posts, but it has made the process of communication much faster.

Photo: Daria Shevtsova

In just a matter of 10 years, we have shifted from a society of reading print magazines, books and newspapers to online news sites and e-books. Many still prefer printed copies. But the trend is purchasing e-books because of its convenience. The exponential growth of the internet has substituted an entire industry and our 100-year-old habit to something that people born before the '60s would have never imagined.

Beyond the Bitcoin Horizon

One of the most amazing benefits of cryptocurrencies is that they are a convertible asset. With regards to the ownership, a person is not required to buy or own a single bitcoin or ether; because these cryptocurrencies are divided into fractions. One hundred millionth of a bitcoin is known as *Satoshi*.[11] While Bitcoin network does not allow cryptocurrencies to be created on its network, the other companies that are building the road towards Web 3.0, such as Ethereum foundation or NEO, have invented game-changing networks, where users are able to create *personalised tokens*, which can instantly be converted into any form of asset. On the same chain, it is possible to store almost any type of information and provide proof of authentication or ownership. It is a convertible form of cryptocurrency. These cryptocurrencies can be traded to provide proof of purchase for a land or even allow access to tamperproof digital identification stored on the chain. Other types of crypto can be used for *asset management* using an automated algorithm that does not require a lawyer to validate a contract or a bank to process the payment.

The question is, could these exchanges of information, data and asset be possible on blockchain without the dependency on cryptocurrency? The answer is yes, it is. In fact, some of these existing technologies are discussed later in the book – how enterprises are using the technology to track assets across a complex supply chain network. However, cryptocurrencies or 'tokens' on a blockchain adds another dimension to the process – i.e. makes it better. Some of these tokens may or may not have an *extrinsic value*, or price, however, the process in which it is designed, would eventually lead to the development of a revolutionary world exchange where gamers can trade their online collectables into coffee shops points, and pay using the same network. Block 9 showcases which companies are working towards such scalability solutions.

Systemisation of The Blockchain Backbone

The entire theory of decentralisation was to enable distributed computing and allow nodes around the world to power the virtual network. According to researchers, an essential factor in the architecture is *the disintermediation*, a process where a centralised authority is entirely replaced by a group of non-trusted or semi-trusted people who can interact with each other, and power the network.[12] How does a group of people who do not trust each other, or even know each other, work together to power a network? This process is achieved by deploying a method of consensus, that is, an algorithm is designed for the nodes, or the participants in the decentralised network to reach an agreement in order to validate the information.

A consensus is defined as an agreement among the nodes that power the network. In order to understand what a consensus algorithm is, we need to know about a broader general categorisation of a blockchain network.[13] The bitcoin network is known as a 'permissionless' blockchain, which is fully decentralised, and therefore anyone can join the network and run a node. The algorithm is designed in this way – all the nodes in a blockchain network, for instance, the Bitcoin proof-of-work, tries to solve a cryptographic puzzle. The node that detects the solution, or wins, is rewarded the ability to add the next block in the chain. Each node in the network obtains a copy of the blockchain ledger; a transaction in the ledger can be verified against all of them to ensure that there is no tampering. It is a shared ledger where all of these nodes do not need to trust or know each other because all the nodes involved in the network have a copy of the same ledger to validate the data that is processed. Therefore, they can monitor and verify the data themselves. If the transaction passes *integrity test*, it is stored as blocks in the network. The blocks in a chain are identified using a term called 'hash'. This is how a hash looks like.[14]

Transaction Hash:	0x57502f19645aa6a7dbf9130934a6e750c9e3f298cc7723808bad4e4f648165bf
Status:	Success
Block:	7349785 1 Block Confirmation
TimeStamp:	46 secs ago (Mar-11-2019 07:37:17 PM +UTC)
From:	0x0bb141c2f7d4d12b1d27e62f86254e6cced5ff9a
To:	0x09cb747254ebba718730ce94f1178405157925fb
Value:	5.791645551292260914 Ether ($771.68)
Transaction Fee:	0.000084 Ether ($0.01)

3.1: Ethereum Hash. Source: etherscan.io

A hash is an ID for a block that stores the transaction. A block may store two or three hundred transactions. All the transactions in a block are identified as 'transaction hash'. This works as a proof for a single transaction, or 'receipt' we send to each other when we use banks. This process is repeated for a chain of blocks, and every time, the nodes need to come to an agreement to approve whether or not the next block should be added on the blockchain. The blockchain can not only store transaction information, but also data. If you scan the next QR code, you can read the peace treaty agreement between North and South Korea, a copy of which has been permanently stored on a public blockchain. The backbone of a blockchain network is the consensus algorithm using which it safely verifies and stores data in the network.

This consensus mechanism design has been a topic of research for decades. When the bitcoin blockchain came into existence, Satoshi Nakamoto described how the consensus mechanism in the network would validate the transactions.[15] Proof-of-work (PoW) is designed to be deployed in a permissionless network. PoW introduced the terms 'miners', where the miners would be the nodes solving the cryptographic puzzles. In this process, the miners provide computational power to verify the integrity of the information and therefore rewarded with new bitcoin if they are successful in solving the puzzle. The difficulty of this puzzle solving mechanism increases over time, which is why it is becoming more and more difficult to mine bitcoin. The difficulty is defined as 'Network difficulty'.

In a simplistic term, the proof-of-work algorithm allows miners to show proof of their work conducted to solve the puzzle and thus receive their fair share of bitcoin. The amount of coins mined is proportional to the number of computational resources provided to the network. It is expensive to mine bitcoin, because similar to gold, it requires a substantial amount of investment, as well as *electricity* to power the computers so that they can work 24/7. Various sources suggest that mining one bitcoin costs approximately USD 800 to 3000.[16] Bitcoin network difficulty looks like this:

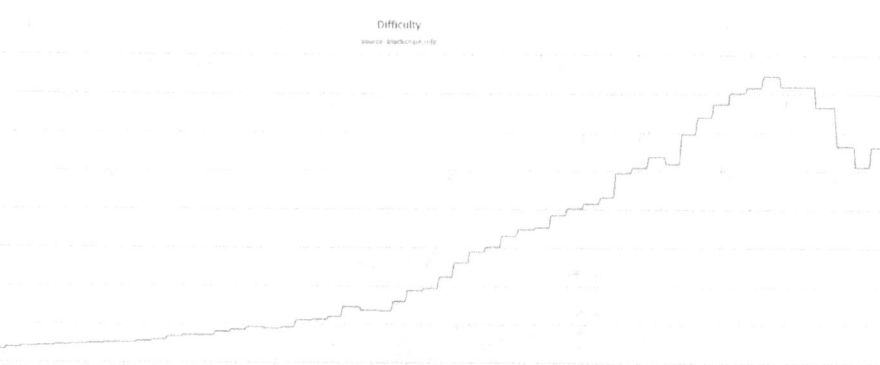

Chart 3.2: Network Difficulty Chart of Bitcoin. Source: blockchain.info

However, the costs may vary based on the prices of electricity in different countries. In order to aggregate resources, miners can join 'mining pools', where a group of miners work together to add new blocks. In Ethereum proof-of-work network, miners can join 'Ethermine' or 'SparkPool', which provides a *turnkey solution* for the miners to run a node from anywhere in the world, and therefore, makes it much easier to mine ether.[17] The share of the reward is distributed via the pools using automated contracts. The reward is proportional to the *hash rate* of a node – a computing unit of how much power is being provided by a single node. The most interesting fact is that the entire process – voting, validating or approving a block happens automatically. The computer processing units (CPUs and GPUs) take care of calculating and solving the complex puzzle.

Another type of blockchain is known as 'permissioned' blockchain. In this type of blockchain, the nodes are identified to a federation or a governing authority, who are in control of the blockchain. A permissioned blockchain can be designed in a way so that it remains private to a particular organisation, for instance, hospitals. In order to process information and validate the authenticity of data, the private nodes are utilised in a permissioned network to agree on the validity of information or a transaction.

Can Blockchain be Taken Down?

It is hard to take a decentralised ledger down. However, similar to the servers on the internet, blockchain technology isn't fully resistant to attacks. Few of the frequent attacks on a proof-of-work (PoW) consensus are -

> Double Spending – This attack happens when criminals try to spend cryptocurrencies twice.[18] Although many believe bitcoin is resistant to double spending, proof-of-work may still be susceptible to double spending, however, it's really expensive.
> 51% attack – 51% network attack happens when a majority of the miners take control of the chain. This type of attack can cause severe disruptions, even alter data and slow down a network.[19]
> DDoS – Distributed Denial of Service. In this process, a server or a network is simultaneously attacked from hundreds of millions of sources, until the point when parts of the network are affected.[20]
> Forks – Not all forks are dangerous for a network – a planned soft or *hard fork* may happen from time to time. However, due to a disagreement between the community and not reaching consensus, a fork may cause a blockchain to split.[21]

Cyber-attacks aren't the end of it – the most disappointing element of PoW consensus method is that the process of 'mining' requires a significant amount of electricity, as well as limitations regarding the *scalability* of a network. In blockchains like Ethereum, thousands of applications would be supposedly storing and processing petabytes of data using one network. Therefore, Ethereum founders proposed a new consensus method that would allow a reduction of wasteful energy resources and planned to deploy a new process of reaching consensus on the Ethereum blockchain.[22]

Known as Proof-of-stake (PoS), the community members in the network would 'stake' a certain amount of ether, which would allow them to run nodes by showing the proof of their staked ether. If any of the nodes commit fraud, go against the rules of staking to attack the network, that node would lose all of its stakes for committing such deception. In this process, the 'miners' are replaced by 'validators'. The network may either randomly choose a validator to assign rights to create another block, or allow validators to vote, and in the end, all the validator come to a

consensus to add the next block on the chain.[23] Few benefits of PoS are:
> Reduced Consumption of Electricity – A validator would not require expensive equipment to run a node in the network
>
> Reduced Risks of Centralised Mining – Goes against the *economies of scale* valid for proof-of-work, where more mining equipment would allow you to mine more cryptocurrencies
>
> Increased Security – Reduces the risks of attack often happens in the proof-of-work algorithm

Another significantly important factor of proof-of-stake algorithm is the ability of random-sampling. It allows Ethereum to shard the blockchain, that would eventually solve scalability issues and increase the ability to process more transactions at the same time. More regarding sharding and the future of blockchain have been discussed on block 9.

Understanding the Components of Blockchain

Web 3.0 is the next version of the internet. This technological evolution utilises a range of peer-to-peer (p2p) *technology architecture* that increases privacy, and *fault tolerance* resulting in better individual protection.[24] One of the first concepts of 'Web 3.0' was proposed by former Ethereum CTO Dr Gavin Wood, where the foundation would consist of the following:

- Encrypted Information Publication System
- Low-level messaging System
- Consensus Engine
- Decentralised Application.[25]

Blockchain technology is based on the foundations of the web 2.0. However, the architectural design of a blockchain network is a little different than that of the internet. The internet consists of multiple components that form the basis of TCP/IP - Transmission Control Protocol (TCP) and Internet Protocol (IP).

The 7-layer model is described here.
> Physical – The first component on the web, however, experts argue that it might not be a part of the actual model. 'Physical' comprises of the hardware.
>
> Data-link Layer – It consists of the individual protocols, for instance, Ethernet. The network could also be cellular 3G/4G, which is used for mobile internet.[26]
>
> Network – It specifies the method for communicating and provides

interoperable packets that are able to use various types of link layer. All our computers have an IP address. IP defines the identity of the computer.

Transport – It is where the data is transported between two nodes. The information is sent and received using a unit of *internet data* known as 'bytes'. The speed of the network can be determined in this layer, the higher the transport capacity, the better and more efficient the transport of the data.

Session – It represents ongoing interaction between applications.

Presentation – It is responsible for converting codes into human-readable format.

Process and Application – This is where the application, software and websites exist. All the processes designed for an application are executed at this level of the internet.[27]

The blockchain is similar to that of the designs of the internet. However, technological components of the blockchains are slightly different from that of the actual internet.

1. Application Layer
   a. Distributed Application – Smart contracts, DApps
   b. App-level Protocols – A protocol based on defined standards
2. Networking Layer
   a. Trust – Consensus mechanism
   b. Transaction – Mining and validation
3. Protocol Layer
   a. Layer 2 – Secondary layer enhancing transactional capacity, allowing off-chain storage and computation
   b. Layer 1 – Distributed blockchain layer, e.g. Ethereum

Another proposed component is the Governance layer.[28] It is noteworthy that the blockchain typically runs on the internet, however, these networks can run without the necessity of an internet connection. Technical experts suggest that a cryptocurrency can be sent or received using hardware such as goTenna.[29] It is also possible to create an SMS-based network that utilises mobile *GSM network* to interact with the blockchain.[30] As the technology evolved, certain improvements and evolutions have occurred that has resulted in the variation of the distribution model. On the basis or foundation of the earlier models of blockchain proposed, the technological components of a blockchain network can be separated in the following ways –

LAYER 1

The layer 1 consists of the primary network or the 'main chain'. For instance, the Ethereum 'main chain' exist on this layer. Fundamental changes made to this layer requires a full-scale network upgrade or a hard-fork.

LAYER 2

The layer 2 is the second layer that exists on top of the primary chain. This layer can be utilised to scale a blockchain network. Any changes to this layer do not require full network upgrade or significant changes to the entire chain. For example, OmiseGo is implementing Plasma, a process of creating child chains on the main chain, a layer-2 scaling solution to exponentially increase the capacity of the network.[31]

TRANSACTION

Another crucial component of the blockchain is processing and validating data. Various consensus algorithm defines how the transactions are processed. Therefore, based on the design of blockchain, the nodes are allocated with blocks, and transactions are handled by routing incoming/outgoing data to its appropriate destination.

Furthermore, this layer may or may not exist depending on the type of network. This infrastructure layer can be created on the Ethereum blockchain, that facilitates the exchange of the tokens or assets among users. This makes it easier for developers to launch an app based on a set of protocols that are designed per proposed standards, e.g. ERC721. It exists on the main chain and focuses on the improvement of functionality. 0x Protocol allows a developer to build token relayers or exchanges on the 0x layer.[32]

TRUST/CONSENSUS

The consensus algorithm used to validate the blocks on the chain and process the transaction. While bitcoin uses proof-of-work, Ethereum plans to move to full proof-of-stake implementation in the future.

APPLICATION

This is top-most layer where the applications exist. A DApp can be built on a network specific protocol. For instance, decentralised relayers such as DDEX are built on 0x protocol.[33] DApps may or may not be built without the dependency on a protocol layer. If a DApp is developed on a protocol layer, the functionality is directly or indirectly connected and dependent on that layer.

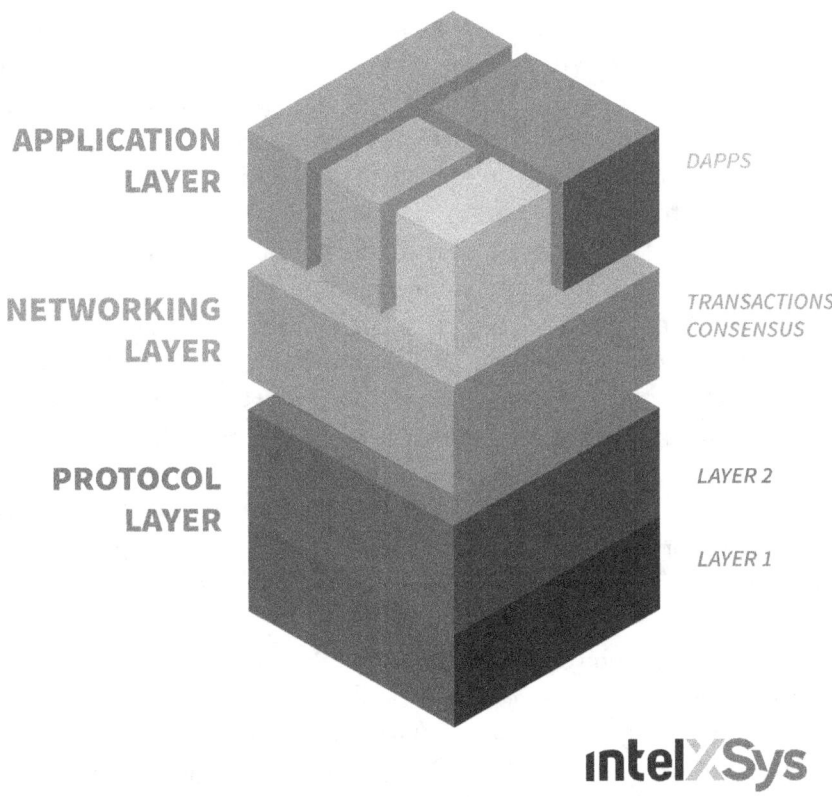

This is an high-level overview of how the blockchain works. The technological components and this description are not peer-reviewed.

 Core components of a blockchain network

Blockchain vs DLT

Although the overall concepts are similar, Blockchain and 'Distributed Ledger Technology' are different to each other. A Distributed Ledger Technology or DLT is a process of storing and accumulating timestamped information and hosted on a distributed database, which may or may not process data using blocks. There could be millions of computers, running nodes to power the network, each hosting a copy of the database to validate the information, however the process in which various DLTs validate information are different to that of blockchain. DLT fundamentally reduces the risk of data tampering and eliminates the risk of centralised data storage.[34]

A website or the application that we use on the internet is typically hosted on a centralised database. These storages are usually known as data centres. Every website, software or mobile application is hosted somewhere in one of the datacentres around the world. Due to the nature of all the data being stored in one place, many large corporations have been hacked previously, compromising millions of people's personal data.[35][36] Larger companies create multiple backups of their database by replicating the information across two, three or four databases. These backups are used in an unlikely scenario if one of their data centres are compromised. DLTs do not store the information in one central database or computer; instead, it encrypts the data and sends it to the network where a copy of that encrypted data is stored across all the computers or nodes involved in that network. DLTs may store data using various methods, such as storing data in a specific order, or randomly storing the data across multiple devices without a specific order. Many DLTs are immune to attacks that could impact a blockchain.

A blockchain is a type of distributed ledger technology that process data in blocks. Examples of blockchain would be Bitcoin, Ethereum or the Stellar Network. Other models of DLTs function differently from the way blockchain functions. Blockchain is a type of DLTs, but all other DLTs aren't blockchain.[37]

Tangle

Tangle works using a function called DAG – Directed Acyclic Graph. Unlike blockchain, it does not consolidate and process information on the chain in 'blocks' which could be 'mined' on a public blockchain, instead, when a tangle transaction is initiated, the network validates and approves two more transactions at the same time.[38] Hence, when a user initiates a payment in the tangle network, the system inquires a small computational power from the user that verifies two more transactions in the network. As a result of this function, micro transactions can be initiated using this network. IOTA is based on tangle, a DLT that was invented to facilitate interoperability and to share data across multiple devices, such as a smartwatch, or smart washing machine or even a sensor. According to IOTA, it is the first DLT being developed to power IoT devices without hindering the data integrity of machines. As a result of how the DLT works, there is no transaction fee, therefore sending IOTA is fee-free.[39]

THE BLOCKCHAIN BOTTLENECK

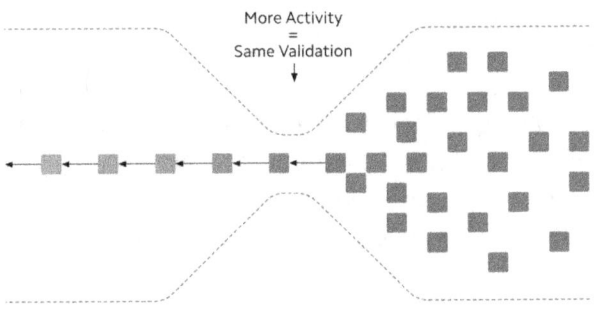

THE IOTA TANGLE SCALES!

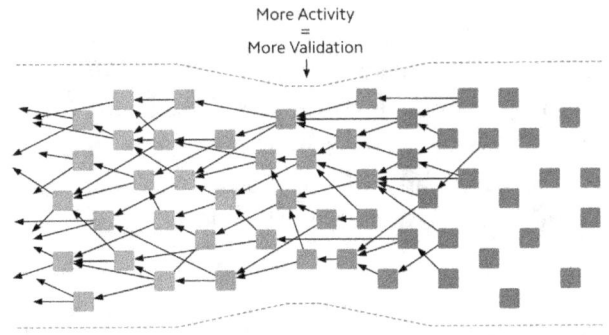

3.3: Blockchain vs IOTA.
Source: wikimedia commons/IOTA/Licensed under CC by 4.0

Hashgraph

It is another type of DLT where the network is run by sharing information among the participants of the network. A node participating on the network shares the information of a particular transaction with multiple other nodes selected randomly. This next node combines the information, with the information it knows and transfers it onto the next node. This aggregated information is passed onto the next randomly chosen node. The process goes along until all the nodes engaging in the process are aware of the information created in the first place. This is an innovative method of consensus, which is termed as *virtual voting*. Similar to blockchain, all other nodes in this type of DLT have a copy of the transaction. However, in this case, the participating nodes are able to pre-calculate each other's reaction, hence they are able to forecast and comprehend the decision without casting any ballot.[40][41]

Business Challenges

Challenge faced by DLTs is an intricate issue to address. A significant number of people mistake the challenge for the *sentiment* of the market. Prices are a challenge, and organisations built around cryptocurrencies and tokenised DLTs, such as Ethereum, Stellar or IOTA will continue to face it. However, there are numerous challenges that DLTs are facing as emerging technologies. Some of them are as follows:

- *Business Challenge*
    >> Cost of Adoption - As a new technology, the cost of user adoption is higher. Users might not be comfortable using the services, or they might be completely unaware of the existence.[42]
    >> User Perception - Due to the dynamics of the cryptocurrency market, users may not be interested in a blockchain-based product. They also may not believe in the future of this technology.
    >> Community Consensus - Keeping the community together is a complex process compared to a centralised business, but its a crucial issue to address in order to succeed in a decentralised institution.

- *Scientific Challenge*
    >> Scalability Issues - In order for millions of applications to run simultaneously, the networks are required to capacitate the influx of users.

High performance GPUs are used to mine cryptos such as Ether, ZCash, Decred and so on. Proof-of-stake consensus will eventually make Ethereum miners redundant, as they will be forced to become 'validators' to earn rewards.

Image: grafvision/envato

>> Standards Development - While Ethereum foundation is using a set of standards to govern the development of applications on its network, the overall industry is required to develop standards around the use of DLTs, cryptocurrencies and blockchain-based applications to ensure cooperation over opposition. Interoperability could be a key towards mass adoption.[43]

• *Financial Challenge*

>> Price Mechanism - Volatility can act as a negative catalyst and deflect traders away. While the next phase of the *bull ride* will attract millions towards buying cryptocurrencies, due to the nature of unstable movements, a tokenised ecosystem may take a little while to be established. Analysts believe that mass adoption of cryptocurrencies is the key to price stability.[44]

>> Regulatory Challenges - Not all the countries around the world have fully comprehended the utilisation of cryptocurrency and blockchain. Although the UK has implemented regulations of cryptocurrency taxation, many countries do not have such clear regulations.[45]

In a press release, one of the largest social trading and asset brokerage company eToro revealed that 43% **Millennials** prefer cryptocurrency trading than stock assets.[46] Also known as **Generation Y**, Millennials are the generation born between 1980 to 1997. Unlike other generations, Millennials have changed the way how they save and spend their money, including their habit of expenditure behind travelling and sharing every part of their experience on socials.[47]

Photo: Darcy McShenrey/Bursi

#HODL

The term HODL first originated in the forum bitcointalk.org. In December 2013, a seemingly intoxicated user of the forum posted with a typo. The user misspelt the word and titled the thread "I AM HODLING".[48] It started off as a meme, then eventually became one of the most famous slang in the world of cryptocurrency.[49] This term has been popular ever since, with bitcoin/altcoin users perpetually apprehending that despite the crash of cryptocurrencies, they would hold it in the long run.

BLOCK 4

CRYPTOCURRENCY MECHANICS

BLOCK INFORMATION

TX# 0x401	TYPES OF CRYPTOCURRENCIES	61
TX# 0x402	HIGH-LEVEL PRICE MECHANISM	62
TX# 0x403	WHERE ARE CRYPTOCURRENCIES TRADED	67
TX# 0x404	VOLATILITY IS STANDARD	69
TX# 0x405	CRYPTO VS MONEY	73

ECONOMICS & FINANCE BLOCK

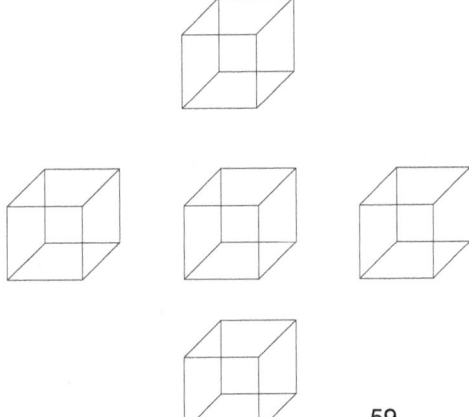

BLOCK 4

CRYPTOCURRENCY MECHANICS

Types of Cryptocurrencies

Although blockchain technology, the infrastructure that powers bitcoin, was invented to eliminate the middleman and transact electronic form of currency, scientists and technologists discovered that the technology could be used in many different ways and provide immense benefit to the masses. Bitcoin or Ethereum network is a type of blockchain powered fully by utilising their own network-dependent cryptocurrency. Cryptocurrencies are the first real-life *use case* of the blockchain, which is why the crypto market dynamics directly or indirectly affects the sentiment of many people towards blockchain technology.

In the crypto world, the more preferred classification would be bitcoin and altcoins. A broader category differentiates cryptocurrencies into following types:
- Bitcoin
- Altcoin
- Stablecoin
- Tokens

Altcoin

Any cryptocurrency that is alternative to the bitcoin is known as 'altcoin'. Such as – ether or ripple. According to cryptocurrency analyst Aziz, altcoins usually possess the characteristics of having its blockchain. It can also be categorised into the following:
- *Bitcoin-derived blockchain* – such as Litecoin
- *Native Blockchain* – such as Ethereum or Ripple Labs[1]

Stablecoin

Stable coins are cryptocurrencies, however, linked to a real world asset-class. Although it could be linked to anything, experts believe that majority are pegged against fiat, e.g. US dollar or British Pound.

Blockchain.com classifies stablecoin into two following categories:
- Collateral-backed
- Algorithmic

Collateral-backed stablecoins are the cryptocurrencies pegged to the value of two types of *asset class*, i) commodities – such as gold, and ii) cash equivalent – such as the US dollar.[2]

Tether, or commonly known as USDT and Paxos Standard (PAX) are stablecoins that are pegged to the value of the dollar. Cryptocurrencies that are pegged to the two asset-class mentioned above can be subject to regulatory approval. New York regulators have approved the circulation of Paxos Standard which is fully collateralised by the US dollar on a *one-to-one basis*.[3] Facebook has developed their own cryptocurrency or stablecoin that would reportedly be used via WhatsApp.[4] Blockchain fundamentalists would argue that it goes against decentralisation ethos. However, there is a strong rationale why stablecoins, backed by fiat, were created – to allow traders to protect themselves in an unpredictable market.

Similar to the stock market, the traders move their funds from stocks to fiat or stable commodities such as gold when the market becomes volatile. With an aim to offer an alternative, instant form of switchable asset in a volatile market, stablecoins came into force. These coins, or a cryptocurrency version of fiat, such as Paxos or USD Tether (USDT), mimics the price of the dollar. These are cryptocurrency versions of fiat money, but on blockchain. Therefore, cryptocurrency users are always able to exchange it to USDC or USDT almost instantly, whenever they are required to do so.

High-level Price Mechanism

Cryptocurrency prices are based on two fundamental principles – the supply-demand thoery, and the sentiment of the public. The pricing mechanism can be compared to that of the stock market. Let's say, there are a limited number of shares issued for a company X that is enlisted in a stock market. If a significant amount of people believe that X is the most influential automobile company in the market, they will keep purchasing X's shares, which will drive the prices up. It is a *domino effect* – as the prices go up, small players get involved which may result in a drastic increase in the share price. The price of a share is not directly dependent on the profitability of a public company – it depends on the sentiment of the shareholders. If a significant number of traders in the crypto market starts to drive the prices up, it acts like dominos and pushes the prices of the overall market. This factor can be explained by using the basics of economics, the supply and demand curve.

Supply vs Demand

In straightforward terms, supply is the amount of a product or commodity available in the market. In the *goods market* or *manufacturing industry*, supply may be increased or decreased based on the demand. In the stock market, however, the supply is increased when a company is required to raise additional funds, and therefore it issues more shares in the market. Demand is the value desired by the consumers in the market. There is a relationship between supply and demand, and it is determined by the supply and demand curve.

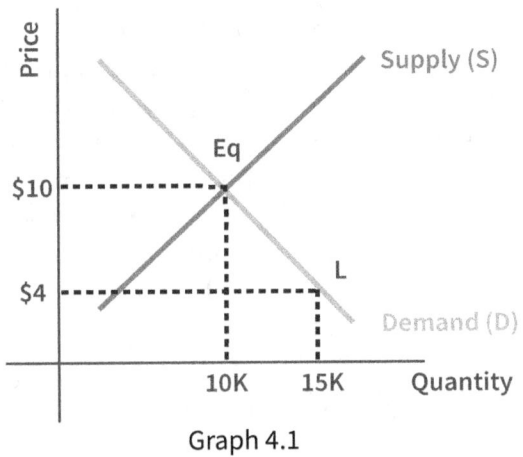

Graph 4.1

In the graph 4.1, the direct relationship between supply and demand has been illustrated. (S) demonstrates supply, and the (D) is the demand. Theoretically, when the demand is high with a shortage of supply, the price goes up. The two lines intersect at Eq, which is known as the market equilibrium. At this point, 10,000 units are produced and sold at a price of USD 10 to meet the demand. Manufacturing companies try to balance the supply and demand to keep the market in equilibrium. If the production quantity exceeds the actual demand of the market and reaches 15,000 units, the price would go down from USD 10 to USD 4. The point L illustrates a higher supply than the product meets its demand.

The supply and demand lines or curves can shift anytime based on market dynamics.

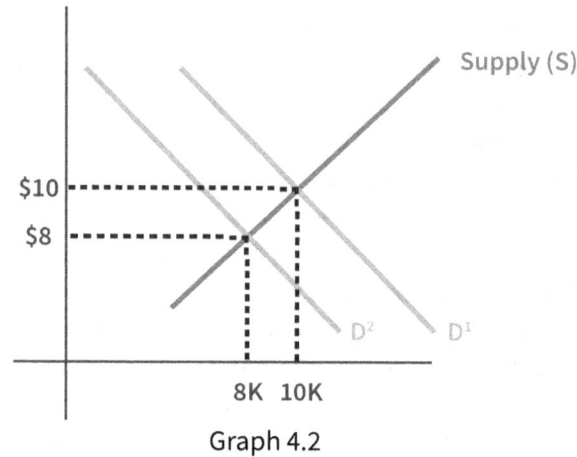

Graph 4.2

In graph 4.2, the demand curve D¹ has shifted leftwards to D². The supply hasn't changed, however, somehow the demand for the product is lower than it was before. In this case, demand would shift leftwards, but if it goes up, the line will shift rightwards.[5] In this scenario, the market equilibrium would move to a new point. Hence, both the quantity and price would go down. In order to keep the market stable, the market demand of 8,000 units are produced and sold at a price of USD 8. If the production quantity isn't lowered, the excess batch of the unsold product will add towards wastage.

The supply and demand relationship with regards to cryptocurrency is different from that of the manufacturing industry or the stock market. The supply for both bitcoin and ether will diminish over time and never react to that of the demand. Due to the nature of its diminishing and fixed supply, the supply curve is vertical and termed as 'inelastic supply' in basic economics.

Inelastic supply means that the supply will not respond to the changes in demand. That is, the supply of bitcoin or ethereum can't be increased if the demand goes up or down. This type of supply has its advantages and disadvantages. The biggest advantage is the potential of their prices moving upwards when there is a sudden surge in demand.

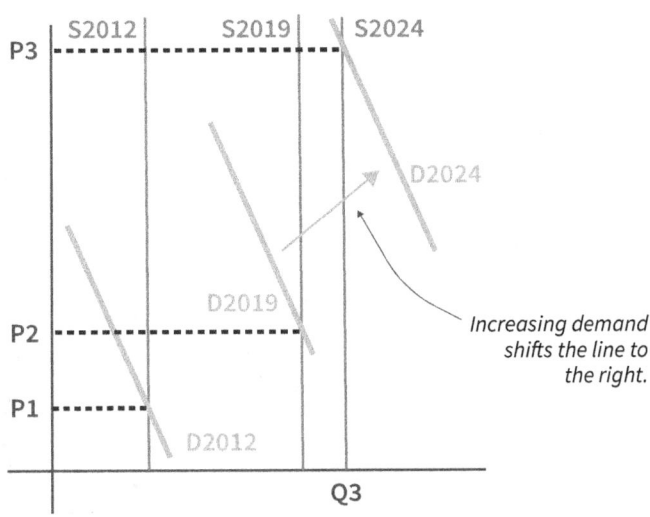

Graph 4.3: Supply vs Demand of bitcoin

Graph 4.3 explains various stages of supply and demand for bitcoin, five years apart. As the amount is fixed and does not react to the changes in demand, any changes to D would shift the market equilibrium dynamically to a new point. The vertical supply curves S2012, S2019 and S2024 demonstrates quantities for bitcoin in 2012, 2019 and 2024 respectively.[6][7] D2012 is the market demand for 2012 when the price of bitcoin was P1. By 2019, the demand has increased, which is demonstrated by D2019. Due to higher demand, the price has risen to P2. By 2024, let's assume there will be more bitcoin users, as a result, the demand will shift rightwards to D2024. This would result in the price increasing to P3. Note that the gap between the three demand lines is equal, i.e., the increase in demand between D2012 and D2019 is almost identical to that of D2019 and D2024.

Let's look at it from a different perspective. Let's assume that the demand for bitcoin in 2012 was 1,000,000, which means the total number of 'active bitcoin users' were 1 million. The demand has shifted to 2 million users in 2019, however, if the demand increases by a difference of 1 million to 3 million users in 2024, the price drastically jumps to P3, even though the time difference is the same. In the chart below, similar increase in demand would push the price beyond P3.

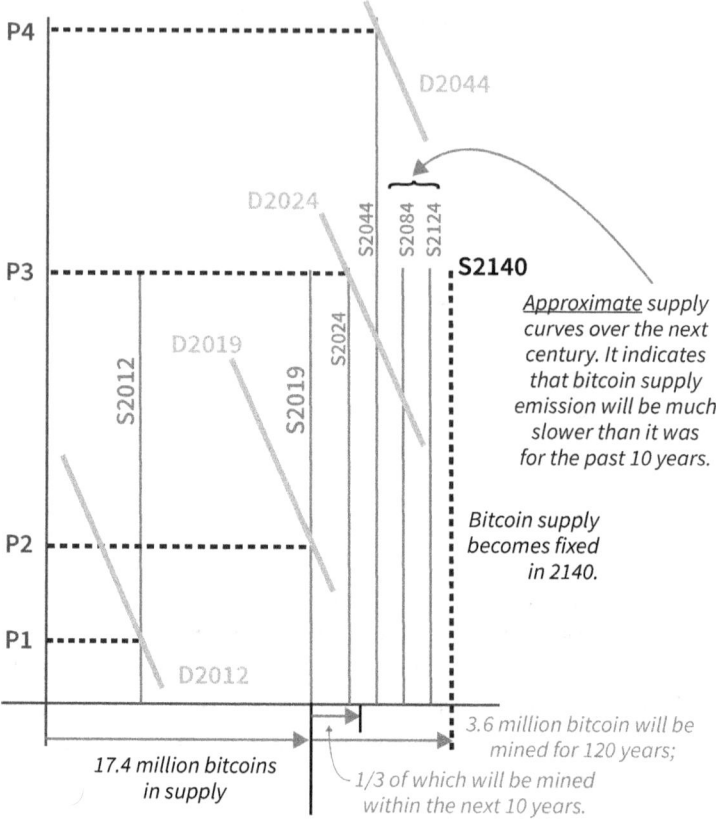

Graph 4.4: Supply vs demand of bitcoin until 2140

According to a research paper published by the University of Cambridge in 2017, the total number of estimated active wallet users are between 2.9 million to 5.8 million.[8] Some analysts forecast that the number of cryptocurrency users will increase over the next few years. If the number of active users increases to 10 million by 2024, the price would be much higher than P3.

The graphs and descriptions also apply to other altcoins with similar diminishing supply curve, such as ether.[9] On the first version of the whitepaper, the founder of Ethereum explained how the supply would gradually slow down and diminish over the next 100 years.[10] Due to this nature of inelastic supply and sudden change of demand, the volatility has been a critical factor in the cryptocurrency market. Based on this very basic theory of economics, analysts have predicted ridiculous targets for the price of bitcoin and ether. Only in this case, their analysis is mathematical and based on the forecast of an expected number of users over the next few years.

Hence if a significant number of crypto adopters move to the market in the next 20 years, which includes developers, users and traders, the price change will be radical and vertical. In comparison to the stock market, certain factors drive prices and demand in a market. Economists believe that the costs of stocks in the financial market depend on factors such as dividend paid to the shareholders, income, competition or forecast of performance.

With the regards to cryptocurrencies, the prices can be dependent on the following factors:
- *Expectations* – Predictions made by industry analysts on the prices of bitcoin and the other altcoins in the market.
- *Development and Scalability* – The development of the platform, better scalability may have positive effects.
- *Regulatory Effects* – Regulations may have a significant effect on the prices. A ban on crypto trading in China had a severe impact on the prices in 2017.[11] Similarly, positive lights from the government institutions can have a positive impact.
- *Competing Financial Markets* – Similar to competing stocks, if stock markets perform better, it would have an impact on the prices in the crypto market. However, if the global financial market hits with a recession and prices of stocks, commodities, cash and cash equivalent fall; bitcoin would be regarded as a better store of value. Therefore, it would drive the prices up due to increased demand.
- *Wealth* – Increase in wealth in different countries may also affect the valuation of the cryptocurrency market.

Where are Cryptocurrencies Traded
Cryptocurrencies can be bought or sold using numerous exchanges around the world. These exchanges are tailored to add cryptocurrencies and use blockchain technology to store user funds securely. Cryptocurrency exchanges are the most profitable business in the blockchain industry. With an average volume of over USD 1 billion and growing, these exchanges are seizing a significant amount of revenue.[12] Various types of exchange offer tailored services to its users. On a typical

cryptocurrency exchange, a user will be required to deposit their funds into the account. If a user wants to make a trade, they will be required to put up a 'sell order' or a 'buy order' for another user to buy or sell it. Users limit their order by placing a reasonable bid. The *median* of the highest bid for a 'buy order' and the lowest bid for a 'sell order' is set as the current price of the cryptocurrency, commonly known as the *mid-market price*.

Let's say the lowest bid for a sell of order of 1 ether is USD 150. Now, if you want to buy 1 ether at a lower price of USD 145, your order will be placed and will show up on the order book among the 'buy orders'. Until the average price goes down to USD 145, your buy order will not be processed. But if you place a 'market order', the system will automatically purchase 1 ether at the lowest bid for sell order on the order book. In many exchanges, you can also set a conditional limit to place an order, for instance, if the prices go down below USD 100, you want to place an order at USD 98.

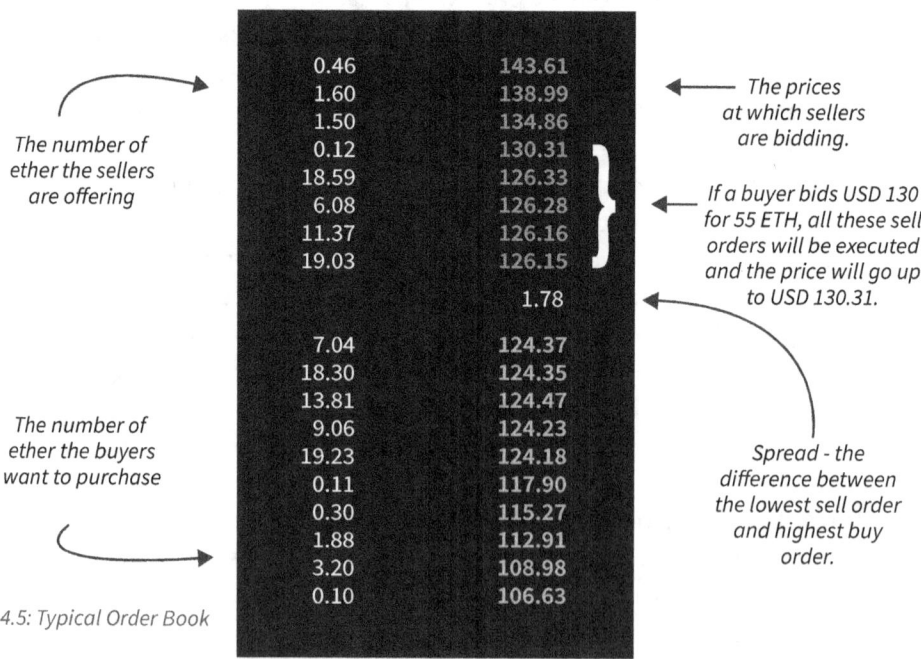

4.5: Typical Order Book

Here's a snapshot of an order book for ETH/USD. The lowest sell order is USD 126.15 for 19.03 ETH, however, other traders have placed a buy order at a lower price of 124.37 and 127.35. Exchanges earn millions of gross profits every month, as the users are charged approximately 0.05% to 0.2% on every trade.¹³ An alternative exchange is Coinbase, where you can buy cryptocurrency directly using a bank card, at a premium. Currently, Coinbase including its sister exchange Coinbase Pro and Binance are two of the most valuable companies in this industry.¹⁴

Users can primarily trade in two types exchanges: centralised or decentralised. Centralised exchanges are faster and have great security mechanisms to ensure user funds are secured. Financial authorities regulate centralised exchanges, and therefore users are required to submit verified IDs or documents to receive and withdraw funds from their account. A decentralised exchange is where the users can trade directly, peer-to-peer from their wallet.

Photo 4.6: A snapshot from the center stage of Ethereum DevCon 4 in Nov 2018/Ethereum Blog/ https://blog.ethereum.org/2018/12/10/devcon4-videos-and-pictures-released/ © 2018, Ethereum.

Volatility is Standard

The volatile nature of the cryptocurrency comes from the term known as 'destabilising speculation'. Every technology goes through phases of *market hype*. Hype is created by speculations of the analysts, investors and industry experts. Economists believe that speculation might have a destabilising effect on the radical fluctuations of price.[15]

Speculation is a key term for any financial market. Due to the nature of blockchain being a new technology, the industry experts and long-term investors have made drastic speculation of the price of bitcoin. As bitcoin has a notable effect on the prices of the entire market, researchers believe that the price movement of the bitcoin in any direction may affect the altcoin market in short-run.[16] Financial analyst Tom Lee, and highly experienced investor Tim Draper have made short and long term speculations on the prices of bitcoin.[17][18] Their thoughts are not arbitrary number generated out of thin air, rather a calculated risk based on the expected 'demand' and the number of users anticipated to be using bitcoin in a given year. Although few speculations are regarded as 'ludicrous', some early bitcoin investors and blockchain analysts have successfully predicted the price of bitcoin in early years of blockchain technology. However, some of these speculations have added up and created a *destabilising effect*. Research conducted in 2014 explains that rapid price movement results from speculations, which has become one of the critical factors for increased volatility and *bubble formation*.[19]

Nevertheless, volatility comes from another factor that blockchain is trying to solve – uncertainty about its existence in the future. Any new technology, whether its augmented reality, artificial intelligence or blockchain, are susceptible to negative feedbacks. Similar to traditional financial markets, if a company or country is hit by bad news or scandal, it is likely to drive the prices down as it increases uncertainty. Geopolitical tension can also affect the market and increase volatility. For instance, the announcement of Brexit had an immediate impact on the price of the British pound. Speculation of uncertainty regarding the future of cryptocurrencies has become the talk of the planet. With an 80% decline in prices, limited knowledge regarding the activity of progress and misuse of cryptocurrencies have resulted in the technology being branded as a 'scam'. All cryptocurrencies like bitcoin have been called scam or fraud due to one of the following reasons:

   i. Due to the nature of its privacy, it has been used to launder money,
   ii. Due to its strong encryption and anonymity, users can hide their assets,
   iii. Banned in certain territories around the world,

iv. No laws or government regulations around the use of cryptocurrencies in some countries,

v. Business influencers have prophesied that the concept will fail.

However, all of these can be counter explained using the following logic:

i) Stopping the use of cryptocurrency will not stop money laundering – this is just another vehicle for criminals. They will invariably find a way to conduct such activities.

ii) Strong encryption is a friend of the public – which is why Apple has become of the largest companies in the world, due to the nature of iPhone's security.

iii) A number of countries previously forbidding cryptocurrencies have devised draft regulation and are slowly allowing trading services to operate legally.

iv) Legal experts around the world are working together to form laws around cryptocurrency – many blockchain tech organisations in the UK have joined forces to draft regulation.[20]

v) All kinds of disruptive technologies have previously been predicted to fail.

Until the technology matures and a significant number of adopters are pushed into the market, the prices are anticipated to be volatile. However, the prices will become increasingly stable as more investors and innovators join the industry. More users will provide researchers with better ideas about how they could improve the technology. Improvement of cryptocurrencies and scalability will require a *substantial* number of users, potentially over hundreds of millions of users, and their continuous feedback, along with a ton of research work from academics, business analysts, financial experts, technologists and developers. Use of the word *substantial* is an understatement.

Are cryptocurrencies like stocks or shares? Not necessarily. The comparison hereabove was to explain, in simpler way, how price dynamics in any financial market works. It is similar to the foreign exchange market. Most of the cryptocurrencies are treated as a currency like the dollar or pound, although deemed as a commodity by certain analysts. Whether or not cryptocurrency is a 'security' can be understood by conducting the Howey Test.[21] According to the theory, crypto will be considered as a security if:

I) If the value is guaranteed to increase over a certain period of time,
II) If the token constitutes any real-world asset, such as a land,
III) If the profit of a company is distributed via the cryptocurrency.

A cryptocurrency can be an asset or security, if the underlying value is determined by the price of a real-world asset, such as a building or an apartment. Financial Conduct Authority (FCA) in the United Kingdom describes that cryptocurrencies are not classified as 'financial instruments' and therefore are not considered to be regulated by the governing laws of the UK and EU.[22] Certain cryptocurrencies can be classified as 'regulated financial instrument' and therefore, are subject to regulations under the laws of the regulatory bodies. Any asset class termed as an 'instrument' are subject to *regulatory approvals* and capable of being financial instruments under MiFID II, 'Markets in Financial Instruments Directive II' under the laws of the European Union. Additionally, Securities and Exchange Commission (SEC) in the US announced in early 2018 that ether or bitcoin are not classified as securities; however, tokens being developed on the Ethereum and other blockchain networks could be classed under regulatory overwatch.[23] In 2017, the chairman of SEC also informed the US Congress that bitcoin is not classified as security and described the cryptocurrencies as *"a replacement for currency that has been determined by most of the people to not be a security"*.[24]

Analysts aim at proposing various factors that define a strong foundation for the success of cryptocurrencies.[25] In the research paper, analysts explained that ease of joining a network to mine cryptocurrencies, having a large and fun community, alongside the factors of privacy and unanimous transfer are few of the elements that define whether the cryptocurrency will be successful. Another comprehensive research on the price dynamics of various top-achieving cryptocurrencies imply that although bitcoin is less volatile in comparison to other currencies, due to its volume and popularity, it may cause collateral damage on all the existing cryptocurrencies.[26] The results of the investigation indicated that the formation of a parabolic curve depicts a bubble; however, the researchers were uncertain about the time-frame for an 'adjusted market'. As of January 2020, the market has adjusted, and due to its domino effect, the prices of almost all the cryptocurrencies have dropped by over 80% from all time high. However, fascinatingly, this situation is a repetition – it happened before, a few times, and the market has somehow managed to recover every single time.

Crypto vs Money

Now that we recognise what money is, it is time we weigh cryptocurrencies with the money we use. Although money has been the principal form of financial settlement for the past few hundred years, it wasn't the only form of settlement in the history. After years of consumer research, economists proposed the formation of a central authority; thus, banks came into existence to regulate global trade. From printed money, after the dot-com revolution, we moved towards an electronic form of payment. Numerous banks in the UK do not even have a single high-street store. Everything is online.

Cryptocurrencies are the next evolution of money – an electronic form of payment that provides several benefits in comparison to fiat. Following are the primary:

Ownership – Paper money belongs to the government. It does not belong to you. Cryptocurrency belongs to the user who purchases it. Every money issued to the public is owned by the central government that issued the currency. For instance, dollar belongs to the central government of the United States and controlled by the Federal Reserve. However, cryptocurrency entirely belongs to its owner. It does not belong to any institution, organisation or entity.

Fast Settlement – Money takes time to settle. Regionally it may take a couple of hours, however, in an international transaction, it might take up to seven days. Cryptocurrencies are much faster as it is technology-dependent. There is no print version of cryptocurrency, and they are dependent on incredibly refined and sophisticated lines of codes that allow cryptocurrencies to be transferred to any part of the world in a matter of seconds.

Minimum Fees on Global Market – Sending money abroad has various limitations – users are required to go through third-party organisations to send money, and it's expensive. Especially, in the third-world countries, global transfer is tough where there are tall walls of limitation set by their governments. Furthermore, it is believed that approximately

1.7 billion adults around the world are still unbanked.[27] These people will be extremely benefitted by these services. Cryptocurrencies have a transaction cost, although, in correlation to the cost and hassle of sending money aboard, it's nothing.

No Geographic Limitation – Money is restricted to the government issuing it. However, there is no geographic limitation for a cryptocurrency. A bitcoin or ether can be transferred and traded anywhere. Although, there are and will be regulations imposed whether cryptocurrencies can be traded in a country or not.

Privacy – To send money, we are compelled to either trust a third-party or a bank. One of the most significant advantages of cryptocurrencies is privacy, that is it's private and anonymous. Unlike credit cards, cryptocurrencies do not share any *line of credit*; only encrypted 'keys' which allows the network to validate the information. Cryptocurrencies can be sent and received by anyone around the world without revealing any information to a money transfer company – because you only need to trust the blockchain network to do its work and verify the person you are sending money to.

No Counterfeit – Money can be forged as it can be printed. Since there is a print version, there can be a counterfeit. There may be many versions of Bitcoin or Ethereum, e.g. Ethereum classic or Bitcoin Cash, but there can only be one Ethereum or one Bitcoin network, and it is not possible to create a counterfeit version of their cryptocurrencies.

Before we discuss the financial dynamics of the blockchain world, we will look into the details of smart contracts on the Ethereum blockchain. Ethereum blockchain uses smart contracts to send and receive cryptocurrencies within its network. But what does a smart contract look like? We will look into the details of various aspects of the code. Besides, traders haven't stopped. Binance, the current leading exchange, exceeded trading volume of USD 20.8 billion during Nov-Dec 2018.[28] We will discuss financial and business aspects, and try to understand why financial experts are making big bets on blockchain networks.

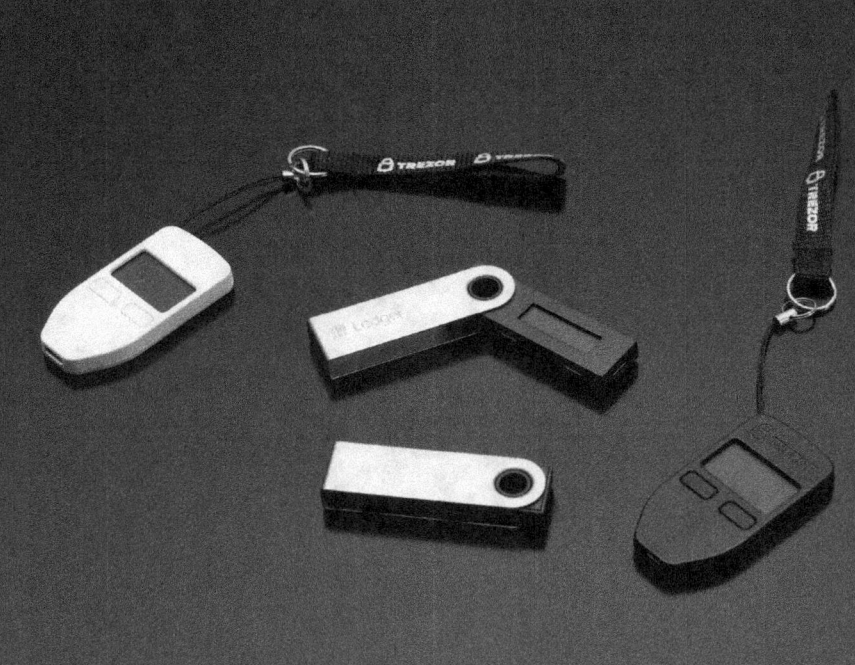

Photo 4.7: Trezor wallet (left and right) and Ledger hardware wallet in the middle. /by Jaro Larnos/licensed under CC by 2.0
© 2017 Jaro Larnos, some rights reserved.

DID YOU KNOW?

There are two primary types of crypto wallet. Hot wallets are online and can be obtained using online sites almost instantly. Cold wallets stay offline, which are typically referred to as hardware wallet. These wallets stay offline and are much safer in terms of storing cryptocurrencies for a long term.

BLOCK 5

BLOCKCHAIN: BEYOND THE SPECULATION OF CRYPTOS

BLOCK INFORMATION

TX# 0x501	SMART CONTRACTS	79
TX# 0x502	HOW DOES SMART CONTRACTS WORK	80
TX# 0x503	ENFORCEABILITY AND AUTOMATION	88
TX# 0x504	COMPETING SMART CONTRACT BASED BLOCKCHAIN	90
TX# 0x505	LARGE ENTERPRISES & SMART CONTRACTS	92

TECHNOLOGY BLOCK

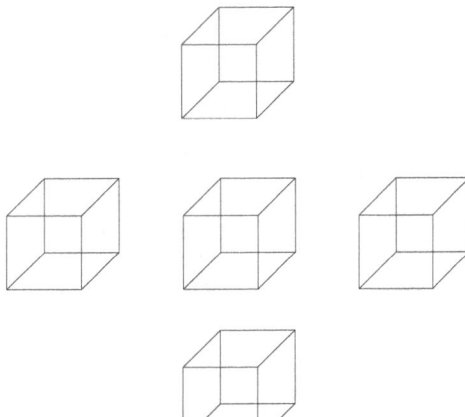

BLOCK 5

BLOCKCHAIN: BEYOND THE SPECULATION OF CRYPTOS

Smart Contracts
Smart contracts are composed of a strict set of functions and variables, that executes a function between two or more users. A simple smart contract may be executed between two, three or four users. However, there may be more complex contracts that would comprise of many more users.

In 1996, Nick Szabo proposed the concept of smart contracts.[1] He demonstrated that a typical smart contract would not require human-intervention and be designed in a way which functions on a peer-to-peer (p2p) basis. A contract may consist of contractual clause and can also be designed to work with application or software so that it is difficult for any parties to breach any terms set aside in it.

The concept has radically transformed over the past few years and practically re-invented in such a way that it now works to execute terms of services defined between two or more parties. Using a set of parameters defined by parties on both sides of a contract, a *smart contract* can automatically enforce rules without the need of a third-party. These contracts are capable of sending or receiving digital currencies, storing encrypted information, keeping money held in an escrow on a *time-bound* frame, send or receive information and also track items as well as assets. A smart contract can be applied to:

  i. Send or receive digital currencies built on blockchain – e.g. tokens of Ethereum network.
  ii. Create a digital legal contract between two parties – e.g. a buyer and a seller.
  iii. Store confidential information – e.g. a passport or an identity card.
  iv. Securely hold currencies in escrow – e.g. money to be paid to a supplier.

v. Raise funds without having to go through traditional methods – e.g. ICO.

vi. To transfer digital assets between two parties, send or receive network-based cryptocurrencies, i.e. tokens on the Ethereum blockchain.

How Does Smart-Contracts Work

Ethereum has transformed the definition of a smart contract and how it can be executed across multiple verticals. Ethereum can be used to explain various layers of a smart contract. A typical smart contract on this network consists of:

- Two or more users
- Their addresses
- The message, or the currency
- Transfer value
- Field of data input

A user interacts with a smart contract by using a *client-side interface* such as MyEtherWallet.[2] Every user is identified on the blockchain using their wallet address, e.g. 0x7A6c6C55205337bE5F51801c97Fc22BD9Aa8B588.[3] Once a user inputs all the variables, such as address, the value of transfer, the currency to transfer or the data to be provided with the contract, it is sent to the blockchain. After the network verifies the information, it is assigned with a unique address known as the *transaction hash*. The wallet address defines a user on the blockchain, while the *transaction hash* is the proof of the deployed contract or transaction.

Explaining The Code

Users are also capable of creating smart contracts to be executed between two parties. A smart-contract code is developed using a high-level language known as Solidity.[4] Once a user inputs the data, a compiler is used to compile the code and thus sent to the blockchain once it returns no error. Similar to the transactions on the blockchain, a contract is also assigned with a *transaction hash*, which acts as a proof of deployment or proof of receipt.

The Ethereum developers have defined a specific set of rules, known as 'ERC standards' for the smart contract developers to follow.[5] Although these standards make the platform more stable, it is still at an early stage of development and not risk-free. Despite the bugs and risks, Ethereum is still the most substantial and widely used platform for DApp development.

> **DID YOU KNOW?**
>
> *Vyper is a Python based, contract-oriented programming language to write smart contracts for Ethereum. The languages has three principles, security, simplicity and auditability.*[6]

This section is a slightly technical, however, the components of the code are split into different sections for greater understanding. Using a standard Ethereum-based 'payroll' contract, the functionality of the smart contract is explained here.

A smart contract is a digital contract, in which a set of conditions can be coded and when those conditions are fulfilled, the functions are executed. An everyday use case would be formulating automatable payment contracts. In this contract explained below, let's assume that an employer is paying three of his or her employees.

Pre-conditions
Transfer of money requires a set of pre-conditions which must be set up so that the contract can be error free. These are:

1. Declaring the wallet address of the employees – where the fund would be sent
2. Function to make the payments,
3. Functions to withdraw,
4. Allowance – how many times are they allowed to withdraw,
5. Distribution – declaring how much each employee would receive.
Pre-conditions are fulfilled by a specific set of functions and loops in the contract.

Important Keywords

Uint: Unsigned integer. This is a declaration for a variable which stores a value, an integer. An integer is a whole number, that can be negative, positive or zero. It cannot be a fraction, such 1 3/4.

Msg.value: This calls the values which are given as inputs manually. It would usually ask a user to put a specific value, for instance, 5 ether.

Bool: The bool keyword is an alias of the Boolean system. It is used to declare variables to store the Boolean values, e.g. true and false.

Employees.length: This is a command for an *array*. In a programming language, array is a *container* that holds value, a list of names for example. The array of this contract holds employee wallet addresses, and 'employees.length' defines how many addresses the array is holding.

Msg .sender: This calls for the wallet address of the employees receiving the payment.

Msg.sender.transfer(amount): This initiates the transfer to the wallet address of the employee.

Contract

We are going to use the following contract for explanation.

```
//code starts here

pragma solidity 0.4.11;

contract payroll{

address[ ] employees =[
0x3dfDE0f73456013442f1cFe34753E45f8AbC2771,
    0x07E39a44eA0A0b19fbeA16534e705Af7DabD45DE,
        0x3aE8A0b53C3327BA0F4b1-
Fea8dbc177E1cF81E55];

uint totalreceived = 0;
mapping(address => uint) withdrawnAmounts;

function payroll() payable{
```

```
    updateTotalReceived();
}

function() payable{
    updateTotalReceived();
}

function updateTotalReceived() internal{
    totalreceived += msg.value;
}

modifier canWithdraw(){


    bool contains=false;

    for(uint i=0 ;i < employees.length; i++)
    {
        if (employees[i]== msg.sender){
            contains = true;
        }
    }
    require(contains);
    _;
}

function withdraw() canWithdraw {

        uint amountAllocated= totalreceived/employees.length;
        uint amountWithdrawn= withdrawnAmounts[msg.sender];
        uint amount= amountAllocated - amountWithdrawn;
        withdrawnAmounts[msg.sender] = amountWithdrawn +amount;

        if (amount>0){

            msg.sender.transfer(amount);

        }
    }
}
//code ends here
```

Description

The 'pragma solidity' keyword is used to enable features of the compiler. It is more like a version declaration where each latest version has the latest features which can help execute functions inside the code.

This code is compiled using the version `0.4.11`. In solidity, the codes are usually backwards compatible. The language, however, is upgraded frequently. If you are to work with an open-sourced code, it should be compiled using the version it was compiled before.

```
pragma solidity 0.4.11;
```

The following line of code is the name of the 'contract'. All the functions and the variables required for the contract are written inside these parentheses:

```
contract payroll{
```

State Variables: In this contract, the addresses of the employees are declared beforehand. It is similar to how we use bank account details to send money to someone. Here, you can see that three addresses which are meant to receive the payment. The wallet addresses are stored in an array, which is defined within the parentheses '[ ]'. Storing the wallet addresses in an array helps the contract retain the addresses efficiently. The employees possessing these wallet addresses can withdraw their payment from this contract.

```
address[ ] employees =[
0x3dfDE0f73456013442f1cFe34753E45f8AbC2771,
0x07E39a44eA0A0b19fbeA16534e705Af7DabD45DE,
0x3aE8A0b53C3327BA0F4b1Fea8dbc177E1cF81E55
];
uint totalreceived = 0;
mapping(address => uint) withdrawnAmounts;
```

As this is a payroll contract, the employer has to deposit currencies inside this contract which would be withdrawn by the employees. Initially the amount is declared to be zero and in another function 'updateTotalReceived()', the amount is incremented according to the amount received.

```
uint totalreceived = 0;
```

'uint' is used to declare the values inside the 'totalreceived' variable. The value is usually in 'Wei', the smallest unit of ether.

Mapping: Mapping is used as a dictionary here to store the information of the accounts. Now, if the employees withdraw their payment, the amount they have withdrawn gets saved to the 'withdrawnAmounts'. When the contract calls this variable, it checks whether the address has a certain amount stored in it.

```
mapping(address => uint) withdrawnAmounts;
```

Constructor Function: This is a constructor function. This function is called when the contract is created. This is usually the same name as the 'contract name'. The 'payable{}' keyword enables the owner of those wallet addresses to withdraw their payment.

```
function payroll() payable{
updateTotalReceived();
}
```

Fallback Function: This function enables employers to pay money to this contract. Hence, whenever the employer puts money to this contract, this function is called. Since this function requires payment from an outside source, there is a 'payable' keyword attached so that it can accept money. Inside this particular function, the updateTotalReceived calls the next function which updates TotalReceived amount in the contract.

```
function() payable{
updateTotalReceived();
}
```

Even though both the functions look the same, the constructor function() payable initiates the contract, and it is called only at the beginning. The fallback function is called whenever an amount is deposited to the contract.

```
function updateTotalReceived() internal{
totalreceived += msg.value; }
```

'msg.value;' defines the value or the 'amount' that can be deposited. If this contract is accessed using a front-end, such as a website or a DApp, it will allow the employer to enter a specific value. Once the money is sent to the contract, the 'totalreceived' value is updated. The keyword 'internal{}' limits the access to only the person who owns and deployed the contract, as such the contents inside cannot be accessed. A public function would allow others to see the value stored in the contract.

Modifier Function: Modifier function adds more conditions to 'canWithdraw()' function. Here, the function modifier is used to verify whether one of those three employees are withdrawing from the contract or not. Here, 'employees.length;' obtains the total number of addresses in the *state variables*. As there are only three addresses, when an employee attempts to withdraw, the function goes back in loop three times to validate the withdrawal attempt. If the address matches or checks 'contains = true;', the modifier shows a green flag and allows the employee to proceed. Typically, a modifier is used in smart contracts to check if certain conditions are met before executing the rest of the code in a function. The symbol _; is used to continue executing the rest of the contract.

```
modifier canWithdraw(){
bool contains=false;
for(uint i=0 ;i < employees.length; i++)
 {
 if (employees[i]== msg.sender){
       contains = true; }
 }
require(contains);
_; }
```

Withdraw Function: This function enables the withdrawal process based on 'uint amountAllocated'.

```
function withdraw() canWithdraw {
    uint amountAllocated= totalreceived/employees.length;
    uint amountWithdrawn= withdrawnAmounts[msg.sender];
    uint amount= amountAllocated - amountWithdrawn;
    withdrawnAmounts[msg.sender] = amountWithdrawn +amount;
    if (amount>0){

        msg.sender.transfer(amount); }
```

The function will process the payment using 'msg.sender.transfer (amount);' as long as the employee requests for any 'amount>0'.

```
uint amountAllocated= totalreceived/employees.length;
```

This defines the 'amountAllocated'. For this contract, three employees are supposed to obtain equal amount of pay. This function can be changed and set based on the complexity of a project.

```
uint amountWithdrawn= withdrawnAmounts[msg.sender];
```

The contract is required to have an option to check whether the person requesting the payment has already withdrawn any money before. The total amount of money withdrawn by each employee is saved in 'amountWithdrawn' variable.

```
withdrawnAmounts[msg.sender] =amountWithdrawn +amount;
```

It updates the 'withdrawnAmounts' variable for future verification. When the contract is called again, and the same employee asks for pay more than once, this determines the request and stops that employee from withdrawing the money.

Interacting with the Contract
Any user can connect to the Ethereum blockchain, write and deploy these type of contracts using open-sourced solidity compiler known as 'Remix Solidity'. All you need a small amount of money in form of ether and the 'MetaMask' browser extension. Hundreds of public GitHub respositories are available for you learn about Solidity and smart contract development.

This is a straightforward and easy contract in comparison to other complex ones such as the contract for an ERC20 or ERC721 token. There are hundreds of different functions that make a smart contract enforceable and automatable without the requirement of any third-party monitoring the transactions. The captivating part is that Solidity is a collaborative open-sourced language, and therefore you can learn all about it from the internet for free.

The contract defines the backend of a system. Although it is possible to interact with this payroll contract using *Remix*, a more advanced code will require an application to index the information on the blockchain, and a frontend interface, such as a web page or a mobile app to use the functions. Learning JavaScript is very helpful for beginners, as you can build simple apps in JS using React Native.[7] Using advanced functions, you can write contracts that will send payments to your suppliers based on milestones, time or other variables declared in the contract. A contract can also allow more than one party to set the desired function. For example, if you are drafting an employer-freelancer *legal contract* along with the option for payments, then both parties will be required to set functions from each side. Furthermore, it is also possible to create reward-based games just by using simple codes.

Enforceability and Automation
Even though smart contracts can trigger automatic function set by multiple parties, there might arise a dispute between two parties if the conditions are not met. For example, a contract between a company and its supplier were enforced using a smart contract. The supplier was paid using that contract automatically. However, the company was not pleased with the overall quality of service after delivery. In these circumstances, there may be human intervention expected to solve the dispute between two parties. The overall idea of decentralisation is to

provide authority to the members of the community, instead of a centralised authority trying to resolve a dispute. However, the circumstances may vary based on the type of platform and where the contract was enforced. Smart contracts are very efficient when used as a form of binding contract between two or more parties to enforce an agreement. Researchers from UCL and Barclays describes smart contracts as an 'automatable and enforceable agreement', which may require human input or control to some extent.[8] With regards to enforceability, they believe that it might be achieved employing two methods, traditional and non-traditional.[9]

Traditional – A traditional method of enforceability would follow binding or non-binding arbitration, and therefore be controlled using the existing jurisdiction of a certain territory. In case of illegal acts, local courts would have the authority to penalise the users. In case of civil litigation, a judge would be able to decide the degree of performance - whether the smart contract was lawfully enforced and rewarded the parties appropriately based on the shreds of evidence. For disputes relating to contracts, the courts have extensive experience of adjudicating on issues of contract wrong-performance or non-performance, of awarding damages or other reliefs as appropriate, and in some cases assist in the enforcement of payment of damages.

Non-traditional – This method would be scripted in the smart contract thus making it automatically enforceable. Smart contracts could be used to make jury selection, making the process transparent and allowing experienced members of the public to join the dispute resolution.

The mining process on a 'permissionless' blockchain network is an ideal example of a fully tamperproof smart contract enforcement. In terms of the current and previous miners on the Ethereum network, technological enforcement cannot fail regardless of malicious acts, network disruption or natural events. The miners would receive exactly what they have contributed. It is possible to enforce dispute resolution and fully automate the process, however, non-traditional methods would require human intervention in many cases. More importantly, some products and service-based marketplaces would also require a system for the users on both end to be able to raise and defend a claim. Suppose, a freelancer named Sophia designed software for her client Amanda.

Amanda was happy for the first few days with the service, although later, she ended up discovering bugs and needed to adjust the code. Since the software developer was paid as soon as the product was delivered, Amanda raises a dispute to solve this issue. This is exactly where tokenised ecosystem would be astonishingly robust. But how?

The token holders of an ecosystem or a DApp can be provided with voting rights and authority in giving their opinion towards an issue.[10][11] This is a digital form of a 'jury' in traditional courts. In case of a dispute resolution, a tribunal can be formed with the users in an ecosystem who stakes the *ecosystem token* to earn the rights. The members of the 'Tribunal of Token Stakers' would be able to process the complaints and reward the party who deserves the chance. Although this requires human intervention, the overall method follows the ideals of decentralisation and thus providing the power to the community to express their opinion. Additionally, most of the process in this method is automated, and therefore the process of the resolution is hardcoded into the smart contracts. This aims to reduce the authority of centralised power.

Competing Smart Contract based Blockchain

After the bitcoin network went live, developers started to create different types of DLTs that support smart contracts. Ethereum and NEO are being two of the platforms, and currently are more popular among developers for building decentralised applications. There are different multiple other platforms which are currently live.

Neo

NEO is similar to the Ethereum and branded as the 'Chinese Ethereum'. While Ethereum focuses on building a platform for 'unstoppable applications' on the blockchain, NEO's focus is on developing the demands of the future 'Smart Economy', that would feature digitisation of assets and objects. Analysts believe that NEO's focus is towards developing a smart digital economy that would be regulatory compliant.[12] While Ethereum is also capable of tracking and storing digital assets on the chain, some interesting DApps are being developed on NEO. Blockchain engineer Nitish Singh explains that NEO smart contracts-based platform allows developers to build an application without the need of learning a new high-level language similar to Solidity.[13] Applications that are currently being built on NEO blockchain focuses on artificial intelligence, identification, e-commerce and media.

NEO also aims to issue digital identities and secure them using the blockchain. NEO's theory of smart economy means collaboration of digital assets, digital identity, and smart contracts to maintain them. Assets can be easily digitised on NEO's platform. If you grew up playing with Pokémon trading card, and you have a couple lying inside your drawers, then they could hold a specific value once digitised. Digital identity would ensure guaranteed authenticity.

Stratis
The Stratis blockchain aims to develop C# blockchain applications on .NET framework. It is similar to Bitcoin but with many advanced features. Stratis was founded in the United Kingdom in June 2016. The developer launched an ICO which raised nearly USD 600,000. The main difference between Stratis and Ethereum lies in the programming language. While Ethereum is created using Solidity, Stratis is created using C#. It has been claimed that Stratis can handle 20,000 requests per second, while Ethereum does somewhere between 8 and 15.[14] Similar to Ethereum, private blockchains can be created on this platform which provides privacy. Stratis is still in early stages of development and expected to gradually move forward in the years to come.

Lisk
Lisk is a sidechain development platform where developers can build DApps using JavaScript.[15] Once it is live, the users could hold their own ICOs based on their currency. Usually, the developers working to create Apps for a centralised platform do not make as much profit as the actual company could potentially earn. Lisk aims to create a platform for the developers where they would receive a fair share for their contribution. Lisk uses *sidechains* for the developers to create DApps. Sidechains are independent ledgers that link to the main chain without creating performance issues to the main chain. It allows developers access to algorithm customisation and asset tracking. The team behind Lisk created a JavaScript-based software developers kit (SDK) which focuses on supporting the developers.[16] Lisk allows developers to focus on the utility of the DApp without creating a new blockchain.

Chainlink

Chainlink is a secure *Oracle* network that is fully decentralised and allows connectivity between smart contracts and external (off-chain) resources. Chainlink was launched in June 2017 with the aim to connect smart contracts in blockchains to access off-chain resources like data feeds, web APIs and bank account payments. Typically on http, 'Oracles' are defined as 'agents' which verify real-world occurrences and sends information to the smart contracts. Smart contracts inside a blockchain cannot access data from outside. Here, oracles form a bridge between the outside and inside of the chain so that data can pass through. Let's assume that a smart contract requires viewing a bank statement in order to execute a specific function. Oracles provide these data to the smart contract. Since oracles are usually third-party services with a centralised point, data passed through them might prove to be wrong or untrustworthy. It would risk the execution of unwanted functions, and the contract could be misused.[17]

Chainlink solves this issue by creating a decentralised oracle network for smart contracts to deal with external data or resources securely. The network has on-chain and off-chain nodes. The off-chain nodes consist of *oracle nodes* which yield responses to off-chain resources. Such a decentralised system could prevent any tampering with the external data and ensures efficient executions on-chain.[18]

Large Enterprises & Smart Contracts

Hyperledger Fabric

Linux Foundation has played a crucial role in advancing various frameworks for blockchain technology. Hyperledger project was founded in 2015 by the Linux Foundation to advance cross-industry use of blockchain technology, encourage smart-contract development and strengthen collaborative efforts between tech enterprises and blockchain companies.[19] Hyperledger Fabric, one of the projects within Hyperledger is a permissioned blockchain framework. IBM blockchain has been built using Hyperledger Fabric.[20] Many public blockchain network cannot support private and confidential contracts. Fabric offers the ability to create channels within the blockchain for a separate ledger for transactions. For instance, a hospital would prefer storing confidential patient data on the blockchain. A public blockchain would allow everyone in the world to access the data of each other, which isn't ideal to store strictly confidential data.

This type of 'visibility' could bring losses to both the supplier and the customer. The Hyperledger Fabric was created to address this issue. Consequently, privacy is one of the priority of this type of blockchain network. Hyperledger Fabric retains the privacy among the concerned parties without passing everything through a central authority.

David Gorman, Blockchain Engagement, IBM, during IBM startup workshops during the opening day of Web Summit 2018 at the Altice Arena in Lisbon, Portugal.

Photo 5.1: 6 November 2018; David Gorman, Blockchain Engagement, IBM/by Sam Barnes/ Web Summit via Sportsfile/licensed under CC by 2.0 Copyright © 2018 Web Summit. Some rights reserved.

Researchers at Tel-Aviv University and MIT Media Lab proposed a solution for blockchain based data access control.[21] In their paper, the researchers demonstrated how blockchain could be utilised to provide full control to the users on the network. Hyperledger has features that allow users to control their information in a similar way, and are beneficial to certain industries. Hyperledger has other blockchain frameworks, including Hyperledger burrow, a type of blockchain explicitly built to the specifications of Ethereum Virtual Machine (EVM).[22]

Quorum
With all the controversy surrounding JPMorgan's position on blockchain, many cannot comprehend why the company was working on their version of blockchain in the background.[23] JPMorgan has already developed their version of the blockchain, in fact, their blockchain is an Ethereum spin-off. The only difference is that the blockchain is not tokenised and it is a permissioned blockchain – JPMorgan in control of the data contained within the network. Quorum is purportedly a smart contract-based enterprise version of Ethereum. JPMorgan claims that the reason for creating Quorum is to provide trust between users without the reliance of an external authority and enforces law using smart contracts.[24] Although private, the development is still open-sourced. Therefore, community contributors around the world can keep up with the updates and also contribute to the development of the blockchain.[24]

As a private and permissioned blockchain, Quorum is a layer on Ethereum blockchain that allow the blockchain to perform transactions using a different consensus algorithm to that of Ethereum.[26] The key advantages of this private network are privacy, and alternative consensus, which replaces existing PoW/PoS consensus mechanism. Based on a high-level design, Quorum's components consist of the Quorum Node which is a fork or spin-off version of the 'Geth' or Go-Ethereum, a transaction manager and an enclave. In this blockchain, proof-of-work is replaced with Quorum Chain, a vote-based consensus. It is designed in a way so that only nodes that are allowed in the network are permitted to create connections to/from a user. Additionally, the transaction cost does not exist in the network.

Although the technology, being developed on the foundation of the Ethereum blockchain, it has been claimed as a scientific experiment, and also that it could have enormous impact on the current banking system.[27] JPMorgan believes that if the idea is implemented successfully, their blockchain could help reduce the time-frame for processing transactions in banks from weeks to hours. In a September 2018 press release, JPMorgan announced their expansion of Interbank Information Network, where more than 75 banks have already signed up.[28] This technological innovation was formerly led by Patrick and Amber, who have made a significant contribution to the development of privacy-focused cryptocurrency ZCash. These blockchain pioneers have recently been featured for the promotion of *"Hidden in plain sight"*, an event in public where they thoroughly destroyed the upgraded code for ZCash using propane and blow torch, due to its nature of sensitivity.[29]

MasterCard Blockchain
Mastercard has recently been involved in developing its own blockchain, however, the company's focus seems to be 'patent-it-all'. MasterCard patented a method to partition a blockchain so that it can store multiple transaction types and formats.[31] MasterCard's new system aims to expand the utility of the blockchain by allowing blocks to receive data from *subnets*. These subnets are the *partitions*. The traditional system of a blockchain interaction includes accessing both 'permissioned' and 'permissionless' parts of the blockchain. The issue here is that any company will have to run multiple blockchains for different purposes and sizes of data. The company also cannot observe transactions in a permissioned blockchain like it would do so in an open one. The patent holders of MasterCard claims that partitioned blockchain can bypass such limitations and provide 'enhanced uses of permissions'. It is likely that the company will integrate blockchain-based hybrid payment methods for cross-border payments.[32]

SAP Leonardo
SAP, German multinational software corporation has recently relaunched their platform known as "SAP Leonardo", a platform that will enable its customers to tap into emerging technologies such as blockchain.[33] Primarily built for the purposes of IoT, SAP now offers products that will enable users to deploy DApp developed on a decentralised architecture in the cloud. Apart from "Blockchain As A Service", SAP offers integration of other advanced technologies e.g. machine learning, big data and data intelligence.[34]

DID YOU KNOW?
Volvo Cars is using private blockchain built by Oracle to trace cobalt used in their electric batteries.[30]

Photo: US Dept. of Energy/flickr

MYTH: *"Institutional investors do not believe in cryptocurrencies."*

FACT 1: Investment firm **NXMH** owns **80%** stake at one of largest crypto exchanges **BitStamp**

NXMH closed the deal on 25 Oct. 2018, as Bitstamp was acquired in an all cash deal at a valuation of USD 60million.[35]

FACT 2: Goldman Sachs backed **Circle** acquired **Poloniex** for USD 400 million in 2018.[36]

BLOCK 6

ETHEREUM STANDARDS AND DAPPS

BLOCK INFORMATION

TX# 0x601	WHY ETHEREUM?	89
TX# 0x602	ETHEREUM IMPROVEMENT PROPOSALS	89
TX# 0x603	DECENTRALISED APPLICATION	94
TX# 0x604	DAPP STRUCTURE	96
TX# 0x605	DECENTRALISATION AND ITS PRINCIPLES	97

TECHNOLOGY BLOCK

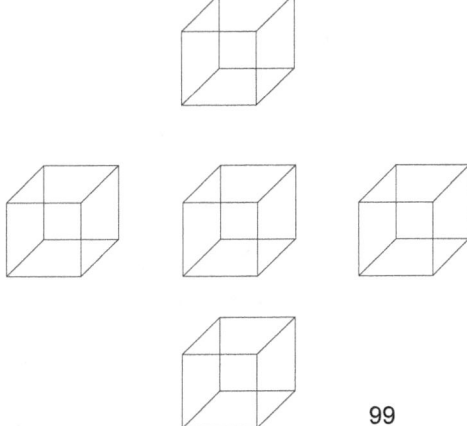

BLOCK 6

ETHEREUM STANDARDS AND DAPPS

Why Ethereum?
While there are other excellent blockchain platforms, Ethereum is the most popular in terms of the number of DApps being developed. Ethereum is also the platform which started the smart contract revolution. It is the gold standard in the world of running a decentralised institution, where the foundation work alongside the community to develop the platform. The ERC standards have made Ethereum more popular and safer platform. Ethereum has altered the way how enterprises work and embedded the concept of decentralisation by involving an enormous community in the development process, and allowing the community to contribute, propose development structures.

Ethereum Request for Comments or ERCs are technical standard imposed for the purpose of token implementation. An Ethereum developer must stick to these rules and add the required boundaries to the token contract based on the ERC standards. 'Standards' here primarily refer to particular *functions* and keywords in the code which must be written on a specific contract.[1]

Ethereum Improvement Proposals
The Ethereum community has a process known as the EIP - Ethereum Improvement Proposal.[2] Developers around the world submit various ERC standard policies through EIP. The community, later on, reviews these policies and comment on them. If the community finds the policies eligible, they later finalise it, and the developers implement it. If not, then the developers may be asked to revise the proposals, or they may be rejected. The proposals can be set as 'Draft'. 'Accepted', 'Final', 'Active', 'Deferred' or 'Superseded'. Therefore, EIP is the proposal given by developers, and after the community make decision over a particular proposal, it becomes an ERC standard.[3]

Ethereum Request for Comments (ERC)

After Ethereum was created in 2015, many independent developers started to develop their own cryptocurrencies based on Ethereum blockchain. As monetary transactions are involved in the blockchain, the community decided to impose some standards to reduce scams and increase compatibility. ERC standards are created to maintain compatibility with different tokens or cryptocurrencies so that the network can be governed, maintained, and transactions can be completed smoothly. Until now several ERC standards have been set. A complete list can be found on the EIP website.[4] The key ones are highlighted here.

ERC20 - ERC20 is the most popular standard, and almost all network tokens have been created based on this standard. The '20' suffix refers to its unique proposal ID. The 'standards' are the functions which must be present inside a token smart contract. ERC20 is defined as a token – an alternative to any other currency. Similar to ether, it has characteristics such as the amount of supply, compatibility with exchanges, tradeability, traceability and so on. This is standard for a digital currency within the DApps built on the Ethereum network. The protocols surrounding ERC20 standard assist in maintaining rules to trace, store, secure and improve transfer efficiency.[5]

An ERC20 standard makes any token created on the Ethereum blockchain transferable and capable of trading.[6] Before this standard was set, there was no specific rule about how a token contract should look like or which functions are necessary for the code to work. In many cases, DApps which were made for a specific token, turned out to be incompatible with other tokens. Therefore, ERC provided interoperability, consenting developers to integrate any ERC20 tokens into almost any DApp built on the Ethereum network. The most significant proposal of ERC20 was to create a fungible token (i.e. single unit of that token is equal to another unit). The following code contains the functions which follow the ERC20 standards. ERC20 is what made 'token' a *currency*.

```
//ERC Token Standard #20 Interface
//https://github.com/ethereum/EIPs/blob/mas-
ter/EIPS/eip-20-token-standard.md
```

```
contract ERC20Interface {
    function totalSupply() public view returns (uint);
    function balanceOf(address tokenOwner) public returns (uint balance);
    function allowance(address tokenOwner, address spender) public returns (uint256 remaining);
    function transfer(address to, uint tokens) public returns (bool success);
    function approve(address spender, uint256 tokens) public returns (bool success);
    function transferFrom(address from, address to, uint256 tokens) public returns (bool success);
    event Transfer(address indexed from, address indexed to, uint tokens);
    event Approval(address indexed owner, address indexed spender, uint256 tokens);
}
```

ERC721 - Ethereum changed the course of history when ERC721 was implemented. In economics, 'fungibility' means interchangeability of any goods. Fungible tokens are the usual ERC20 tokens, such as Civic, Waves, Status and so on. However, non-fungible tokens can be compared to an asset which has a specific value, a value that may come from either a tangible or non-tangible asset. A tangible asset is a physical, such as a piece of land, and non-tangible assets aren't physical but holds an intrinsic value, similar to a university certificate. Collectables like coins, stamps, cars, figures etc. which hold a specific value but are not currencies itself, can also be compared to non-fungible tokens.

Let's say you are an avid online gamer. You receive rewards for completing a mission. However, the coins earned are limited to the boundaries of the game. Imagine, what if you could bring those out of your game and exchange it with something like money?

ERC721 is a standard for non-fungible tokens. The first viral use case was 'CryptoKitties', a game based on such standard. In this game, users can buy, sell, create and breed kitten characters. After its launch in November 2017, the player spent millions of US dollars' worth of ethers.[7] Players buy digital kittens at a low rate and later breed, and can sell them at a higher price. This is a live implementation of ERC721 standard. Users can sell these non-fungible virtual kitties and prove ownership by storing them on an Ethereum wallet. Although it sounds weird for people to spend thousands on a kitten, it projects the idea of how people in real life buy and sell artefacts or rare-collectables. This game has provided the foundation for how ERC721 can be used and implemented across multiple verticals to create non-financial and financial use cases, to transfer high-value assets, such as certificates, work experience, land registry and so on.

6.1: One of the cryptokitties I currently own. Source: cryptokitties.co

ERC721 standard can be used to tokenise almost every asset available. There is a scope of exchanging these assets inside the blockchain using this standard. An ERC721 based smart contract is just like any other contract in real life. Hence, potentially, it could bring back the barter system where people can exchange almost everything with anything. ERC20 and ERC721 are the most popular standards in the current world of blockchain. There are many other standards and also expansions of these two standards available:

ERC1155 - ERC1155 is an expansion to ERC721. In the ERC721 standard, each collectable item has its serial number. Due to its limitation of functions, CryptoKitties can be deployed using only a few smart contracts. It cannot be implemented for the mainstream games where non-fungible resources may exist. With the existing token standards, for each collectable, a separate contract would be required. Multiplayer games like World of Warcraft, Fortnight and Counterstrike have thousands of collectable items, and the developers would need an individual contract for every single type of object. To create and deploy contracts for each and every one of those items would be very difficult and result in data wastage.

ERC1155 brings forth a new way to store multiple items in a single contract, with the least amount of data. Only the data required to distinguish each piece is added to the contract.[8] This makes ERC1155 a combination of both ERC20 and ERC721 standards. In ERC1155, any number of items to one or more recipients can be transferred in a single transaction.[9] This reduces the cost of transaction and congestion on the network.

ERC1155 standards will help initiate transfers among non-fungible and fungible tokens, which is an update to existing token standards. 'Enjin' is a company working on this concept and working to implement the ERC721 token in transactions using in-game collectables.[10]

ERC223 - This proposal was created to solve one of the most important issues with the ERC20 contract – reversibility. ERC20 is not reversible; therefore, if you send your money to the wrong address, it might get stuck forever.[11] ERC223 has a separate function called *TokenFallback*, which makes it reversible. Additionally, ERC223 requires less 'gas' than that of an ERC20 token. As of 2018, ERC223 is still a proposal. To accept the plan, the exchanges would be required to do significant modifications to support ERC223 tokens.

```
//sample code
contract ERC223 {
  function transfer(address to, uint value, bytes data) {
        uint codeLength;
        assembly {
            codeLength := extcodesize(_to)
        }

        balances[msg.sender] = balances[msg.sender].sub(_value);
        balances[_to] = balances[_to].add(_value);
```

```
            if(codeLength>0) {
                // Require proper transaction han-
dling.
                ERC223Receiver receiver = ERC223Re-
ceiver(_to);
                receiver.tokenFallback(msg.sender,
_value, _data);
            }
        }
}
```

ERC827 - ERC827 is an extension to ERC20. It is similar to ERC223, with an addition of flexibility to transfer data, along with tokens, using smart contracts. It is more likely to replace the ERC223 concept as it is comparatively advanced. The additional function of ERC223 allow tokens to be used by a third-party. This ERC standard primarily focuses on 'security'. This is just an extension to ERC20, and the standard is still a 'work in progress'.[12]

```
  function transferFromAndCall(
      address _from, address _to, uint256 _value,
bytes _data
            ) public payable returns (bool) {
    require(_to != address(this));
    require(super.transferFrom(_from, _to,
_value));
    require(_to.call(_data));
    return true; }
```

Ethereum blockchain is built upon defined rules, and there is a system in place for every execution. To make the whole ecosystem user-friendly and free from bugs, ERC standards are essential. There are many other ERC standards not described here. As a DApp or smart contract developer, the standards are fundamental to understand, because they provide the basic framework for how to build on Ethereum. As more EIPs are put forward by the developers, more ERC standards will be approved, and more functions will be added in the future. Use of ERC standards will certify that the tokens you are about to create, are compatible across all the devices that support Ethereum network, such as the functionality of storing that token in a Trezor wallet.[13]

Decentralised Application

Apps built on decentralised platforms are known as DApps. Unlike a centralised application, a decentralised application does not have a central point of failure or central storage where the application information is hosted, stored or processed. The idea of DApp was proposed by Dr Gavin Wood in 2014, one of the co-founders and former CTO of Ethereum.[14]

The concept of decentralisation is not new. Users on the internet have been using decentralised application for a while now, for instance, the ideation of *torrent*. Although the word *torrent* has been used mostly to generate and spread pirated content, torrent is a good way of sharing open-sourced and free information to tens of thousands of users from one network.

Researchers suggest that there are differences between a decentralised and distributed application.[15] A decentralised application is where the processes are executed by multiple nodes across the network although the nodes are independent of their network. Therefore, if any of the nodes stop working, it will not have any effect on the network. A distributed network is different, as all the nodes are connected to each other. Typically, a distributed system is used to fasten up calculations - application processes and latency. Both centralised and decentralised applications can have a distributed architecture. An application could also have a hybrid architecture, where some of the data is stored and processed using a centralised server, while parts of the processes are run on a decentralised network.

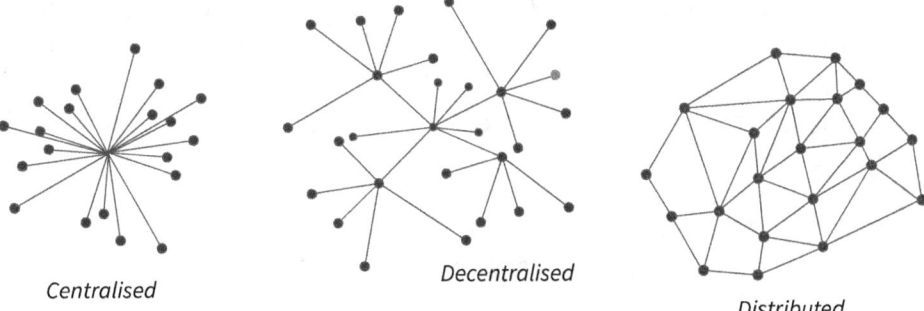

Centralised *Decentralised* *Distributed*

6.2: Comparison of different architectures.
Adapted from source: commons.wikimedia.org/Licensed under CC by 3.0

DApps can also be built on the permissioned blockchain. Developers can also use Amazon Web Services or Microsoft Azure to make hybrid DApp that is powered by both centralised and decentralised architecture. Large software corporations are working on various types of decentralised networks to provide a gateway for a typical application developer to find their development path towards *road to decentralisation*. Azure, in fact, provides Blockchain-as-a-Service (BaaS), by writing smart contracts on Quorum.[16]

Decentralised application development is an emerging field in the world of technology. DApps are built and managed on DLTs. Most of the existing DApps are experimental, and their business model has the potential to disrupt various verticals. However, a combination of multiple emerging fields, a hybrid business model has the most potential of disrupting the area of innovation. Some of these hybrid models would consist of the following business application structure:
- Virtual Reality, Augmented Reality and Blockchain
- Artificial Intelligence and Blockchain
- Biotechnology and Blockchain
- IOT and Blockchain
- Genetic Engineering and Blockchain

The process of decentralisation not only involves using decentralised architecture, such as a DLT to power an application, but also the notion of providing the control of information, ownership, and the right to users to contribute in the process. There are several decentralised business models, such as decentralised exchanges (DEX). Coinbase recently acquired a decentralised exchange to expand their business model.[17] DEX can provide the opportunity to the community to vote and have their opinion in operating an organisation. EthFinex, a decentralised exchange, lets its users to vote on development progress using their native ecosystem token.[18]

DID YOU KNOW?
Global financial firm Goldman Sachs have a very interactive source for beginners to learn blockchain. Search: The New Technology of Trust - Goldman Sachs[19]

DApp Structure

Decentralised application (DApp) on a blockchain is an application built using the foundations of decentralisation, using smart contracts run on a DLT network, such as blockchain. A typical Ethereum based DApp can be written in programming languages such as JavaScript or Python. Based on the standards proposed by blockchain researchers, a typical decentralised server and a DApp consists of the following.[20]

Frontend: A front-end or the 'client-side', a user interface (UI) using which the users can interact with the application, such as a webpage, or a mobile app.[21]

Backend: A back-end is the server-side or network-side built using languages such as Web3 or JavaScript (JS). The backend can be accessed using both command tool, application development software or even the browser.

RPC Connection: Remote Procedure Call or RPC connection is a process that establishes a connection between the server and the browser. In terms of Ethereum, the connection uses a format known as JSON RPC. JavaScript Object Notion (JSON), a commonly used form that can transmit human-readable data between an application and server. It is a current internet standard for language-independent data interchange format.[22]

Network: This where the nodes on the blockchain exist. The *Ethereum Node* is known as the Ethereum Virtual Machine or EVM. It is also termed as the World Computer.[23]

Decentralisation and Its Principles

Automated Validation and Fault Tolerance – The idea is to create a platform to reduce human intervention and steps that involve an intermediary. By digitising contracts, blockchain automatically validates user data. The decentralised architecture uses automated methods to identify intentional or accidental fraud and take required steps necessary.[24]

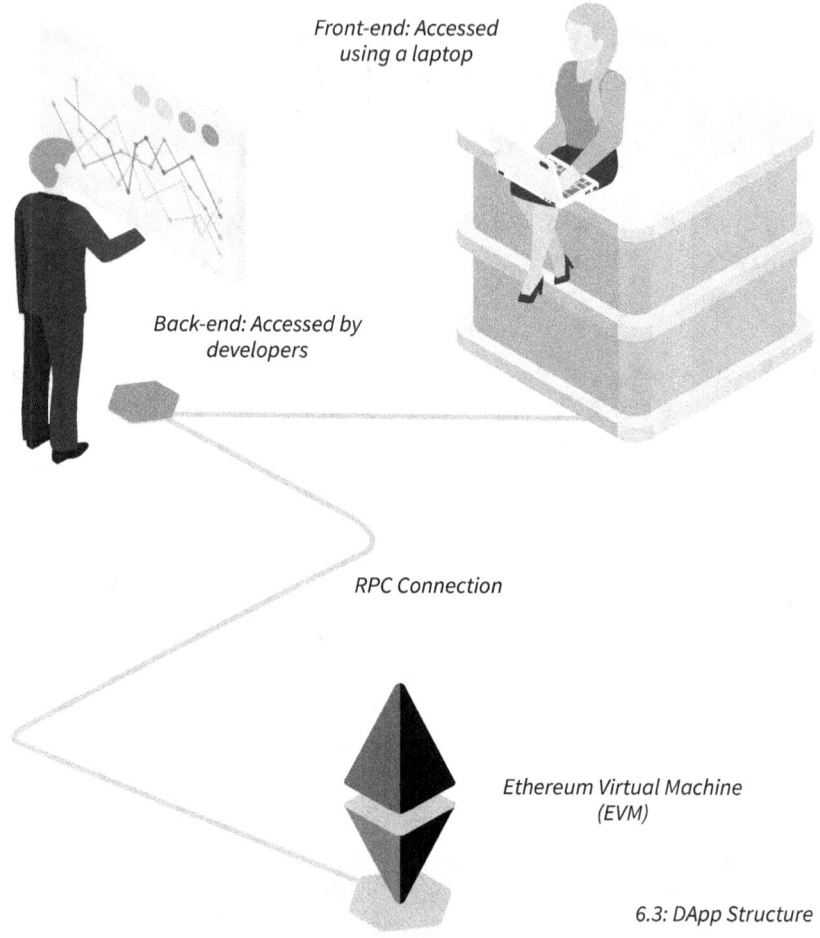

6.3: DApp Structure

Security and Encryption – Transaction and information stored on a decentralised network reduce the susceptibility of theft as these data are encrypted and distributed among millions of computers in the world. To take a blockchain network down, hackers will be required to attack almost millions of computers at a time. It isn't impossible, however, DLTs make it hard and expensive for the criminals.

Disintermediation – The model provides the idea of moving away from a centralised, top-down organisation to a community-driven model. Centralised third parties and middleman have replaced a group of semi-trusted or non-trusted people, being able to trust each other by depending on the consensus of the network. Trust the protocol and its agreement, not the middleman.

Value Driven Incentivisation – Earning rewards for providing computation power requires the users to run a node. By providing the necessary ability to run nodes, miners and validators can earn money by either providing the proof of the computation work or staking. There are many other processes using which tokenised blockchain users can get involved in a permissionless network and earn their fair share of rewards.

Open Sourced – The development remains open-sourced and community driven.

Control of Data – User remains in full control of their asset using DEXs, while also being in complete control of their confidential data encrypted on the blockchain. A user will be able to decide what they are comfortable to share.

Decentralised Governance – Using blockchain technology to increase community participation, voting process tracked on a decentralised ledger. Tokenised ecosystems are the ideal example of decentralised governance by an organisation.

BLOCK

DISCOVERING A NEW CHAPTER IN ECONOMICS

BLOCK INFORMATION

TX# 0x701	CROWDFUNDING 3.0	115
TX# 0x702	INITIAL COIN OFFERING	116
TX# 0x703	ICO FACTS	122
TX# 0x704	TOKENISATION OF EVERYTHING	124
TX# 0x705	WHY TOKENS FOR INDIVIDUAL NETWORK OR APPLICATIONS	125
TX# 0x706	TOKEN AS AN ASSET CLASS	126
TX# 0x707	FINANCE OF TOKEN SUPPLY	128
TX# 0x708	FIXED SUPPLY VS VALUATION	130
TX# 0x709	DISTRIBUTION MODELS	131

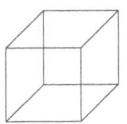 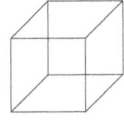 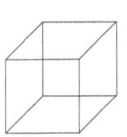
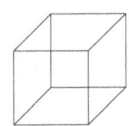

ECONOMICS & FINANCE BLOCK

BLOCK 7

DISCOVERING A NEW CHAPTER IN ECONOMICS

Crowdfunding 3.0
The world of finance is incredibly dynamic, with trillions of worth assets including cash being moved around the world every day. Financial technology received a facelift on the front end after the integration of digital systems, although the rules haven't changed for over 70 years. While five big accounting firms monopolistically drive the accounting world, credit or debit card processing systems are owned and dominated by three or four. The reason for this kind of monopolistic operation is due to their significant control over the design and deployment of systems, mostly its intellectual properties and patents. Leading fintech companies are at the top of their game due to patented processes that others cannot copy.

It's not like that the internet didn't have an impact on the financial world – we are watching the banking world being profoundly shaken by the fintech startups. First came the phase of venture capital funding. Billions were poured into technology startups giving birth to global technology hubs such as Silicon Valley in California and Shoreditch in London back in the late 90s. A competition between investors resulted in thousands of companies raising billions of dollars of capital investment around the world without the requirement of generating any revenue. Nevertheless, that wasn't the end of it.

The launch of crowdfunding sites such as Kickstarter or Indiegogo gave birth to an era of fundraising and finance.[1] The process of corporate investment has eased over the past decade, with fintech startups like eToro enabling users to buy company shares and cryptocurrency CfDs with just a few clicks.[2] Crowdfunding sites provided the opportunity to give seed capital to tech companies who are keen to launch their products. Some companies offer a special version of their product for pre-ordering, while others offer perks in return for seed capital.

CfD – A "Contract for Difference" is contract between a trader and a broker, instead of buying shares directly. As a trader, you are able to open a 'buy' or 'sell' position, therefore you can make a profit even if the price of the asset goes down. It won't allow you to buy the asset, however, you are allowed to leverage the prices. The higher the leverage, the higher the risk of loss or the chances of making a profit.

Crowdfunding sites such as *Crowdcube* allowed booming startups like *HyperSciences* to share a small portion of their equity with the public, and therefore help to raise micro-equity capital.[3] Hundreds of companies raised billions over the past few years. The process of getting approved on a crowdfunding site started to become more and more difficult due to increased competition. Nonetheless, another movement was going on in the background - the launch of a new blockchain startup and its unique form of fundraising. The success flooded in when Ethereum launched their initial coin offering.[4] The offering was for a limited number of participants who received ethers. The coin offering flew through the roof, as the company managed to raise over 3700 bitcoins, which was an estimated USD 15 million at the time of raising the funds.[5]

On a blog post published in 2014, the co-founder of Ethereum, Gavin Wood, proposed his vision of DApps. This was a fundamental point where the blockchain technology provided a new meaning. The real-world use case was not only providing the ability to facilitate a better process for monetary transactions, but also build web 3.0 and ecosystem based on *consensus engines*, that would be dependent on the opinion of the community.[6] While the traditional market only allowed middleman and corporate institutions to be able to raise funds from the members of the public – ICOs allowed the opportunity to remove the middleman and go directly to the contributors.

Initial Coin Offering

Initial Coin Offering is a means of raising funds from the public to fund a startup. In return, the contributors would receive a type of cryptocurrency, utility or security token that may or may not be used in the application the founders of the startup are proposing to develop. Many companies have promoted their ICO as Initial Token or Security Offering.

Founder of Ethereum Vitalik Buterin during TechCrunch Disrupt London 2015 - Day 2 at Copper Box Arena on December 8, 2015 in London, England.
Photo 7.1: Founder of Ethereum Vitalik Buterin during TechCrunch Disrupt London 2015/by John Phillips /Getty Images for TechCrunch/licensed under CC by 2.0

The companies offering profit, equity or company shares offered STO, Security Token Offering.[7] In a typical Ethereum network based ICO, a user would be required to create an Ethereum wallet and register for the ICO on the company's website. The company offering the ICO will then add the registered addresses to their 'whitelist', a process in which the users are vetted to be allowed to participate in the ICO. The users are then provided with the access to a terminal or ICO fundraising platform, where the users are required to send the desired amount of ethers to the company's wallet.

There are multiple methods in which companies have raised funds via ICO:

    a. Raising funds via automated Crowdsale Contract – There are open sourced crowdsale contracts available on GitHub, using which companies raise funds and use a time-lock to release the funds. If the funding goal isn't reached, the agreement would automatically return all the funds to their owners.

b. Raising funds via *Turnkey Solution Provider* – Using hardware wallet and external platform to process the transactions. In this scenario, a turnkey solution provider, e.g. *TokenGet* would provide a platform to a company.[8] The users are required to register on the platform, get KYC approved and then be able to participate in the fundraising. Due to operation logs attested using smart contracts, the system keeps track of all the users and funds raised via the platform.

After the funds were raised, the tokens were distributed using either of the following processes:

a. Immediately transferred to users once participated in the ICO, however, in many cases, the tokens were locked until a specific date, for instance, until it was listed in an exchange.

b. Transferred to the user wallet after ICO, once the users have provided appropriate verification documents.

The process of verification and transaction recording is an intricate mechanism. A smart contract allowed the startups to automate the processes, thus removing any institutional middleman from the process. The birth of this process has shaken up the fintech industry, as it fundamentally changed the way investors looked at financial markets. In other words, ICO and blockchain technology startups reinvented finance and fundraising process.

Secondary statistics reveal that the companies raising funds from 2014 to 2016 have been able to raise between USD 7 to 20 million.[9] One of the most significant changes happened when DAO, the 'Decentralised Autonomous Organisation' raised over USD 150 million.[10] Regulatory authorities launched an investigation when the security of the independent organisation was compromised and resulted in a major hack. The industry learned its lesson, but that did not stop companies from bringing new ideas and raising funds via ICO. From April 2017, came an entirely new era of fundraising – ICO 2.0, when ICOs raised millions in a matter of minutes. Companies such as *Filecoin* raised over USD 200 million, while *Status*, an Ethereum based blockchain messaging app, raised USD 100 million in just under a week.[11] While ether was hitting the peak and hovering around $1200, ICOs successfully launched and raising hundreds of millions in a matter of days. Many ICOs have successfully raised over USD 50 million between April 2017 till March 2018.[12]

However, with the launch of bitcoin futures contracts on CBOE and its price hitting $19000, the industry came under attack by many *corporate finance* experts, regarding how cryptocurrencies are being misused to conduct civil and criminal activities. It's not possible to pin down whether the comments made by these industry experts were deliberate attacks to push the prices down, or genuinely meant against the decentralisation of financial services. News outlets suggested that all the institutional investors were investing in cryptocurrencies and ICOs, while the public were backing off due to the downtrend of the market.[13] As the market started to indicate a long bearish trend, more institutional firms and investors moved into the market. Meanwhile, Coinbase launched its own OTC trading desk to provide better benefits to professional investors.[14] Over-the-trade counter allows traders to trade stocks, securities and cryptocurrencies directly with private dealers, unlike a typical exchange where trades take place among third-party traders.

The downtrend has affected almost every startup and institution raising funds via ICOs. As the value of Ethereum went down by 90%, consequently nearly all the startups lost 70 to 90% of the funds raised.[15] While many startups moved their asset over to stablecoins and fiat currencies, the downturn has wiped almost all the value of the companies who were holding their funds in cryptocurrencies. This has severely damaged their plans for operations, as well as aims of delivering targets. Even much larger companies like Consensys announced restructuring to provide efficiency.

The idea of ICO has given a makeover to the finance industry by introducing captivating new ways of funding startups. High-flying days of raising millions may never come back, but the circumstances will improve once the governments around the world declare their regulations regarding ICOs. This renovation also added pressure on traditional financial institutions. Nonetheless, banks and institutions stepped up their games and jumped head over heels to start a race, and become the first adopter. *JPMorgan* and *Credit Suisse* began working in collaboration with Ethereum, whereas other high-street banks began to conduct and investigate the process of acquiring exchanges in a bid to diversify their portfolio.[16] Due to volatility, high-street banks were not keen to support bitcoin or Ethereum transactions, however, in the UK, FCA approved fintech institutions to allow trading, buying and selling of cryptocurrencies using banks, such as *Wirex* and *Revolut*.[17] Revolut was one of the first banks in the world to offer cryptocurrency payments to the public. Over the past three years, non-high street banks with an option for cryptocurrencies have taken over the world by storm, with Revolut being valued at over 1.8 billion.[18] Question is, why did investors pour tens of billions in blockchain applications?

7 November 2017; Nikolay Storonsky, Founder & CEO, Revolut, on MoneyConf Stage during the opening day of Web Summit 2017 at Altice Arena in Lisbon.

Photo 7.2: Nikolay Storonsky, Founder & CEO, Revolut /by Stephen McCarthy/Web Summit via Sportsfile/licensed under CC by 2.0 © 2017 TechCrunch, some rights reserved.

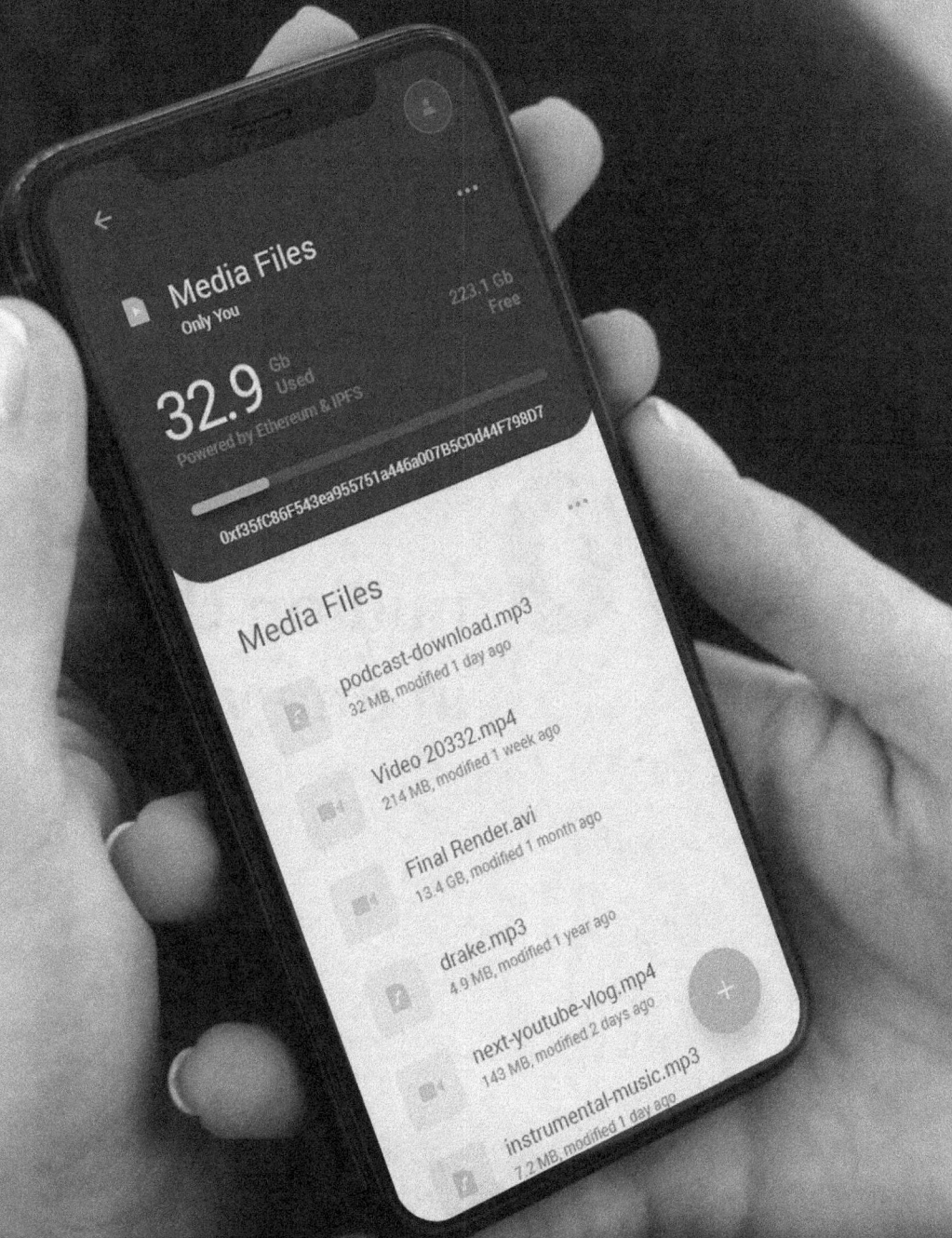

A sample UI of a blockchain-based file sharing DApp

Filecoin raised

257 million USD[19]

EOS raised

200 million USD in one year[20]

CIVIC raised

21 million USD in one month[21]

NAGA raised

30 million USD, a public company in Germany[22]

BAT raised

35 million USD in 30 ~~DAYS~~ **SECONDS**[23]

Tokenisation of Everything

There is no traditional definition of token economics. Analyst Cox suggest that token economics is the process designing a token for an ecosystem that will attract the investors, provide an advantage to the users, its early adopters and also inspire expansion of the idea.[24]

As mentioned earlier, economists have been conducting research to create better and advanced economic models — one of the researchers to propose the innovative idea for token economics was John Kagel from Texas A & M University. In his research paper published in 1972, John discusses several experimental designs for token economies and summarises the experiments that may be conducted in the future.[25] He describes that in token economics, users would receive salaries or charge their customers in tokens.

The current exploratory idea of token economics follows this principle – having a token for an application or ecosystem that will allow users to utilise the token within it. Ethereum is an excellent example for a token-based network, where miners receive ether in return for powering the network. Ether used in the network as a form of transaction fee to send or receive money, create and deploy contracts. Consequently, applications built on the network will be required to have ether as a form of payment for using the network. Ethereum not only itself is a bright example of how token-based economies work, but it also allows developers to build a token-dependent application on its network.

The idea of tokenisation exploded when blockchain startups followed the process of raising funds via initial coin offering using their tokens. As the sector progressed, the analysts and investors realised that the tokens cannot be used solely for the purpose of raising funds. A token created on the Ethereum network must have some intrinsic as well as an extrinsic value that allows the participants of the system, investors and end users to reap advantages. Without an intrinsic value of the token, such as a utility within the application, creating a token for the sake of raising funds does not make sense.

This chapter addresses various types of tokens, the methods of creating the tokens, focuses on different token standards on the Ethereum blockchain. As first-movers in the token economy, most of the decentralised applications and ecosystems are being built on its network. Based on these models, the next chapter looks into the details of the real-life use cases in different verticals.

Why Tokens for Individual Network or Applications

Tokenised application isn't something new. A use case of a tokenised ecosystem will be loyalty points, for instance, *Emirates* reward points or *Nectar points*. Typically, users of an individual network have to their scheme of benefits – Nectar for BP and Shell points for using Shell service stations. Users also receive Nectar points for shopping in *Sainsbury's*.[26] These nectar points are registered against a nectar card of a user, who would be able to use the nectar points to buy products. Within the nectar ecosystem, there are various retailers, such as BP. Users will therefore receive nectar points for both shopping and refuelling. Once enough points are collected, these points could be spent on selected retailers. Currently, over 500 brands are a part of this network ecosystem. Having a similar type of loyalty scheme on tokenised blockchain means that the loyalty points can be withdrawn and used as a currency. It can also be swapped with other kinds of tokens almost instantly within the Ethereum network. Loyalty points are just one example of a tokenised economy.

Tokens for a blockchain or a decentralised application have numerous other use cases. All of these tokens can be integrated with exchanges. Therefore, all the tokens or cryptocurrencies have an extrinsic value, and directly tied to the factor of instant liquidity - the opportunity to convert the tokens into fiat or other cryptocurrencies at any given point of time. For instance, KNC is the token for the Kyber network, while XRP is for Ripple Labs. All these tokens can be traded in various cryptocurrency exchanges and can, therefore, be recognised as a digital form of money. Instant liquidity is deemed to be an attractive factor in blockchain-based tokenised economy, and understanding liquidity in a crypto market is a key to becoming a successful investor.[27]

While blockchains can have their network currencies, a decentralised application built on the Ethereum blockchain can create their own token for their applications. Token engineering experts believe that when combined with the utility of smart contract, tokenisation can provide amazing benefits, including rights to the community for decentralised governance, as well as a provision of ownership in various assets, such as properties or lands.[28] As discussed earlier, with smart contracts making methods automatable, a tamper-proof loyalty scheme can be created using tokenised economy. It is believed that costs of representing real-world asset will go down significantly, as public blockchain gains better acceptance among people, hence accelerating e-commerce.[29]

Token as an Asset Class

Before understanding the differences between various tokens, it is vital to understand the basics of investment – understanding the meaning of various asset class. Experts have provided various models of 'asset class', in which investors capitalise to gain returns.[30] To summarise, there are primarily five asset class that investors are interested in:

- Shares
- Properties
- Debt Securities – such as Government Bonds
- Commodities – such as Gold, Platinum
- Cash or Cash Equivalent, e.g. Currency[31]

Although cash is not considered as a form of investment, it is still classified as an asset class and provides security for funds when the market crashes. It is also essential for us to understand the term 'security'. The term has varying definition in different jurisdictions. In the UK, securities are classes equities, debentures, pension schemes and investments.[32] In the United States, 'security' is classed as a tradable asset and categorised into:

- Debt
- Equity
- Derivatives[33]

Any organisation issuing debt security, investment packages to the public, and platform offering derivatives must be registered via security regulatory bodies.[34]

With the progression of token development, and a significant increase in token-based blockchain startup funding, innovators have come up with many different ideas. The types of tokens can be segregated into categories based on whether the purchase of a token provides a promised return on investment, or offers a mere access-right to a

network. Grounded on various models and draft regulations proposed by regulatory bodies such as the SEC, tokens of startups offering fixed or variable return on investments are classed as a security. Hence, cryptocurrencies can be primarily classified in the three following categories:
- Security Tokens
- Utility Tokens
- Network Tokens

Security Tokens – These tokens are backed by various securities that provide a guarantee or a return on investment, ownership to a physical asset, or profit from an organisation. Based on the fundamentals of finance, security tokens can be further classified into the following categories:
- *Equity Tokens:* Shares, or Company Shares
- *Debt Security Token:* Government Bonds
- *Physical Asset-Backed Token:* Property Shares

If a particular token is backed by the shares of the company, promises a timely dividend and also provides ownership to the company issuing the token, it will be classified as a security token. A token can also be backed by the ownership of a property or any physical asset, that might offer a perceived increase in return on investment. A 'Debt Security Token' can be backed by *debentures* or *bonds* issued by the government.

Utility Tokens – Utility is similar to loyalty points in a network, a type of cryptocurrency that provides value to the users of the application or ecosystem. This type of token can be compared to the fundamentals of consumer behaviour, a value that a customer receives based on *task-relation* and *consumption behaviour*.[35] These tokens have various other intrinsic values – such as membership benefits similar to year-long discounts, loyalty rewards for using the application, as well as voting or governance rights in an individual organisation.

Network Tokens – These tokens are used as a method to grant rights to individual networks. These tokens could also be used as a form of payment within the system. Bancor Network Token (BNT) can be classified as a network token.[36]

Commodity and Currency Backed Tokens – Any tokens that mimic price of commodities or currency, such as Platinum can be classified into this subcategory. However, there are no defined regulations on whether startups issuing commodities-backed tokens should be regulated or not. *Wrapped Ether* or WETH, an ether-pegged token was created for the 0x ecosystem. *Goldmint* is a token backed by the price of Gold.

Commodity-backed and currency-backed tokens are collectively termed as 'Stablecoins'. There are multiple stablecoins built on the Ethereum blockchain, including TrueUSD, Dai Stablecoin, Gemini dollar, Paxos Standard and so on.[37]

With regards to the regulations, certain jurisdictions such the US would impose and classify commodity-backed tokens to be strictly regulated by SEC and *Commodity Future Trading Commission (CFTC)*. In an ongoing court case against a company and its cryptocurrency backed by Gold, a federal judge upheld the decision that the currencies meeting the definition of a commodity and falls under regulatory approval.[38] Financial governing bodies such as FINMA and SEC have provided investors with regulations of which type of tokens can be considered as securities.[39]

Finance of Token Supply

Token supply is an essential term in the world of cryptocurrency, as the sustainability of the ecosystem is dependent on the supply of the token, as well as the method in which they are supplied. Supply of a cryptocurrency is designed after considering several determinants, including mechanism of allocation, the process in which the tokens are sold to the public, and token velocity.[40] The process of determining economics of token supply and calculation of market capitalisation is a little different than the publicly listed companies in the stock market. In finance, these are the following terms that define the valuation of a company –

Market Capitalisation – The total cash or cash equivalent value of a public company, calculated using the following formula:

```
Price of Shares X Outstanding Shares = Market
                  Capitalisation
```

Outstanding Shares – Outstanding shares are all the shares owned by the investors, including institutional investors and the restricted shares held by the company employees and officers.[41] The 'maximum number of outstanding shares' is referred to as 'Capital Stock' in Accounting.[42]

In the cryptocurrency market, the following terms define the size and valuation of a coin or token:
Total Token Supply – The total number of tokens in supply.
Circulation Supply – The number of total tokens in circulation, held by traders, investors and being traded in the cryptocurrency exchanges.
Market Capitalisation – The total value of a cryptocurrency, blockchain network or a token ecosystem. The valuation formula is different to that of the stock market –

```
Price of Crypto X Circulation Supply of Crypto =
              Market Capitalisation
```

For instance, on November 12 2018, the circulation supply of ether was 103,599,014. Therefore, the total market capitalisation of the Ethereum was:

```
$111.23 X 103,599,014 = $11.5 billion
```
[43]

This market capitalisation refers to the value of the cryptocurrency. Regarding tokens, the market capitalisation may not apply to the actual valuation of the company. If a token represents equity or shares of a particular company, then the total value may provide an idea of the valuation of the company. If the token is a utility, the actual valuation of a company may be calculated using a different model – such as the model provided by traditional venture capital investors.

Can a company go public? Yes. Raising funds via initial coin/token offering and getting listed in exchanges provides an extrinsic value for the token, and therefore generating an overall market value of a cryptocurrency. A company which did not issue any shares can also get listed in a stock market, and raise additional funds from traditional investors by going through an Initial Public Offering (IPO). In this case, the market capitalisation in the stock market would provide the actual value of the company, while the market capitalisation in the cryptocurrency market would offer an ideal cap of the cryptocurrency used within that token ecosystem.

The management of the token, the process in which the tokens are being generated is essential to understand, as this may be defined as one of the pillars of success for a crypto-based blockchain network. Based on the research information, the token supply be:

Controlled – The tokens are systematically released in the market. For example, Ethereum and Bitcoin follows the principle of diminishing supply, in which the supply of the token decays over time, where the 'supply *tends to zero*' in the long run.[44] If the supply is fixed, the number of tokens can never be increased, similar to how Bitcoin works.

Flexible Supply – The total number of tokens supplied in the market can be flexible, and similar to how central banks print 'new money'. Administrators of a token can 'mint' new tokens in order to stabilise price and increase liquidity. In a typical market, governments use a method known as quantitative easing to print new money by purchasing back assets such as bonds.[45]

The following are also taken under consideration:

Pre-mined – All or a partial number of tokens are pre-mined and stored for future reserve. Many utility token ecosystems pre-mine their total supply and release the tokens to the public periodically.[46]

To be Mined – It is the process in which the contributors of the network mine the tokens themselves. In this method, the miners contribute their computational power and receive the cryptocurrency as a form of reward. An example would be the total supply of bitcoin.

Fixed Supply Vs Valuation

In terms of a tokenised ecosystem, a significant number of experts prefer the fixed supply method, as it may result in the potential increase in the valuation of the token, when the demand increases over time.[47] Based on tokenised ecosystems on the Ethereum blockchain, it can be concluded that many token issuers keep a certain number of tokens in reserve to either raise additional funds in the future or utilise the tokens for marketing and PR purposes. For instance, Ethereum-based blockchain startup Crypto.com, formerly known as Monaco initially issued some of the tokens from their total circulation supply.[48] Many tokens were used for promotional purposes to drag the attention of the traders via exchanges and resulting in increased liquidity in the market. Fixed supply may lead to a price surge once all the tokens have been released in the market. With reference to the supply and demand curves explained in one of the previous chapters, the growth of a company or demand for its product may lead to this surge. If the activity in a network or the DApp increases, it also increases the possibility for higher number of transaction of that token for using them in the DApp. Since the supply of the token is fixed, it has to be bought from a third-party seller from an exchange. Due to the increased demand, the traders would, therefore, ask for a higher bid, leading to a price surge. The opposite might also happen if the demand drops. A reserve allocation is kept to:

    a. Periodically release some tokens to utilise for marketing purposes, which helps in increasing overall liquidity in the market,

    b. Releasing some tokens from a reserve in a controlled manner to reduce the volatility of price.

Some sceptics and blockchain promoters believe that the infinite supply of a token goes against the foundational theories of a decentralised ecosystem.[49] A company with unlimited token supply might possess full control of minting tokens, that is, they are capable of issuing more tokens whenever required, which results in inflation. Large networks use an automated algorithm to release or control the supply of tokens. The supply of tokens can also be dependent on the consensus of the community in a vast, decentralised network, or it could be algorithmic, where the supply of the token diminishes over time and results in fixed supply, in the long run, a principle framework followed by the Ethereum foundation.

Distribution Models

The model for the distribution of the tokens varies from company to company. In a traditional market, 5-20% of a company token is sold when raising funds via crowdfunding platforms.[50] However, if the token does not constitute the principles of equity or security, companies can raise money by issuing tokens to the public without having to distribute any capital. Based on a research sample of blockchain networks and ten tokenised ecosystems on the Ethereum, the companies have followed the framework for the distribution of the tokens discussed below.[51]

1) *Token Sales* – The tokens were distributed during the initial offering. The token sales process can also be divided into the following:

a) Tokens Minted During The ICO – Some blockchain startups utilised the model framework proposed by the Ethereum foundation and used a crowdfunding contract to generate the exact number of tokens sold during the ICO. Bancor, a token liquidity network, created a 'token generation event', where the tokens were minted and instantly transferred to the users right after users participated.

b) Tokens Pre-Mined Before the ICO – Total number of tokens were fully deployed in the blockchain network. A specific allocation of the tokens offered in the ICO were distributed during the fundraising process or after the ICO was completed.

2) *Airdrops* – Airdrop is the process of distribution of tokens to a potential group of DApp users as a form of promotion. It is similar to providing complimentary balance such as free credit offers. Typically, your 'USD 20 credit' can only be used within one app, and it cannot be cashed out. In the case of tokens, it can be liquidated anytime. Token airdrops were conducted using the following methods –

a) Pre-ICO Airdrop – This process is where the blockchain companies offered complimentary tokens ranging from a value of USD 3 to USD 50, to build a list of potential users of the network. TRX, the network token for TRON completed an airdrop to almost all the users of Ethereum in 2017. POLY token of Polymath completed a successful airdrop of 9.5 million POLY tokens to 38,224 users.[52] This airdrop resulted in over 40 thousand pre-registrations for the Polymath Network.

b) Post-ICO Airdrop – This process is where the companies airdropped a certain allocation of token after getting enlisted in an exchange. This assisted in an increase of demand for the token as well as overall increased volume and liquidity. Many exchanges conduct a smaller form of these airdrops – such as by promoting a social media competition on Twitter. In this scenario, a token pool is shared with only a restricted number of participants, which results in the distribution of a higher percentage of allocation per user.

c) Physical Airdrop – Some companies encourage users to participate in physical events organised in various countries. Once users join the event, they are entitled to receive free tokens. Many companies conducted this unique form of airdrop in order to gather followers and attract users in their exhibition booth at an international conference. *Mainframe*, a company which raised 27,000 Ethereum from investors, distributed USD 1 million worth airdrop in a physical airdrop event named *Token2049*, where the MFT tokens were literally dropped from a balloon.[53]

3) *Bounty* – Bounty programs have been one of the most productive ways of airdropping tokens in return for promoting a DApp or ICO. Typically, a startup would launch a bounty campaign for the promotion of their token offering, allocating a range of 0.5-2% of the total distribution towards the bounty participants.[54] The participants usually follow various pages of the company on different social media channels and receive accolades for completing tasks, such as translation of whitepaper. It is an incredibly effective strategy to advertise, as it serves both the company and its followers.

4) *Partnerships* – Tokens may also be distributed as a form of payment or business, where a contract with a corporate alliance benefits both users. In this process, tokens can be provided to various companies offering services in return for a certain amount of tokens. The companies usually sign contracts for offering exchange listing or other services.

Companies which raise venture capital from traditional investors may opt out from offering tokens via ICO or ITO, and therefore distribute their allocation only via airdrops. Blockchain network may also airdrop their currencies to promote adoption. *Stellar Foundation* conducted the largest airdrop to date. With an aim to boost the number of users on the network, a partnership between *Blockchain Wallet* and *Stellar* knocked out a promotion plan of airdropping USD 125 million worth XLM tokens. This stunt generated a substantial amount of PR and deemed as the largest airdrop in the history.[55][56]

The ICO hype has ended and it's highly unlikely that the craze of 2017-2018 would return anytime soon. More than 90% of the companies will be affected due to market crash and lack of liquidity. However, the process has paved way for a decentralised capital raising process without the involvement of the middleman. Over the period of this new decade, we will witness much better methods of implementing ICOs and STOs.

BLOCK 8

USE CASES OF BLOCKCHAIN

BLOCK INFORMATION

TX# 0x801	SMART CONTRACT BUSINESS CASES	137
TX# 0x802	FEASIBILITY OF BLOCKCHAIN	142
TX# 0x803	PLAYERS IN BLOCKCHAIN TRANSFORMATION	144
TX# 0x804	IMPLEMENTED PLATFORMS	146

BUSINESS BLOCK

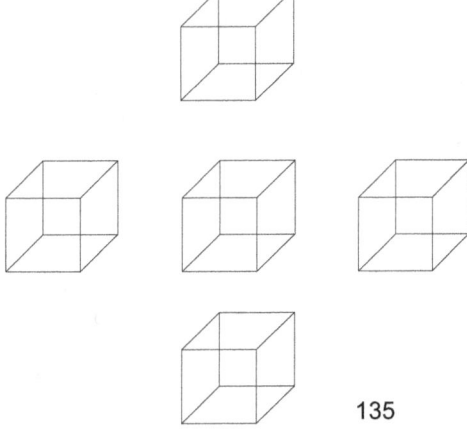

BLOCK 8

USE CASES OF BLOCKCHAIN

Smart Contract Business Cases

Utility token could serve various market requirements. A token can be created to be utilised on specific *market verticals* or could also be beneficial across a *parallel market*. The utility of the token will be dependent on the business model of the startup. *Niche startups* serving a well-defined 'customer requirement' or a 'customer set' can be defined as *vertical market*, for instance, tokens that are created to provide benefits to the patients.[1] An example would be We Power (WPR) token, a utility token designed to create a *renewable* energy pool.

Cryptocurrency

Cryptocurrency is the most popular use case for smart contracts. Cryptocurrencies like Ethereum, Binance Coin and all others are used to fund different projects and have proven useful in trading and exchanging. Utility tokens in comparison to bitcoin offer various benefits, such as fast and low transfer fees. Bitcoin is a useful form of payment and accepted in many places. But some altcoins offer much lower transaction fees. Besides, most ERC20 tokens have an intrinsic value - those which are required to access their native DApp features. While the tokens can be used to make purchases within their network or DApp, these can also be used as legitimate currencies outside the perimeter of the system. Coinpayments, a cryptocurrency payment processing merchant, enables users to make payments with ERC20 tokens such as Binance Coin or Gemini Dollar.[2] The tokens are created using 'Ethereum standards', therefore allow better integration with external applications compatible with ether and the Ethereum network. Being in a decentralised system with necessary standards (ERC) make a network more secure and extra reliable in trading as well as payment processing. These rules have made tokens and DApps compatible across multiple platforms.

Supply Chain Management/Manufacturing
A supply chain usually works based on the network established between various suppliers and sellers. Lack of transparency is a widely visible problem in the supply chain industry. Using blockchain technology and smart contracts, every single product can be given their own identity. Therefore, the apple you eat can be traceable to its original source. You will also be able to know exactly where your coffee beans came from. Since peers connected to the chain can see every transaction inside the blockchain, each deal is transparent, resulting in a customer being able to verify and track their products. This also cuts down management and maintenance costs. Each smart contract issued can be checked and followed from within the blockchain. It provides more transparency to suppliers, sellers and consumers. *OriginTrail* is working on such a project to bring data sharing to global supply chains using blockchain technology.[3] *Vechain* is also another platform to enhance the supply chain processes.[4]

Digital Identity
Smart contracts provide individuals to control their own identity containing data and assets. They can choose to show or hide the necessary information to the concerned parties. The sellers can thus verify the information without the necessity of asking for documents. Besides, the decentralised nature of blockchain will help protect the data of individuals from hacking. A user can store various personal information without the risk of getting lost. Users can securely store many confidential information, such as verified national insurance, medical records and social media credentials. *Civic* provides facilities to store ID, and tools to control and protect identities.[5] It can allow users more control of their private data to transact securely online. Moreover, billions of unbanked people could benefit from such a system. These users can obtain a credit score without having to open an account in a traditional high-street bank.

Healthcare
In the world of medical science, a patient's records hold the key to different research and provide guidance towards future insurance of a patient. Usually, the health records of a patient are stored in a secure network that doctors and hospitals have access to, however, using

blockchain, a system can be developed where the patients have control over such confidential data. Different organisations such as hospitals, laboratories and pharmacists can request permission to access a patient's record to serve their purpose and record transactions on the distributed ledger. *MedicalChain*, for instance, provides facilities to store health records and provide utilisation of the records by allowing the patients to communicate with the doctors and share the stored health records.[6] Analysts suggest that large blocks of medical data could be stored in off-chain storage, while the data hash references could be stored on-chain.[7] This process will increase performance and allow such system to be deployed using the current processing power of blockchain.

Insurance

The current insurance system consists of processes which usually takes a number of steps to generate a quote. Price comparison sites in the UK have made buying insurance easier, although the process of insurance claim is still manual in developed countries, which makes it inefficient. Therefore, the customers have to face plenty of troubles, and claims take a really long time to be processed. Insurance companies can automate policies by writing them into smart contracts. Since a smart contract can be programmed according to needs, each customer can be dealt with ease. The smart contracts would check the claim, and if the conditions meet the requirements for the insurance, the repair could be approved within a couple of hours. Using the same blockchain, the vehicle can be tracked to detect various aspects of the claim. This reduces the administrative costs and ensures the transparency of each transaction. *AXA*, the insurance giant, launched an insurance product that utilises smart contracts on Ethereum blockchain.[8] The system works by detecting the delayed flights and pays compensation if the flight is delayed for more than two hours. The flight data is provided by third parties and linked with smart contracts.

Copyrighted Content

In the media industry, ownership and distribution of rights is a huge market. The material put out in the market are protected by copyright privileges, which allow the copyright holder to receive a royalty fee, every time their content is used.[9] A smart contract built on a blockchain would keep track of all ownership rights. It ensures the actual owner that any changes made in the contract require the consensus of all the parties involved. The royalty payments would also be more efficient.

Internet of Things

We are rapidly shifting into the world of IoT, where every device in our home could be connected to one hub. Introducing smart contracts in this system radically changes the dynamics of how devices interact with each other. *IOTA* is working developing the next generation DLT for IoT devices. With security of devices being at the centre of discussion, smart contracts and DLTs can provide a solution by hosting the processes on a decentralised network, thus reducing the susceptibility of cyber-attacks. Evidently, large corporations control electricity or other energy supply in almost every country. Blockchain can be adopted to implement smart metering. Decentralising the energy market will mean transparency of proper usage ensuring that every consumer will pay for what they consume. Let's say you have an IoT enabled renewable energy device, such as solar panels. By having the data usage on a DLT and using smart contracts to monitor the energy, you would be able to buy and sell renewable energy on the chain.[10] Sounds implausible, however, such models are already being tested.[11] GRIDPLUS Energy is one of the world's first hardware enforced, automated crypto payment system.[12] They aim to cut out the financial middlemen and make the whole system more transparent and efficient. Scientists have studied 140 research and commercial initiative in the energy sector to comprehend the viability and discussed challenges in implementation.[13] They concluded:

> *"…blockchain or distributed ledger technologies can clearly benefit energy system operations, markets and consumers. They offer disintermediation, transparency and tamper-proof transactions, but most importantly, blockchains offer novel solutions for empowering consumers and small renewable generators to play a more active role in the energy market and monetise their assets. Blockchains have enabled applications of sharing-economy in the energy sector, which has prompted several authors to speak about novel market models and energy democratisation."*

International finance and technology consulting firm *McKinsey & Co* believes that blockchain's primary impact will be driving operational efficiency. Additionally, the firm explains that certain industries would be more suited to solutions offered by blockchain technology.[14]

The value at stake from blockchain varies across industries.

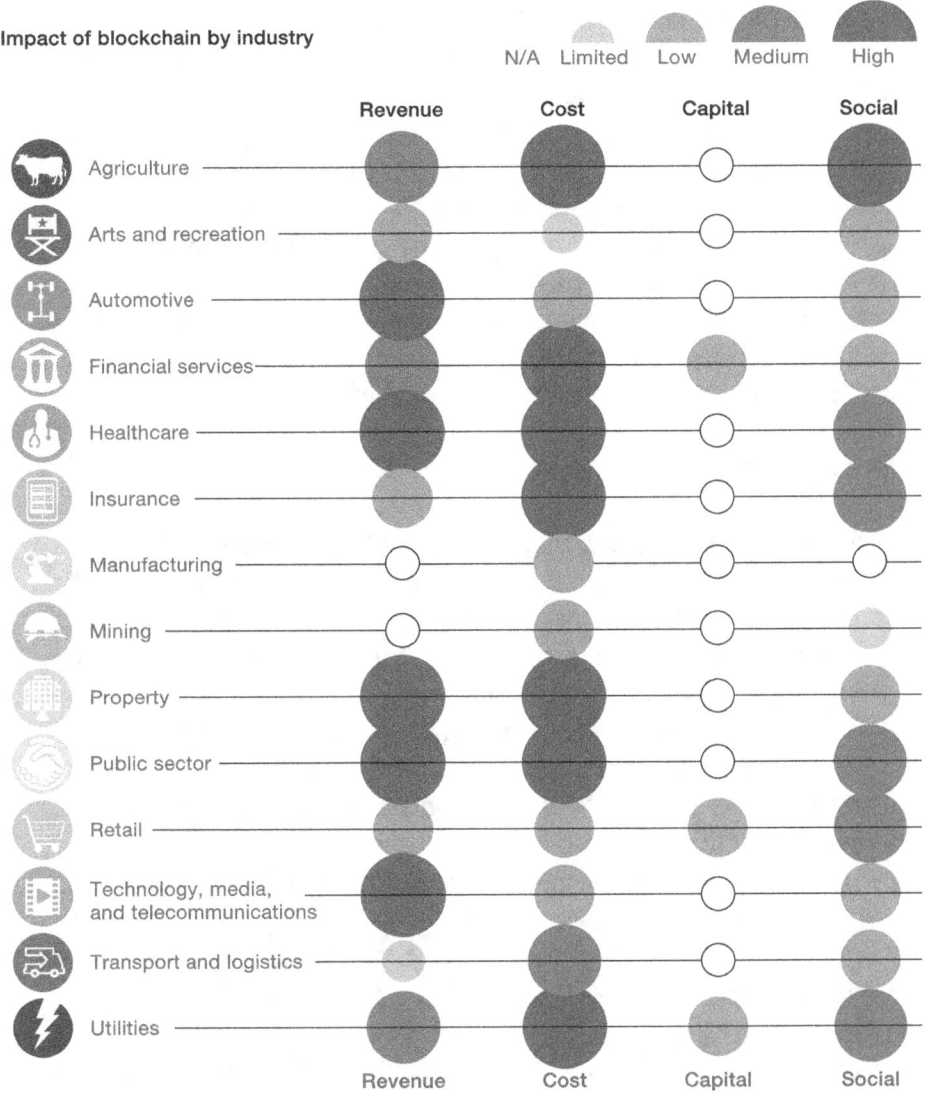

8.1: Exhibit from "Blockchain beyond the hype: What is the strategic business value?", June 2018, McKinsey & Company, www.mckinsey.com. Copyright (c) 2019 McKinsey & Company. All rights reserved. Reprinted by permission.

Feasibilty of Blockchain

In multi-million-dollar manufacting projects, there are complex hierarchies, as well as information management process, that involves a substantial number of people exchanging data among numerous branches of several companies. Researchers believe that communication patterns among the participants of a project show peer-to-peer nature of communication and relationship.[15] It is where blockchain will be extremely innovative – to make the transfer of information immediate and efficient. It can be used as a decentralised trustless infrastructure to assist in creating an efficient decision-making process. With blockchain, companies will be able to streamline payments and make procurement processes smarter. They can hold supplier funds in escrow using smart-contracts – once a particular parameter has been achieved, the fee is automatically released to the supplier.

The construction industry, for instance, could be benefitted from such technological upgrades. Analysts believe that poor productivity in the construction industry is caused by underinvestment in technology.[16] In the mean time, the manufacturing industry is utilising blockchain and catching up on tech upgrades.[17] Blockchain could radically improve the productivity of both of these industries. Using smart contracts, it is possible to reduce the number of intermediaries, as user-defined parameters would execute specific functions that would not require human intervention. In terms of managing private files, blockchain could be used to store and exchange confidential data efficiently, trace asset purchased on the chain, use smart contracts to automate those payments and track input of project managers involved in the decision-making process.

However, blockchain may be not equally feasible for all type of industries. Analysis conducted by *McKinsey & Co* illustrated that they are four primary factors which determine the viability of the use case: ecosystem, standards and regulations, technology and asset. Use case of blockchain as a 'technology' is more feasible in agriculture compared to other industries, such as transport or logistics. Blockchain for 'assets' is more feasible in industries such as financial services, property, retail, media and so on. For example, land registry and title certificate on blockchain is an excellent way of validating ownership.

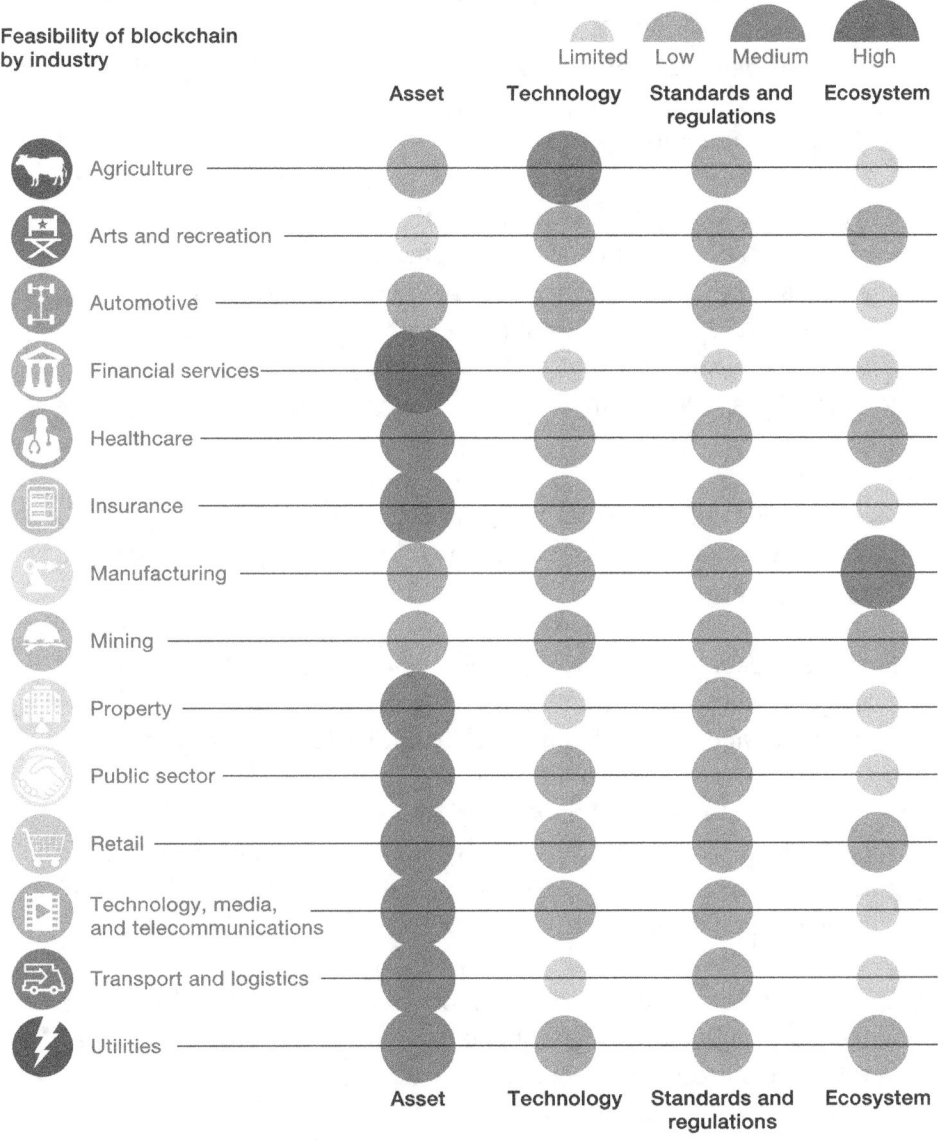

8.2: Exhibit from "Blockchain beyond the hype: What is the strategic business value?", June 2018, McKinsey & Company, www.mckinsey.com. Copyright (c) 2019 McKinsey & Company. All rights reserved. Reprinted by permission.

Likewise, blockchain based data ownership tracking and verification could have an extensive impact on the public sector. Using blockchain would significantly reduce costs in terms of paperwork, and allow councils around the country to be administered and automated under one common network. This type of use-case implementation would require a permissioned blockchain, where only the government organisations and selective institutions would have access to such records and information.

Players in Blockchain Transformation

In a bid to adopt blockchain and harness the potential, significant changes are needed to be made for such corporations. Harnessing full potential would mean automating almost everything – starting from payments to eventually registering the asset. However, to take a step towards the adoption, small changes could be made to integrate the technology:

Skill Development – Transforming the process of how employees are trained. Blockchain could be introduced into training materials to spread the information extensively.

Business Model – Introducing blockchain solutions architects and managers who could consult and assist an existing construction company to adopt technical and business development, provide plans on creating a transformational model.

Supply Chain and Procurement – By presenting smart contracts to automate procurement. Alibaba and DHL are using blockchain to streamline supply chain.[18][19]

Legal – By providing access to the information stored on the database. Since blockchain allows a user to control and share it to third parties, lawyers could access raw data in the event of a legal issue.

Blockchain has been a fundamental revolution to increase trust between two parties. A significant number of decisions in agile multiparty complex projects involves several intermediaries. Blockchain could be used to remove some of them and thus make the process much more efficient. In this case, a major incident occurred that shook the UK in

2016, the Grenfell Tower fire, can be highlighted. Initial examination suggested that the cladding was of poor quality, which led to the fire going in an upward direction and burn the building much faster. It took almost a year to investigate that the council, with an aim to save GBP 1.3m, awarded the bid to a different company than initially proposed.[20] It is a direct result of *destructive competition*, which highlights a major flaw in the supply chain and projects the dangers of a centralised system. If the information was stored on the blockchain, it could have been shared with appropriate authority to find the right balance between profit-margin and potential risk factor. Besides, it would have been much easier to track down the person involved with that decision to approve the purchase of poor-quality cladding. It is impossible to alter these types of data when using blockchain. Hence, in the event of a legal battle, blockchain can be utilised to validate information, which later will provide the foundation of any legal documents to be prepared. It could significantly increase trust by storing and sharing robust data.

Small Medium Enterprises (SMEs) in other non-tech industries could greatly benefit by utilising smart contracts. Smart-contract based jobs could remove third-parties, such as bank managers, who may take longer to process large payments. Additionally, payments could be automatically released to a supplier once that firm completes the job. Question is whether human intervention is still a necessity – for instance, is a project manager required to verify the completion of signing off the payment? Yes, of course. Nevertheless, a field manager working in a remote location does not require the authorisation of the accounts department or pass this information around, while the supplier waits for payment. Furthermore, a tokenised community of suppliers could largely benefit 'small players' in the game.

These institutions mentioned above would have an important role in controlling and democratising. Creating an ecosystem means contribution and support from all type of roles to make a business process viable. However, the following may carry a more significant role:
- Government – creating policies for better adoption of blockchain in local councils
- Financiers – invest in companies that are adaptable to disruptive innovation
- Consultants – assist in implementing and help to share information

on distributed database
- Suppliers – Adhere to the technological upgrades and policies for better efficiency
- Manufacturers – Adopting blockchain to create a larger collaborative ecosystem on a global scale.

Implemented Platforms

It has been common in the history of technological waves that mainstream media would focus most prominently on the disadvantages of the technology. Some of the brightest minds have made the worst predictions of technology. In 2006, experts thought how e-commerce *"wouldn't be a thing"* in the future after the strong emergence of Amazon. In 2010, when social media wasn't a preferred platform for *content advertising*, marketing experts suggested various reasons for social media branded a lousy platform for marketing with respect to the return on marketing investment.[21] One of the most significant shifts was the change from the printed newspapers to social news websites. It did affect the magazine publishing business, however, the news publishing sites were eventually able to cope with the idea, and generate hundreds of millions in revenue from online advertising.[22] All these predictions were made by sceptics who were not sure about the growing technology, and the worldwide media were taking full advantage of it. While the critics were busy making comments, and publishers busy writing the negative feedbacks to generate more revenue, thousands and millions of developers, managers, marketers, entrepreneurs, innovators and researchers worked tirelessly to build what the internet and social media have now become. Although the *performance* might look different in the eyes of the global media, the *foundation* of a technology is built based on the work conducted in the background.

> **DID YOU KNOW?**
>
> *Pharmaceutical giant Pfizer has partnered with a blockchain startup to utilise the technology to improve supply chain logistics.*[23]

Blockchain technology and cryptocurrencies are under constant scrutiny, and materialised as a vehicle for the perpetrators. It is time to consider what's going on in the background, what has happened over the past few years, and who are working on solving the scalability issues. Since the focus of this book has been on Ethereum network, we will first look at some of the Ethereum-based DApps that has developed disruptive business models.

Marketplace Protocols – As blockchain allow a peer to peer trading, the developers have utilised Ethereum blockchain to build protocols on the chain. Origin, a peer-to-peer marketplace development tool, was founded in 2017, in California. The startup has already raised over USD 30 million.[24] Origin aims to provide developers with easy-to-access, open-sourced codes, for developing decentralised marketplaces. Using origin protocol, companies can build markets that will allow users to buy and sell without any intermediaries. Other marketplaces are focusing on digital assets, such as NameBazaar, KnownOrigin and so on.[25][26] Here are the primary differences between eBay and a decentralised marketplace –

a) Smart contract based payments enable better security encryption and direct payment from one person to another. A centralised authority will not control the payment protocol,

b) Identity and reputation management allow decentralised marketplaces to securely store data and let users from different corners of the world to trust each other and initiate trade,

c) Data storage is decentralised, therefore, confidential information is less susceptible to cyber threats,

d) An open sourced platform allows almost any developer with little knowledge of blockchain development to launch their marketplaces.

Blockchain Storage – IPFS, or Interplanetary File System is a blockchain-based protocol designed to store data in distributed file system using a peer-to-peer method. It's similar to how BitTorrent operates. When data is stored on IPFS, every file is hashed with an encrypted key. Data isn't stored centrally in one server, rather distributed across the blockchain in various nodes. Multiple nodes keep a copy of the cache. The architecture of IPFS is very secure and powerful. It's an immutable storage of documents, therefore, once a copy of a file is stored, it cannot be tampered. However, users can upload an updated file, although the previous version won't be replaced. The changes will be tracked, and history will be accessible to other nodes.[27] IPFS is currently being used by multiple blockchain DApps, including Civic, Decentraland, Augur, Request Network and Dether.[28]

Intelligence Prediction Market – Stox, an Ethereum DApp have developed a prediction market. The users on the platform can use their native token to make a prediction and earn money.[29]

Asset Tracking, Trading and Storage – Asset tracking is one the primary use cases of Ethereum-based DApp. In a recent tweet, Vitalik mentioned that non-financial DApp would form the most of the Ethereum based platforms.[30] Cryptokitties are an ideal example of how assets on blockchain can be stored immutably and transparently. If you replace the concept of kitties with other assets, such as graduation certificates, or entitlement certificates, or even certificate for original artefacts, the possibilities are tremendously endless. Similar to Cryptokitties, other blockchain startups working on asset-based platforms are:
    Blockchain Cuties – Similar to CryptoKitties, but are more diverse in terms of animal species and categories,
    Decentraland – a blockchain based platform where users can buy and sell virtual land on the blockchain,
    MLB Crypto Baseball – A game for baseball fans, where the baseball action figures are the collectables.

Online gaming is a billion-dollar industry with a staggering growth rate. In online gaming, storing and collecting game collectable is an important part of the challenges. Some gaming companies including Mark Cuban backed *Unikrn* has announced the integration of blockchain, and therefore potentially tokenise the collectables to be able to trade on the network.[31] Open sourced asset sharing platform *OpenSea* is another great concept of sharing blockchain based assets.[32] On this platform, users around the world can bring their tokenised game assets out of their game and trade it on the marketplace. It is the first time that an open platform has allowed interoperability – the ability for multiple applications to build on the same network to agree on interchange and exchange of assets. Now, would a user be comfortable in sharing data with the public on the internet? Maybe not. A permissioned network would be a solution to such a problem. Not only can the network be

PERMISSIONED vs PERMISSIONLESS

	PERMISSIONED	**PERMISSIONLESS**
PUBLIC	1. Nodes open to the public 2. Node operators need to reveal their identities 3. Only authorised users can create node and commit to the network 4. Slow but scalable 5. Transparent and open ledger, anyone can read tx payload 6. High security	1. Nodes open to the public 2. Users do not need to reveal their identities 3. Anyone can commit to the network 4. Highly transparent and open ledger, anyone can see the transaction payload and data 5. Less scalable that permissioned blockchain 6. Immutable and high security
PRIVATE	1. Nodes open for authorised users to read, need to reveal their identities 3. Only network operators can commit to changes 3. High scalability, low transparency 4. Can be operated by a limited number of nodes 6. High privacy, great for storing confidential information	1. Nodes open for authorised users to read and write, do not need to reveal their identities 2. Authorised users can commit 3. Can be hosted on private servers 4. High scalability 5. Good for community-based development for enterprises requiring privacy

Source: IntelXSys Research, licensed under CC-by-ND 4.0 International

tailored to the requirement of the company, but it can also allow a blockchain user to be in full control of their data. Here's how.

Confidential Data Storage – Research published on *IEEE Explore* in 2015 described of how blockchain can be utilised to grant access to multi-parties and ensure user ownership and control over data at the same time.[33] It will be a game changer in the healthcare field. As technology scales, many hospitals can store their report on the chain, allowing doctors to share patient data securely with any other healthcare institution sharing the same network. Patients can also access the same network and will have the ability to share their confidential information with a particular doctor or hospital when requested. The data never leaves the blockchain or can never be tampered. When the information is updated, all logs will be timestamped and stored on the chain. One of the use cases would be Nebula Genomics – a Genome sequencing startup. Nebula aims to use blockchain technology to store highly sensitive data to create a database where researchers, pharmaceutical institutions and research organisations can access and analyse them.[34] While the blockchain eliminates the middleman, the users can choose whether they would keep their information private or share it with researchers to contribute in research and development progress.[35] The same idea can be replicated across the healthcare and other industries with an aim to revolutionise big data. The potential of such a system is limitless. Hundreds of hospitals can be brought under the same permissioned network, where patient data can not only be securely stored, but also shared with doctors and researchers in need of a particular data. By using blockchain, it would be impossible to alter any information, allowing users to have access to safe and untampered data.

Collaterals – Blockchain technology is also being used to promote financial collateralisation. Peer-to-peer lending platforms such as Salt and EthLend allow borrowers to lend money directly from the lenders.[36] A smart contracts-based system automatically tracks interest as well as payment records. As the data are securely recorded and shared with blockchain based credit reference agencies, in case of any fraud, the users will be flagged on the system and thus will not be allowed to participate. BBVA, one of the leading financial institutions, has completed transactions for USD 80 million corporate loans using Ethereum blockchain and IBM's Hyperledger.[37]

Interoperability is one of the strongest unique selling points (USP) for using tokenised ecosystem on a blockchain. In the next block, we will talk about the future of DLT, blockchain and tokenised ecosystem. Tests and research are being conducted on the feasibility of such a network, with great success achieved by many blockchain companies. However, to get to the peak of the mountain, blockchain world will need to get past the most significant obstacle – scalability. Presumably, 1 million DApps operating in the same network, each having 100,000 active users would demand an extensive amount of computational performance and a much higher transactional capacity compared to 15TPS. How would the leading blockchain platform solve these scalability problems to be able to process petabytes of data and billions of transactions in a day?

OmiseGO Founder and CEO Jun Hasegawa (L) and Bancor Protocol Co-Founder and Head of Product Eyal Hertzog speak onstage during TechCrunch Disrupt SF 2017 at Pier 48 on September 18, 2017. Jun has plans to implement a network that could be able to capacitate 1 million transactions per second or more.[38]

Photo 8.3: OmiseGO Founder and CEO Jun Hasegawa (L) and Bancor Protocol Co-Founder and Head of Product Eyal Hertzog/by Steve Jennings/Getty Imagesfor TechCrunch/licensed under CC by 2.0. © 2017 TechCrunch, some rights reserved.

BLOCK 9

FUTURE OF ETHEREUM & SCALABILITY

BLOCK INFORMATION

TX# 0x901	WHY IS THERE A SCALABILITY ISSUE?	155
TX# 0x902	UPGRADING THE NETWORK CONSENSUS ALGORITHM	156
TX# 0x903	WHAT ON EARTH IS SHARDING	158
TX# 0x904	EXPLAINING ZKSNARKS	159
TX# 0x905	50,000 TRANSACTIONS PER SECOND	162
TX# 0x906	THE GROWTH OF DECENTRALISED EXCHANGES	168
TX# 0x907	A RACE TO WIN DOMINANCE	170
TX# 0x908	FUTURE PROOFING VS CRYPTO MARKET	171

TECHNOLOGY BLOCK

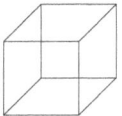
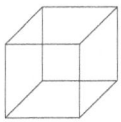
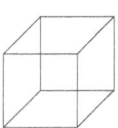
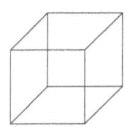

BLOCK 9

FUTURE OF ETHEREUM AND SCALABILITY

Why is there a Scalability Issue?
Blockchain is designed to secure transactions and data stored within the network. On a typical blockchain network, the new data does not replace the old data. Instead, the new data is stored in a new block by conducting an automated crosscheck to ensure the information is tamperproof. Being one the most popular platforms for developing a decentralised application, there are lots of expectations around the development of the Ethereum blockchain. Currently, one of the most discussed terms presently inside and outside the scope of blockchain development is whether blockchain is scalable enough. Scalability issues are substantial, and it requires significant upgrades to the network. More simply, you can look at it as if the computer you own will require a clean installation of the new *Windows* to get rid of redundant features and upgrade its security.

Ethereum, the leading blockchain for DApp development was launched based on similar principles of consensus used to run the bitcoin network. There is a block limit on the bitcoin network and hard-coded frequency for the miners to be able to add a new block. One of the significant reasons why these earlier versions of blockchain cannot process a lot of data is their security protocol – every single transaction are checked and validated against every database stored on every node on the chain. This validation step ensures the transactions are untampered and uniform. You can compare Ethereum blockchain 1.0 to a linear shape, e.g. a chain in a straight line. The challenge in a proof-of-work consensus is either increasing block size or creating faster block times to increase transactional capacity. Contrary to the popular belief, Ethereum founder believes that faster block may not compromise the security of the chain.[1] Although the lighting network upgrade of bitcoin increased efficiency, till this date, Bitcoin blockchain is not efficient enough to handle a thousand transactions in one second.² Nevertheless, due to demand and overall market capitalisation, bitcoin is considered as a store of value.³

Due to the involvement of the miners, the transaction costs are higher in proof-of-work consensus. *Ethereum blockchain 1.0* cannot process thousands of transactions per second, however, the foundation has a better idea to solve this issue.

Upgrading the Network Consensus Algorithm

The plan is changing the design of the blockchain to the shape of a tree. Theoretically, the primary branch will be the tree trunk, and there will be secondary 'branches' growing from the trunk. This will create a hierarchy, where the main chain will be supervising the overall activity of everything being broadcasted to the network. The branches will individually be able to store and process the transactions. Only in the case of Ethereum blockchain, the branches will be known as 'shards', and the design will be implemented on layer 1. However, to deploy this new design effectively, the blockchain will need to move completely to a new consensus algorithm, known as proof-of-stake (PoS). Ethereum's milestone is designed in a way that it will force miners to shift from the old chain to the new and upgraded one.

Ethereum laid out its plan from the beginning, showing four stages of these upgrades. These upgrades on the network can be compared to the updates of the operating system we use. When the operating system of a computer is upgraded, some new features are added, and new security protocols are implemented. Additionally, codes are added to make the workflow processes faster. Ethereum planned four stages of upgrades - *Frontier, Homestead, Metropolis, Serenity*. Blockchain networks require *hard fork* when layer 1 is upgraded. You might confuse hard fork with the probability of creating a new coin, but hard fork does not necessarily mean that a new coin will be created. The team has recently annouced in that they are confident about the launch of the next update by mid 2020.⁴

Why wouldn't a new coin might be created when Ethereum upgrades its network in the near future? The answer lies in the community consensus. Although every major *network upgrade* on the proposed milestone will require a hard fork, the Ethereum foundation and the community came to the consensus that the engineers and miners will support the new chain. As explained earlier, the network is not controlled by a single entity, instead, run and managed by the consensus of a large pool of engineers, business management board on the foundation, network developers and miners working to keep the decentralised network alive. The question is, will these hard forks and shift towards proof-of-stake affect miners who are an integral part of keeping it thriving? Without miners, the network would not merely exist. Therefore, miners are as important as the other contributors to the network. With regards to Ethereum, the decisions regarding the upgrade of the network were unanimously agreed among everyone including miners. The plan was proposed in their earlier version of EIPs and accepted by the community. Therefore, everyone within the boundaries of this network knows what to expect. The miners and validators are expected to keep supporting the hard forks until the final upgrade 'Serenity' is implemented.

It was agreed that the move from Ethereum Homestead to Ethereum Metropolis would be conducted in two stages, Byzantium and Constantinople.[5] The Byzantium hard fork was activated in October 2017, which raised the difficulty of mining Ethereum using proof-of-work algorithm and added many additional features to the network. Once Constantinople hard fork was deployed, the difficulty has been increased to an extent where it would be impossible for the miners to stay in the old chain, therefore, to earn ether by providing their computation power, it will be mandatory for them to shift to the upgraded chain. The difficulty of mining process was not increased overnight, rather gradually, and is expected to 'explode', after which all the nodes are expected to shift to the new consensus algorithm. Constantinople upgrade means implementation of a hybrid of proof-of-work and proof-of-stake consensus.

Think, if you were a miner, why go through all this hassle to shift to a completely new system? The answer goes back to the concept of building a network that can process millions of transactions every minute. Currently, Ethereum 1.0 is capable of processing approximately 6-15 transactions per second.[6] In 1.0, the nodes in the network participate in processing every transaction in the history of blockchain to create a new block. Every transaction can also hold up to 200 transfers of ERC20 tokens and contract deployments. Ethereum planned to scale its network in such a way so that the entire blockchain is capable of capacitating over 50,000 or more transactions per second. The first reason for upgrade was to deploy new code to implement sharding and completely upgrade the Layer 1 of Ethereum network.

The second and the essential feature was to move to a proof-of-stake network. Sharding will require PoS implementation. It is where the game completely changes. Unlike proof-of-work, the miners will not be required to spend a significant amount of money to participate in the process of earning ether. In PoS, the miners become validators. As a validator, a user can stake and lock a minimum of 32 ETH to join the validation process in the network.[7] By staking the ether, the validators verify the blocks and get rewarded proportionally to the ether staked. One of the three main features of the PoS are:
 • No equipment or energy inefficiency
 • Less susceptible to 51% attack - makes it incredibly expensive to execute
 • Reduction of transactional error – malicious blocks can't be mined, as it will invalidate the stake and will be taken away
 • Reduced transaction costs compared to PoW

What on Earth Is Sharding
When sharding in implemented, the blockchain will be divided and split into multiple subsets, or shards. These shards can process or store transactions individually. The nodes would be able to participate in one or more shard, therefore allowing to validate transactions on the blockchain without having to provide a significant amount of computational power. Companies like Google, processing and analysing billions of data points, use sharding in their centralised databases to increase computational power and increase capacity with lower latency.[8]

Parallelisation
By allowing the chain to be split and stored into multiple subsets from the main chain, the blockchain would be capable of storing a significant amount of data in the shards. The sharding process allows the network to create a chain-of-command, where individual shards are capable of storing and processing multiple transactions. Thus, the main chain will not be required to store every single data on the blockchain. It allows the

main chain to handle a higher number of operations at the same time in parallel.

Remember, miners are being cited to as 'validators'. In proof-of-stake, the validators may be chosen at random to participate, and in turn, they add a block. As the shards are individually capable of storing and processing data, instead of asking the nodes to process data on the main chain, they are allocated with the shards. The method of allocation is random sampling, in which the validators are not able to choose which shard they want to process or know from beforehand regarding the which shard they are about to be allocated. Proof-of-stake is a requirement for sharding, as this consensus algorithm would allow the network to allocate random shards to the nodes, and as a result, increase security and efficiency of the network.[9] Ethereum is not the only blockchain to use sharding to scale. *Ziliqa* is another blockchain that uses sharding.[10] Analysts believe this process significantly increases capacity, with Vitalik claiming that sharding will increase the capacity by to 100 times.

Explaining ZkSnarks

The metropolis upgrade will also see the implementation of ZkSnarks – Zero Knowledge Succinct Non-Interactive Argument of Knowledge. ZCash is currently using zero-knowledge proofs to secure their transactions.[11] The concept was first described in a research paper published by Joe Killian from NEC Research Institute at Princeton in 1992.[12] In theory, zero-knowledge is required to satisfy the following parameters to verify a transaction:

- *Correctness:* Allowing precision of the calculation
- *Succinct:* Using a mathematical process of random sampling to reduce the size of proof and verification time[13]
- *Non-Interactive:* Without the requirement of having to execute any interaction
- *Zero-Knowledge:* Without the need of revealing any information to a third-party

In a non-technical explanation, this design will assist in benefitting a contract between multiple parties without the need to reveal all or any information. The issuer of the contract will be able to prove that the person is trustworthy without revealing some or any of the details of the contract. Imagine that you would like to speak to a manager named Adrian at a car company. Every time you would make a call, the company is legally required to verify your credentials by asking you confidential information, such as date of birth, nationality, driver's license, home address and so on. ZkSnarks reduces this workflow by allowing a batch of data to be instantly verified by the blockchain without revealing such information to the other party.[14] Let's assume that Ella wants to speak to Adrian regarding her new car. Ella opens the app to contact her manager. The app verifies the information via the mobile application and its smart contracts. Using ZkSnarks, the data is compressed, sent to blockchain to be verified. Within seconds, Ella's information is verified automatically. Thus the app connects the call to Adrian, without the need for Adrian to verify Ella's identify or give access to any of the confidential information. This implementation can radically change the way users are by several customer services of different brands.

An intuitive model can be explained using decentralised personal identity storage application. Large metro cities such as London is famous for its nightlife. Going out without an ID could be a hassle, and in many cases, you might be barred from entering a bar or a club. Besides, when you're out with your friends, the risk of losing essential documents such as that passport always prevails. Blockchain-based storage service would allow users to securely store their government-issued ID.

As a user, you will need to download the DApp and upload your driving licence or passport to store the data within blockchain. When requested for an ID at the entrance, all you need to do is scan the code generated from your DApp. In this process, the system will automatically verify the ID data stored on the blockchain. Therefore, the admins will not be required to see your full identification or personal data, because once the encrypted keys are verified using the system, they will know that it's you. By allowing zero-knowledge proof to validate the data, you are neither required to carry your ID nor reveal the confidential information to anyone. The system on both sides of the architecture will exchange secure keys to verify the data without having to pull the data out of the blockchain, or compromise any or all of the data stored within the chain. This process also eliminates the method of scanning your confidential information, hence a third-party wouldn't be required to save a copy of your private data on their servers. The same process applies to any other institutions such as solicitor firms. You can prove the existence of a bank account without having to show your bank statement. If all of these

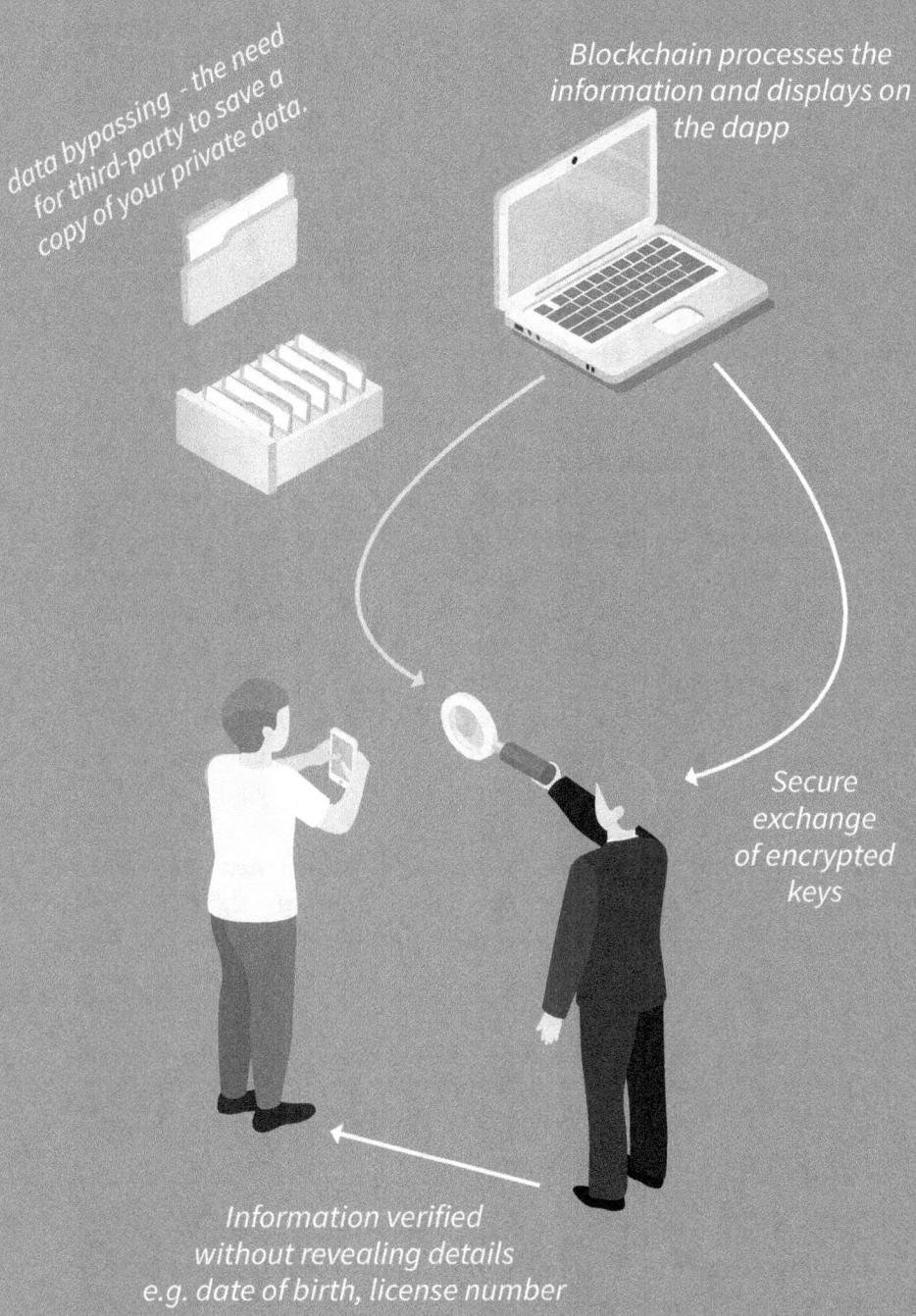

9.1: ZkSnarks use case.

institutions from various industries are brought under the same network, then it would make ID verification process incredibly straightforward and efficient.

ZkSnarks will not only keep the data encrypted on the blockchain but also automatically permit a large batch of transactions to be compressed and processed at the same time. This implementation will provide better processing capability. Ethereum foundation claims that ZkSnarks could increase Ethereum blockchain's capacity to 500tps without the need to implement more advanced or *layer 2 scalability solution*.[15]

50,000 Transactions Per Second

As networks like Ethereum has allowed thousands of developers to build more application on the network, the blockchain is continuously under pressure to increase the competence of its transactional services. Ethereum's development plans include several updates including the idea of "Sharding", nevertheless, there is one company working to solve the scalability of this network and has successfully tested their version of a scalable solution. The proposal was designed by the founder of Ethereum Vitalik and Joseph Poon, one of the leading engineers at OmiseGo.

Enter the world of Plasma. A thoroughly researched idea and a framework which is claimed to be scalable *"to a significant amount of state updates per second"*. According to the technical whitepaper published by OmiseGo,

"We propose a method for decentralised autonomous applications to scale to process not only financial activity but also construct economic incentives for globally persistent data services, which may produce an alternative to centralised server farms." [16]

This solution is termed as 'Layer 2' scalability solution. Other 'Layer 2' scalability solution would be Lighting Network on Bitcoin and Loom network.[17] In terms of OmiseGo, in much simpler terms, the idea is to create child chain, a second layer on the primary chain, where the blockchain would work as a hierarchy and treat individual branch of the tree as a child, which would enhance computational performance. It is also known as an off-chain computation which reduces the pressure of processing transaction on the main blockchain. The idea is to allow anyone to create a plasma chain using OMG as their vendor. This will initiate a series of smart contracts that will enable many smaller versions of the blockchain run in parallel within the main Ethereum chain. The main chain will only get involved and intercept a transaction when there is a proof-of-fraud.[18] The implementation of the Plasma by OmiseGo has already been laid out in the following milestones:

Tesuji Plasma: This is the initial test-net model of the plan, a milestone where multiple wallets are tested along with OmiseGo as vender or an operator with proof-of-authority (PoA) consensus.

Tenjen Plasma: This is aimed at the final product with support of proof-of-stake (PoS) consensus protocol when implemented. The validators in the PoS network will be rewarded with fees for providing computational power.

OmiseGo has already made their first version of their product open-sourced in order to receive support from the community. The developers of plasma chain will have full access to the tools and source codes to create their own child chain that will work independently, i.e. without the dependency on the root chain. It can be compared to a company with its own hierarchy. A corporate organisation has its chief executive, who is in charge of its entire operations. There are multiple departments, each department in charge of individual operations. For instance, the market department is led by CMO, or the chief marketing officer, who is responsible for overseeing marketing projects. Similarly, other department heads are responsible for creating and approving various proposals and work through the operations. Under the chief executives of different departments, are the managers, who are running the day to day operations of an individual area. In retail, for instance, under the head of operations, are the individual retail branch manager. The branch manager leads department managers, such produce or bakery. The bakery manager is liable for keeping track of everything going into the bakery department of that store, including stock count. Nevertheless, there are staff to assist him to keep track of all the stock required in a particular week.

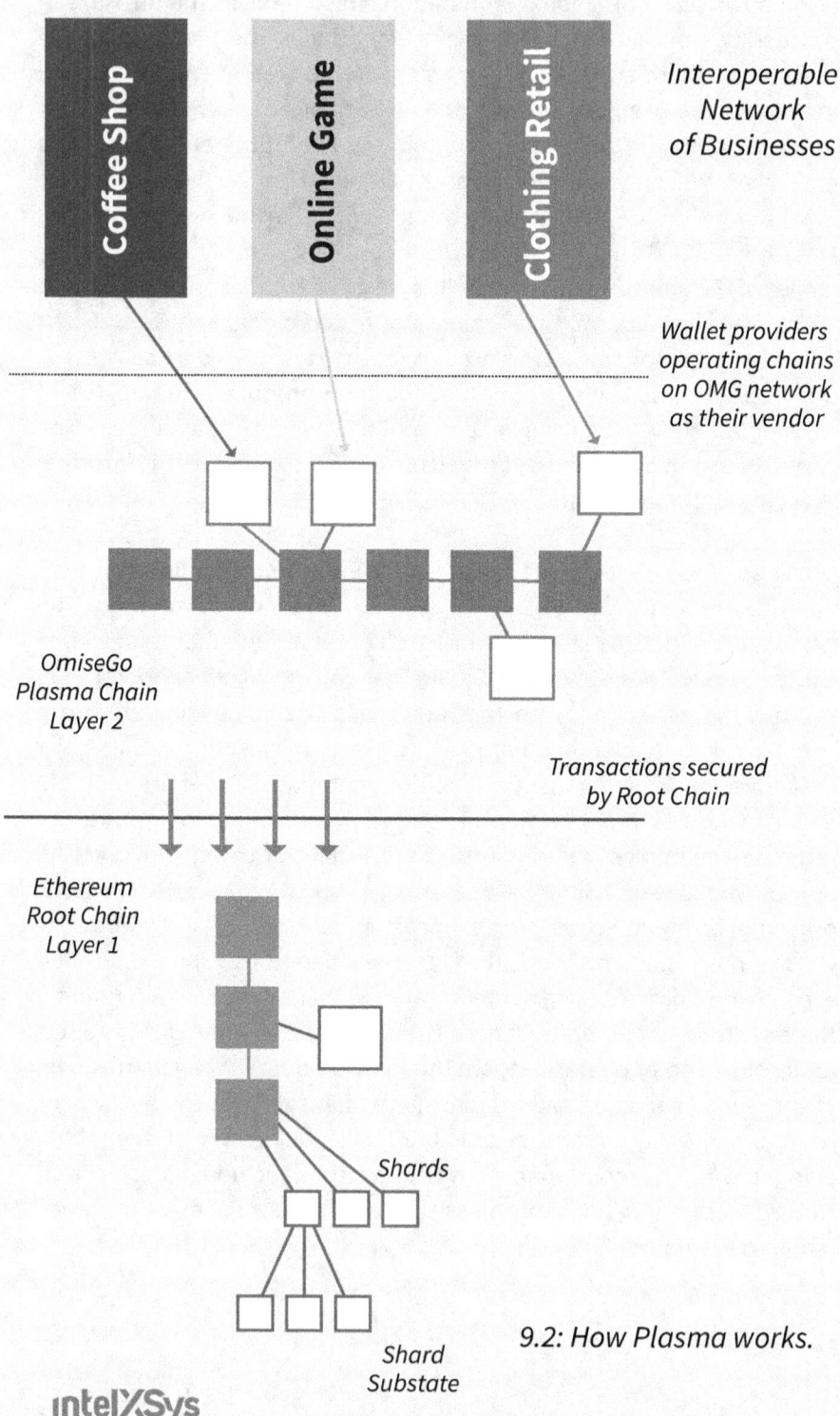

9.2: How Plasma works.

Now let's get straight back to the head of operations analogy. The COO is neither required to authorise, nor expected to know the details of every single work going on all the branches around the country. It is unnecessary. Instead, a department requests the brand manager, and the brand manager then follows up with the procurement to ensure enough stock has been delivered. Once the data has been processed, the procurement officers then fulfil the requests based on the stock requirement. The chief operating officer is only responsible for handling emergency queries or keeping track of the overall operations. The operational procedure of a blockchain will be similar.

Although the root chain would be aware of millions of transactions, it will neither be required to process nor store all these transactions on the main chain. All the functions are stored, processed and maintained on the individual chains. In case of disputes in transactional validity, each chain would have its own rules and regulations, yet, still be connected to the main chain 24/7. This process allows billions of users to coexist within just one blockchain. OmiseGo is building the infrastructure to convert almost any asset to any other asset within the same network.

There are lots of questions around whether Anna would be entitled to refunds in case of a product she doesn't want. Other concerns could be the validity of the individual chain and whether they are reliable. This process is solved by creating a series of proof-of-fraud. A customer can exit funds in the event of a block not responding or being withheld. The customer will be required to broadcast proof of transaction to the root chain, which will allow her to withdraw the funds after a series of validation. Therefore, within this entire hierarchy of chains, if any of the child chains stop working, withholds fund, or commits fraud, the customer is entitled to validate their information by broadcasting message to the root chain. The root chain will only validate blocks from time-to-time, in order to make sure that the child chains aren't committing fraud; by using PoS consensus, and execute business logic by following ecosystem laws and regulations.

This explanation is a high-level overview of how the implementation of plasma will work. The idea is still being tested on the test net, and not yet been implemented on the main. Will OmiseGo be able to create a full Plasma? It should be. The business is moving in the right direction with an incredibly talented group of innovators on-board. Until then, Ethereum will be able to increase capacity by deploying layer 1 scalability, such as ZkSnarks and also sharding.

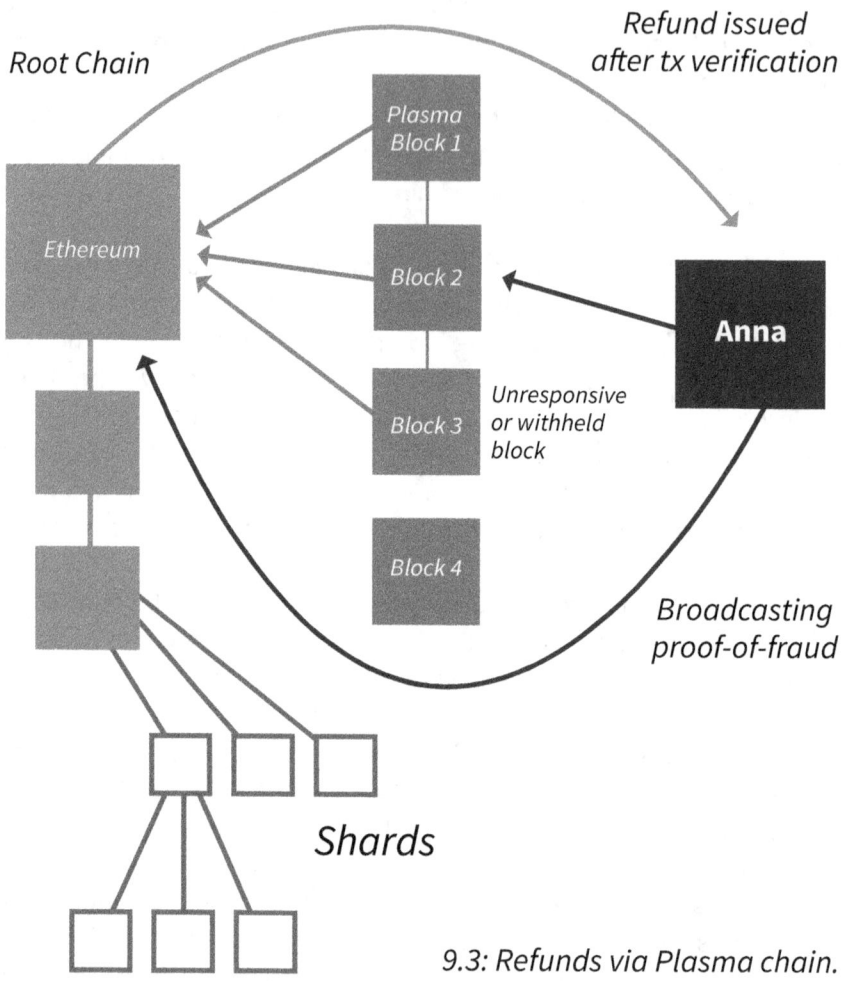

9.3: Refunds via Plasma chain.

Even if Ethereum achieves its target, an increased capacity of 10tps to 500tps will be a 50-fold increase in transactional volume.[19] That's a potential capacity of 43 million transactions, compared to just over half a million transactions recorded in December 2018.

A fashion retail shop 'Boutique X' and bookshop 'Millennial Books' run plasma chains with OmiseGo as a validator. The shops will be responsible for maintaining their plasma chains, which will monitor and process all the necessary transaction. Let's say Anna is one of their loyal customers. All of Anna's loyalty tokens from Boutique X will be tracked on the chain. Now, if Anna desires to exchange those loyalty tokens with her favourite books, she can go to Millennial Books and make purchases directly. With thousands of shops under one validator, Anna can interchange tokens earned from games straight in coffee shops! The OmiseGo network allows interoperability. Therefore, Anna would not need a separate wallet to convert various tokens and make her purchase in the book shop.

Photo: Praew Stock/Shutterstock

In hindsight, let's look at how the technology has been overcoming the obstacle and grew:

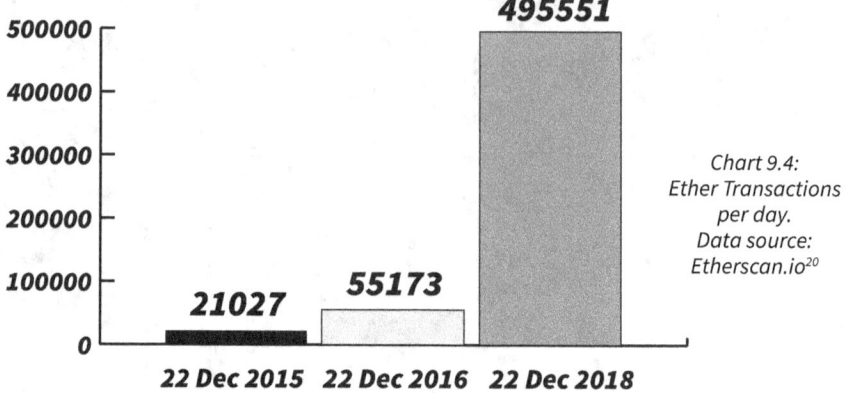

Chart 9.4: Ether Transactions per day. Data source: Etherscan.io[20]

The problem here is that *Plasma* is still a new-born technology and has only achieved certain milestones on the test net. Plasma is a solution to many problems, but it isn't there yet. For the technology to survive, it will need many factors to support the growth. To start with, OmiseGo needs to stay financially afloat to ensure that significant research and development takes place before the technology is released to the mass public. There will be lots of barriers and problems to overcome to get to 'million TPS' stage of scalability. It might take one, three, or even five years. If OMG can integrate their idea with Ethereum blockchain, the founders believe that the network could be scaled up to millions of transactions per second. The possibilities of an infinitesimally scalable platform, where billions of unbanked people can connect and interact with others, will be possible with this significant step. Interestingly, the development of layer 2 scalabilities will not be limited to OmiseGo, in fact, over the next ten years, more startups will come up with even better solutions. The winner will be the entrepreneurs who could design, test and fully implement the platform. In a recent update, OmiseGo announced *plasma cash*, their *point-of-sale* as well as merchant app.[21]

The Growth of Decentralised Exchanges

One of the fastest growing trends in 2018 was the creation of decentralised exchanges (DEX). Cryptocurrency traders most often use centralised exchanges. The advantages of having centralised exchanges are that centralised servers are utilised to increase the its computation power to process transaction, therefore allowing millions of users to trade much faster. A user would be required to create a new wallet account with these exchanges and at times get verified. The cryptocurrencies are stored in various types of wallet, and protected by multi-party signatures to protect the funds from getting hacked. That's where the disadvantages come in - since the funds are stored centrally in the exchange wallet that stays online, it is susceptible to be attacked by the criminals. Previous incidents include the hack of Mt. Gox and other major exchanges such as Bitstamp.[22] In 2017, Ethereum's multi-signature wallet Parity, used by hundreds of startups, was hacked.[23] Recently, a Japanese exchange was also hacked where the hackers were able to steal approximately USD 59 million.[24] Although many exchanges recovered from their hack and improved the security of code, a few went into liquidation, resulting in millions losing their belongings. It resulted in innovators come up with the idea of a decentralised exchange or DEX. The trading mechanism of a DEX is similar to a centralised exchange; however, the users are in full control of their funds. Instead of sending the funds over to an exchange account, the users can directly trade from a personal wallet. *0x Protocol* developed an open platform for decentralised exchanges, that will allow developers to set up an exchange without much hassle of developing it from scratch. The open protocol facilitates the trading of any ERC20 token and permits any developer to build a DEX on 0x protocol. The idea is fascinating as developers with minimal experience would be capable of creating a DEX on their protocol.[25] 0x host some of the most sophisticated DEXs, including EthFinex, the decentralised-spinoff of the parent company BitFinex; along with other DEXs e.g. DDEX, Radar Relay and so on. EthFinex uses a trustless system and a decentralised governance mechanism, where the users holding EthFinex native currency *Nectar* can participate in many critical voting processes for the development of the organisation. The idea is not only limited to exchanges – 0x believes that their platform can be utilised to buy and sell cryptocurrencies in conventional websites, develop prediction market platforms, trade collectables and also offer financial collaterals.[26]

Many exchanges are hesitant to move towards decentralised exchange-based business model, but that move will increase security. It is a compromise between transactional capacity and the security. Any website in the entire world is susceptible to cyber attack. Billion-dollar companies like Carphone Warehouse and Equifax gets hacked even after having cyber defence teams on board.[27] However, top exchanges such as Binance has deployed three to four-layer security, including password, two-factor authentication (2FA), withdrawal confirmation via 2FA and email. Shifting towards DEX will ensure the users are entirely in control of their funds, as the funds are never required to be moved out of their hardware or software wallet. With increased blockchain capacity and better technologies such as sharding and ZkSnarks, developers will be able to create much improved and high-performance DEX.

In a bid to step forward towards decentralisation, Binance CEO Zhao also explained that DEXs would provide better freedom, and once the technology can capacitate more transactions, DEXs will rule over the next five to ten years.[28] The company also announced that they are developing their own DEX.[29] Four out of five of the top six DEXs are built on the 0x ecosystem, and with millions of existing users, it is rapidly growing. One of the primary reasons why entry-level developers often prefer 0x as they offer the right tool to lower the barrier who are interested in monetising their skillset.[30] Additionally, by providing an open-sourced protocol to incorporate exchange functionality, up and coming DApp developers will find it easier the develop cost-effective products by building on a defined set of standards.[31]

A Race to Win Dominance
While blockchain companies valued at billions are establishing the system of creating more and more open sourced projects, a number of corporations are racing towards patents. Historically a technology would start a patent war, with companies such as IBM racing towards filing patents. A patent ensures an exclusive right to a certain design of a technology or hardware, in return for the company to reveal its invention to the public. One of the reasons why existing dominating technology companies race to win patent is to ensure that their core model and revenue stream are not threatened.

The battleground has already triggered controversy among blockchain pioneers, although, it technically diminishes the ultimate goal of decentralisation. In order to stay ahead of the invention process, companies such as Bank of America, IBM, Alibaba, Mastercard are racing towards attaining the highest number of patents. Barclays also filed a patent application with the US patent office, with regards to the transfer of digital asset, and blockchain based encryption data storage.[32] Besides, after the launch of Mastercard Blockchain, the corporation was awarded patent for blockchain-based multicurrency exchange on a permissioned blockchain.[33] A number of sources have published their finding on how the patent war has intensified in 2018. With 89 patents under the IBM brand, a number of Chinese companies are chasing to become the top company to win the patent battleground.[34] More corporations are expected to join the race over the next few years. This patent war is likely to continue if blockchain becomes a established and widely used technology.

A bearish market attracts corporate investors to take advantage of low prices, and that is what encouraging the multinational corporations to shift towards blockchain. While many traditional brands such as Kodak used blockchain for PR, investment companies such as Goldman Sachs are actively investing in blockchain companies. Goldman Sachs led the USD 25 million investment round into blockchain based money transfer startup Veem.[35] Goldman Sachs also aims to open a dedicated corporate trading desk for bitcoin and other cryptocurrencies. Additionally, NXMH's aquisition of Bitstamp has gained attention of a large number of corporate finance institutions looking to diversify their portfolio.[36]

Coporate Involvement in Blockchain Development

Dragonchain – Owned by Walt-Disney, Dragonchain raised over USD 2 million via ICO. Dragonchain has developed their blockchain and aiming to commercialise the platform.[37]

Amazon Chain – In 2017, AWS CEO announced he was not interest in blockchain or cryptocurrency-based services.[38] In 2018, after receiving a patent, AWS has also launched a managed service, where developers can choose between Hyperledger and Ethereum to develop smart contract based DApp.[39]

Future Proofing and Crypto Market

The involvement of existing popular software and hardware companies with millions of existing users is the key to mass adoption for users in the blockchain. The founder of Mozilla Foundation and Firefox has launched his decentralised browser that will permit users to browser DApp directly from browser. Currently, a browser extension *Metamask* allow any user to connect to web 3.0 application. Users can browse web 3.0 sites, connect to DApps, as well as trade on decentralised exchanges directly from their hardware wallet using this simple extension. The development of MetaMask was the first gateway to bridge the gap between web 2.0 and web 3.0, but that wasn't the only attempt to launch the process of mass adoption.

The *Brave* browser is similar to Firefox Privacy, a privacy-focused browser. Basic Attention Token (BAT) is an Ethereum based utility token, a native cryptocurrency for the *Brave* browser.[40] Using Ethereum blockchain, Brave browser opens a new world of opportunities to internet users and publishers, who would be rewarded with BAT tokens in return for opted-in advertising. In short, Brave users will be rewarded for browsing the internet. The token will also act as a utility token among the three critical users in the triangle, internet users, publishers and advertisers. The advertisers can connect directly with publishers to advertise on their website, resulting in a peer-to-peer ad network. It has many benefits including more revenue share for publishers as well as reduced advertising cost due to the elimination of middleman platforms. Using Ethereum platform, Brave will be able to anonymously and cryptographically track users and publisher information to serve better targeted ads. With plenty of industry experience of developing one of the most famous browsers on the internet, Brave will open the door to an enormous number of users to 'earn while you browse' when the full version of the ads program is launched.

Opera, another privacy-focused browser has now released an update, which includes an integrated Ethereum wallet. Therefore, any Opera user will now be able to access DApps using built-in wallet. This update is another gateway to better adoption, as many non-blockchain users will be able to access decentralised platforms and trade on exchanges using mobile phone browser.

Although there are hundreds and thousands of developers actively developing the foundation of the technology, is it really for billions of people? The bright and straightforward answer is no. Before the ultimate goal of blockchain – 'banking for the unbanked' is achieved, it is bound to pass through the various phases of adoption. Gartner's *hype cycle* shows how various technologies can go through a sequence of hype, followed by the *trough of disillusionment* and ultimately reaching the *plateau of productivity*.[41] Blockchain, like other technologies, is going through the same cycle. Don't confuse the *hype cycle* with the financial trends in the cryptocurrency market. Evidently, the sustainability of the technology in the eyes of the public are proportionately determined by the condition of the market and price of bitcoin. However, in reality, it's very different. The market dynamics affect the persona, but that does not stop companies from developing the technology. The question here is whether cryptocurrency has passed the stage of hype – and to be fair, it is difficult to predict that. The chart 9.5 shows the state of cryptocurrency index –

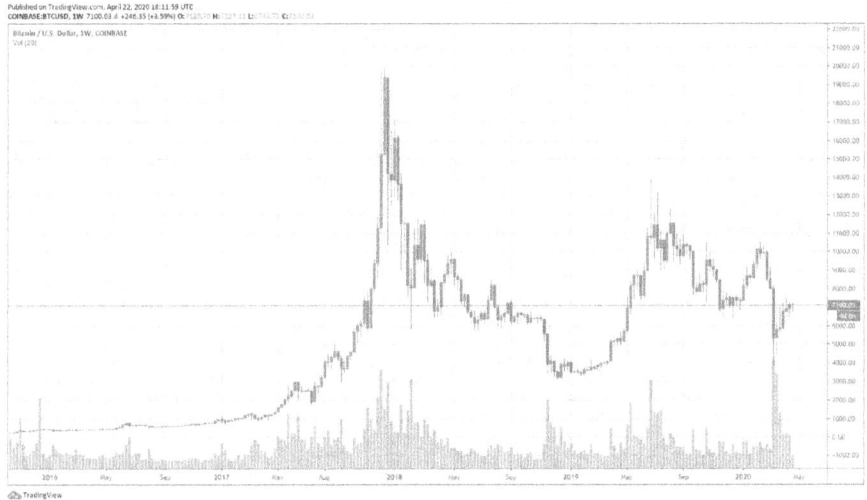

Chart 9.5: BTC price since 2015. Source: tradingview.com

Now let's have a look at three critical junctions of the cryptocurrency market.
        a. Chart 9.6 represents the first time bitcoin hit USD 30,
        b. Chart 9.7, represents the time when it had hit USD 1000,
        c. Chart 9.8 indicates the time the bitcoin reached almost USD 20,000 (April 2020).

The first chart represents the time between September 2010 and January 2013. The bearish market lasted approximately twelve months during this period.

Chart 9.6: Bitcoin hitting $30 in June 2011. Source: buybitcoinworldwide.com

The second chart represents the time between April 2014 and November 2017. The highlighted period in the middle shows the bearish market between 2014 and 2016, during which the bear lasted approximately twelve months.

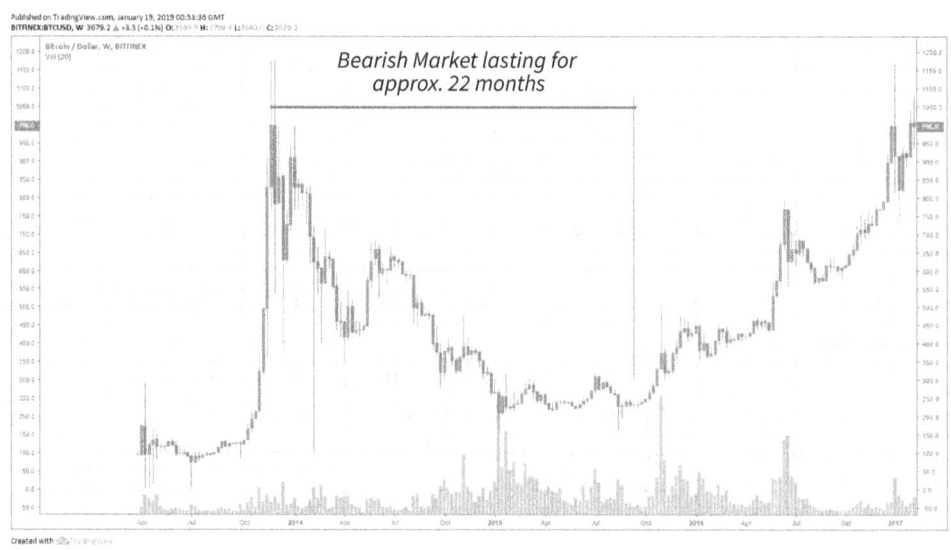

Although the market recovered a little after October 2016, it started to form proper bullish curve after April 2017. Can you compare charts 9.6 and 9.7 with 9.5, i.e. to the overall market? It demonstrates that every

time the market retracted, the bullish ride following the crash was even more prominent - the growth was higher, and broke any previous record.

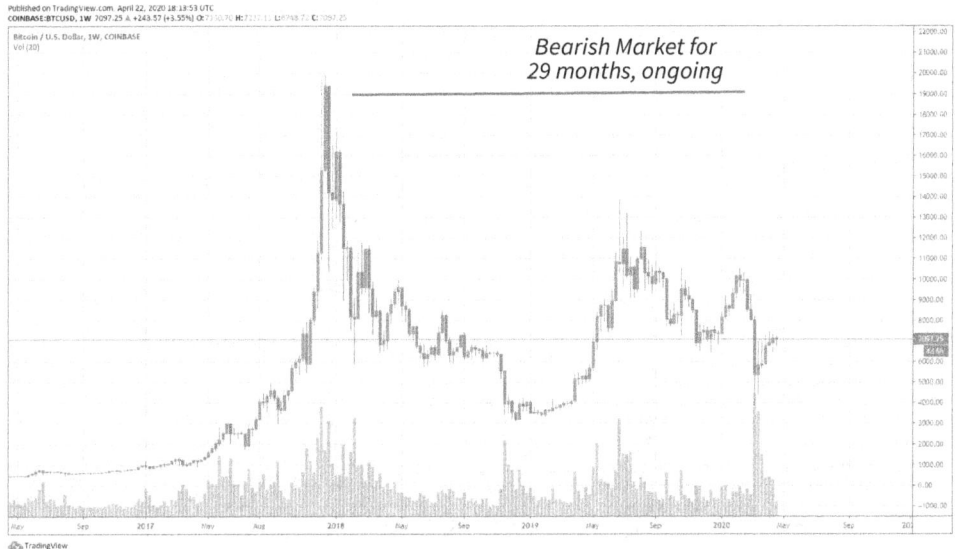

Chart 9.8: Bitcoin hitting USD 19000. Source: tradingview.com[42]

Chart 9.8.1: Previous chart 9.7 overlapped on 9.8. The bullish and bearish formation patterns look very similar. (n.b.: chart 9.7 has been cropped)

The hype phases are very contextual because the graph looks very similar to the curve in the chart (PTO).

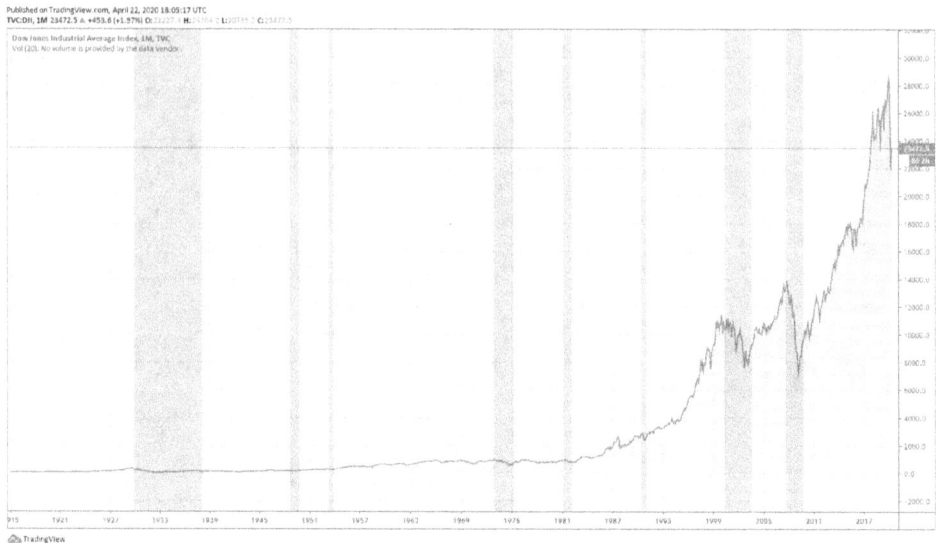

Chart 9.9: Dow Jones since 1915. Source: tradingview.com[43]

This chart represents Dow Jones Industrial Average (DJI) or the pulse of the US stock market. It defines the overall market dynamics in the United States, representing the price of top thirty large US companies based on 'weighted average'. The grey areas represent the *recession* and *depression* phases of the market. However, the market pulled back and broke previous records as new technologies and industries emerged after the recession.

It is not an indication that the entire stock market has been forming a bubble for the past 250 years. Instead, it is evident that no matter how a market crashes, entrepreneurs, innovators, technologists, researchers work together to tackle the issue and pull the market back by following one principle – 'head down and build'. Based on previous statistics, it is likely that the market will retract and form a bullish curve anytime within the next two years. Analysts are expecting that bitcoin will break USD 20,000 and might reach USD 50,000 within the next three to six years. Ethereum is also expected to break USD 1424 resistance at some point in time. It is impossible to say exactly when, although there is a logical explanation of why the market would recover.

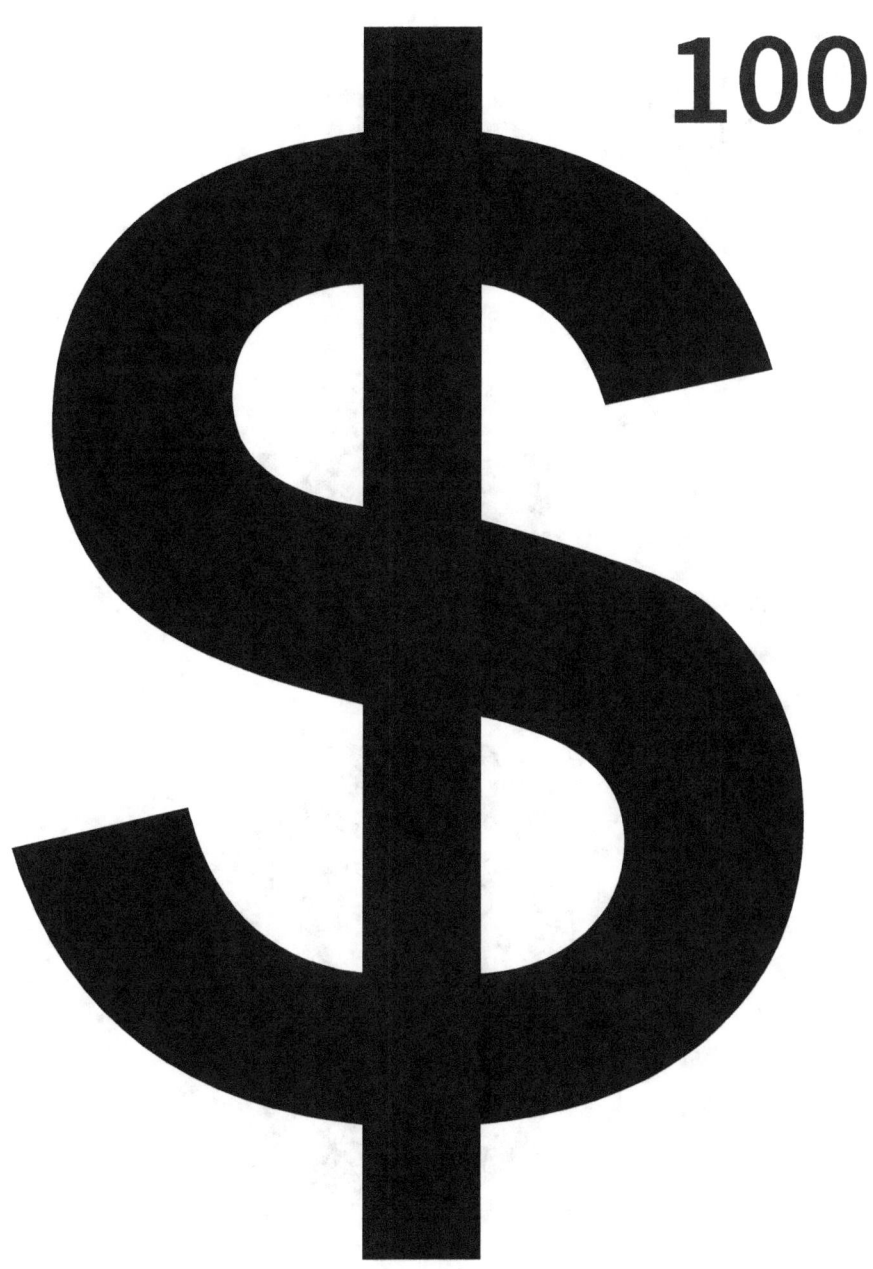

worth bitcoin in 2010 would have been worth over USD 12,000,000 today. Why do you think it happened? Do you regret not learning about this technology earlier?

BLOCK 10

WHY IT IS TIME TO GET INVOLVED

BLOCK INFORMATION

TX# 0x1001	IT ISN'T WHAT WE EXPECTED	181
TX# 0x1002	YOU CAN FIND THE NEXT BIG IDEA	183
TX# 0x1003	2044 IS CLOSER THAN YOU THINK	187
TX# 0x1004	A PEEK INTO THE NEAR FUTURE	192

OPINION BLOCK

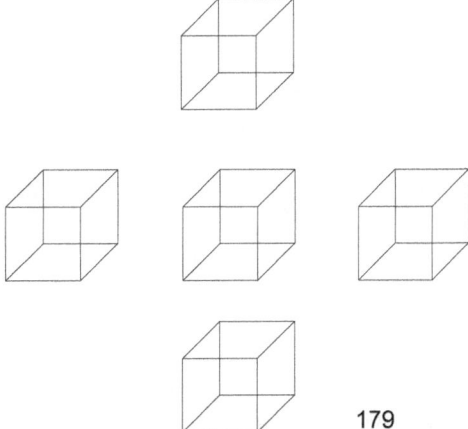

BLOCK 10

WHY IT IS TIME TO GET INVOLVED

It Isn't What We Expected
#1
I have been involved in the background of this industry for a few years now. I have always been an avid crypto enthusiast. Now imagine working very hard to learn about a technology for many years, then making over a thousand percent gains on crypto trades, over a year or two. When you reveal these proofs to other people interested in portfolio diversification, they would want your expertise and presume that they themselves would not need to "learn a lot" to understand how it works. But when the inevitable happens, that is the market collapses, the very same people would start doubting the sustainability of the technology. What you would apprehend is that people tend to avoid learning how or why they should get involved, and what could be the risks if everything goes wrong. Short-term thinking doesn't work when it comes to disruptive technology.

Companies, investors and startups have lost a significant amount of money due to this 'predictable price correction' of the market.[1] To be honest, it was expected that the market will go through correction at some point. Similar to how everything was overbought in 2017, during the entire year of 2018, all of them were oversold. Similar patterns can be observed in 2015, 2013 and also 2011, as shown earlier.[2] Being a *blockchain believer*, it is not figuratively possible for me to avoid the problems and issues around the industry. While it is easier to come across incredible talents, who are contributing to their fullest, there are many labelled as experts who barely recognise the differences between a blockchain and a distributed ledger. One of the reasons why blockchain is not being branded as great technology is the fact that it has attracted the attention of a significant number of opportunists taking advantage of short-term gains. In other words, the wrong kind of people. Besides, a large number of companies have raised funds, however, disappeared before the companies even distributed their tokens after raising the funds.[3] But this did not stop the bubble from growing. In fact, imagine attending a paid event worth hundreds of dollars, and then finding speakers who neither have an in-depth knowledge, nor the capacity to publicly speak about the benefits. One of the worst cases of misinformation was the fact that people around the industry were deceitful about their work and educational experiences. They were not aiding the technology – they were a supplement to the *growth of fraudulent activities*. All of these worked as a catalyst towards bubble formation.

#2
Unmistakably, the quick *bullish formation* of the market led a mass public towards a deception – joining the cryptocurrency world means making a thousand times over a few months. Any investor would primarily protect themselves from losing money, but the problem is that people with minimal experience with investments absolutely flooded the industry. Buying tokens to make few thousands of percent gains over a few months is fundamentally wrong. A professional and experienced investor would never take such a risk. Instead, they would continue to have faith in the team and technology they invested in – it's called long-term investment.

The bull-ride in 2017 also attracted the attention of many more thousand people who still have absolutely no clue of how the technology works. These pre-conceptions of making 'quick-buck' has aided in the formation of a bubble. The concept of arranging bank loans and taking in mortgages to buy bitcoin is profoundly incorrect. Development of any technology requires time, possibly decades. If it is pushed for time to receive a better return on investment, the outcome of the product wouldn't be as good as its promised.

#3
These are the worst kind of frauds – using anonymity to conduct criminal activities. Just like money, the internet, social media, bitcoin and other cryptocurrencies are being used to conduct fraud and illegal activities. A DW documentary shows how police in the Philippines are tackling this kind of cybercrimes. One of the most attractive schemes are short-term

financial gains by 'investing' in bitcoin.[4] This type of project attract a lot of gamblers, as many people made a lot of money in a short space of time.

Back in 2017, Ethereum founder once said that he is fed-up of all the cryptocurrency companies asking him to be their advisor and worrying whether or not the cryptocurrency market capitalisation is truly worth 0.5 trillion.[5] In essence, while disruption, decentralisation, and power to the community was the aim of creating this technology, attracting tricksters wasn't the aim of Nakamoto. Although you can't get rid of opportunists, what you can do is commemorate the milestones and achievements of the true innovators, who have successfully contributed and continue to prosper. Thousands of entrepreneurs and developers are working 24/7 to build the foundation for a decentralised society. Working with new technologies requires an entrepreneur to go past a significant number of hurdles. The innovators who worked towards the development of Google or Amazon, the investors who believed in those technologies in the early years of this millennium are now sitting at the peak of their achievement status. Just as these companies drove forward the development of Web 2.0, many new blockchain technology companies are working extremely hard towards the development of the next phase of the internet. Failure of many startups is inevitable. There will be job cuts and disappointments. But the people with perseverance will eventually lead the movement and change the course of history. That's why almost every major financial firm is now invovled with at least one or more blockchain product or startup.

You Can Find the Next Big Idea
Bearish financial markets typically wipe out short-term players, as well as provide a better opportunity for newcomers to get into the market. It's similar to a fresh start. It is gut-wrenchingly disappointing that the condition of the cryptocurrency market is defining the technology. Without a reasonably scaled network, and without the right type of people in the industry, it wouldn't be possible to have billions of users trading, playing, and exchanging *data* as well as a *value* on the chain. While the leaders in blockchain are working towards the scalability issues, it is time for newcomers and disruptive thinkers, idea creators, and the new generation of innovators to start working; building and contributing towards the development of web 3.0. If you believe in

long-term return, if you believe in the cause of developing a genuinely reformed system, if you are hardworking and willing to learn, then please come forward. Forecasts suggest that the market would recover soon, however, utilising a bear market to learn the language, develop a business idea is the best way to contribute in the industry. The technology is here to stay. There are hundreds of courses, open-sourced *GitHub repositories* and free materials to learn. Learn to develop, contribute and scale up. If you don't, someone else will.

The blockchain is at the early stages of adoption and has been branded as a hype. However, neither experienced investors nor top technology companies believe blockchain is hype, as a result of which billions of dollars are being invested in cryptocurrencies, even in a bear market. Whenever a particular financial market crashes, it attracts a large number of corporate and institutional investors, as bad market acts as leverage for making profits. Hundreds of millions are being funded in blockchain companies, as well the race towards the acquisition of patents.[6] Although, blockchain technologists believe that IP shouldn't be a goal in a decentralised world, as open-sourced collaboration from all kinds of companies would assist in scaling the network faster.

Do you have solid business acumen, ideas, skills as well as the aim to chase something big? Then you can be the founder of the next Coinbase or Ethereum. The industry demands you – who have the patience to compartmentalise and want to develop an idea. More community members, developers, traders, business magnets, innovators and users must be a part of this new disruption. Any early stage of technology is the best time to be involved. Further development and research require more hardworking innovators to be a part of this ground-breaking technology. Technologists, educators, business development consultants and blockchain specialists are also a necessity for a broader adoption. Most importantly, researchers are an integral part of the ecosystem – more data analysis will assist companies to understand the power of blockchain and assist in materialisation.

Many countries are sprinting towards better adoption of blockchain tech to make the best out of the business opportunities. While few of the largest conferences are being organised in UK and US, countries like Singapore, Malta, Switzerland and Estonia are working towards proper regulations in the blockchain industry in general.[7] While Switzerland has already proposed rules around initial coin offering and cryptocurrency trading, Malta has approved regulatory framework making it one of the most blockchain-friendly countries in the world. Furthermore, Japan, and South Korea also working towards better adoption of cryptocurrency. While a significant number of people are hindering themselves from taking advantage of the technology only due to the poor conditions of the market, technologists are racing towards utilising this technology with an aim to make the world a better place. Swiss Federal Councillor Johann believes that the industry requires more blockchain experts.[8] If your interest is in trading cryptocurrencies, evidently it's the right time to slowly learn, as the situation is going to get better from this decade.

Freetrade chief executive Adam Dodds suggests that bitcoin has been a better version of 'gateway drug' for millennials, as it attracted them to the trading world.[9]
Photo: Matthew Henry/Burst

Analysts suggest that the role of blockchain developer is increasingly becoming an emerging role in LinkedIn's emerging job list.[10] Blockchain jobs for developers, architects and business experts are currently offering up to USD 175,000 per annum.[11][12] These figures represent what the companies are willing to pay to recruit the right kind of talent. While there are many developers in the blockchain space, most of the innovators have either joined a team or working to develop their own idea. Some of the ideas are genuinely disruptive, which is why they drove a significant amount of investment funding even during the bear market of 2018 and 2019.[13]

While there are millions of amateur and professional traders working in the cryptocurrency market, the technology is in need of something different. What the market requires are long-term *devoted players* – business managers, solution managers, highly skilled marketing professionals, blockchain architects, application developers, small to large investors as well as late or early-stage contributors – such as students currently chasing a university degree.[14] This is specifically why top tier universities are launching more and more research work into this particular sector.

The number of cryptocurrency and blockchain professionals are expected to increase over the next few years, as more universities start to offer blockchain courses and degrees.

It isn't surprising that the best universities the world are the first to offer blockchain academic degree, and publish peer-reviewed reports on the technology.[15] *Imperial College London* has created a department known as the 'Imperial Dept of Cryptocurrency' to accelerate the growth of the crypto market.[16] University professors from the top universities such as *Stanford* and *Harvard* are participating in research into this sector. Additionally, *Nicosia University* are already offering certification programmes that will assist in attracting thousands of new generation blockchain enthusiast.[7] This will continue pushing the industry as more universities start conducting full-scale research and development work in the industry.

2044 is Closer Than You Think

In 25 years, the world is going to look very different. Technology is progressing faster than ever, with various nascent tech being used in almost every aspect of our lives. Self-driving cars, mobility, smart automation, artificial intelligence, IoT, smart-cities, genetic engineering, augmented and virtual reality will influence our daily lives.[20] Interestingly, all of these promising technologies can be benefitted by the integration of blockchain technology. Combination of one or more of these technologies powered by blockchain can become revolutionary. By using blockchain, many industries will achieve automation by 2044. For instance, an entire accounting department of a multinational conglomerate can run without the necessities of humans, using a combination of a hybrid blockchain network and artificial intelligence. Errors in accounting practices will be reduced to fractions, as more and more companies adopt such process of automation.[21] Manufacturing industries will also see a significant portion of supply chain and procurement automated using smart contracts. Corporate governance will be disrupted with better models, where various stakeholders of a business will have rights to vote over decision making process.[22] Furthermore, blockchain based green technology is already paving ways for efficient utilisation of energy resources. Blockchain can assist streamline the technology by enabling millions of users around the world to have access to smart energy using a tokenised system. This will reduce waste and empower people in many remote areas of the planet to get access to cleaner and efficient energy. Meanwhile, the financial services and intermediaries controlling almost every aspect of our financial lives will be heavily disrupted by the technology. While discussing the Equifax hack that affected 145.5 million people's data,

Researchers suggest that Bitcoin and Blockchain Technology is expected to reach the tipping point by 2027. The data projects that by 2027, **10% of Global GDP** *will be stored on the blockchain.*[18]

Scan this QR code to read the report by WEF.

Let's put that into perspective. In 2018, Global GDP was approx. USD 80 trillion*. **In 2027**, the figure is expected to reach USD **120 trillion****. In that scenario, blockchain would **potentially store** and process approx. USD* **12 TRILLION** *worth of various asset class globally. Just let that sink in.*

*Data collected from the World Economic Forum.
**Estimated forecast calculated based on the average World GDP growth rate 3.5727% between 2012 - 2018, and forecasts between 2019 - 2022.[19]

Wharton Professor Werbach explained how blockchain can make credit scoring process automated and reduce dependency on highly centralised credit bureau.[23]

As artificial intelligence evolves, biosynthetic technology and smart devices will become more intelligent in 25 years. With 100 million devices sold, Alexa has already paved a way towards 'personal AI'.[24] Google recently showcased its AI making a phone call to a hairdresser and book an appointment.[25] This demonstration is a fraction of what AI could be capable of in 2044. It's 2019, and sensor-based devices have already taken over many aspects of our lives – smart meters, smart watches, and all kind of smart devices connected to one smart hub.[26] By blending blockchain and utilising decentralised computation, IoT devices can be encrypted and secured.[27]

Besides, *fashion technology* will advance to the next level. Our clothes are going to become connected smart devices. Phones and payments cards will be integrated into the fabric of our clothes.[28] We will even start to see extensive use *biosynthetic materials* and self-repairing smart materials using nanotechnology.[29] With these incredibly powerful and emerging technologies at the growth of explosion and almost everything connected to the internet, companies and startups are already at risk of two things – device security and user privacy.

A machine learning algorithm makes it easier for companies to securely and efficiently process such massive volumes of data.[30] Having said that, current models of AI and IoT devices are vulnerable – one attack on these servers can leak a significant amount of data.[31] By using a decentralised network, artificial intelligence will become harder to be messed with, as it can store and process data using cryptography. Employing a hybrid of decentralised and centralised architecture could significantly increase device security, as well as enable higher computational power to handle larger chunks of data in milliseconds. However, for blockchain based AI to process that much data, scalability issues will need to be resolved in the next few years.

More personal data floating around the internet means increased user privacy concerns.[32] In 25 years, almost every aspect of our lives can be stored on the internet - starting from health records to the DNA data. Let's focus on our DNA for two minutes. Millions of users around the world are taking DNA tests, and by 2044, there will be billions more.[33] These records would allow medical researchers to create technologies straight out of Sci-Fi films, well known as CRISPR System – editing genes before the birth of a child, which can reportedly stop a hereditary disease from continuity and enable altering physical characteristics of a new-born baby.[34] CRISPR/Cas9 genome editing has already been achieved, and the technology will substantially advance from this point onwards.[35] Question is, who owns all these data? Do we possess the proprietorship of our own DNAs, or are we simply giving it away to large corporations for their benefit? Just like our personal information, genomes can be misused by criminals. Academics from Vanderbilt University have conducted an extensive research on 47,974 participants regarding privacy concerns over genetic information.[36]

"People varied widely in how much control they wanted over the use of data. They were more concerned about use by employers, insurers, and the government than they were about researchers and commercial entities."

In numerous ways, your DNA can be leveraged by data analytics companies for further research, as well as corporate benefits. In a bid to utilise DNA data, pharmaceutical giant GlaxoSmithKline invested over USD 300 million in a biotech startup to develop drugs using DNA data shared by millions of users.[37] If these genome engineering companies get hacked, all these data would be compromised, leading to catastrophic consequences.[38]

Scientists have conducted wide-ranging studies on how DNA can be used as long-term storage. Researchers from the *University of Washington* and Microsoft have successfully trialled storing data in DNA strands.[39] Jonathan Cox from the *University of Bath* suggested that DNA could be used as a stable long-term repository – for thousands, in fact, millions of years.[40] Moreover, scientists have already proposed *model architecture* for storing data in genes using *molecular nanonetworks*.[41] By 2040, scientists would figure out a way to increase storage capacity in our DNAs and start preserving history. Popular Canadian Sci-Fi TV show on Netflix 'Travelers' showcase a fantastic way of how personal data could be stored in our DNA.[42] The data stored in the DNAs are preserved in the 21st century in such a way that it can be passed from one generation to others, which eventually becomes beneficial in hundreds of years in the future.[43] Blockchain can provide a gateway to store ownership and identities of DNAs permanently, a path to give rightful ownership of these data, and a method of encrypting it to the highest possible standards.[44] Decentralised servers will continue to expand as scalability issues are fixed in the near future, therefore, this architecture is a feasible method of storing untampered data indefinitely, without having to give away control of information to a single centralised authority.

CRISPR gene editing is just the tip of the iceberg. We need to start owning our data before the situation goes out of control.

In 25 years, we will start to see these technologies emerge. However, DNA data needs to be protected at the first place, and we need to have control over ownership to that data – starting from now. Biotechnology startups collecting and analysing DNAs should start tapping into blockchain to provide us with the rightful property of our data. In this way, you will be able to decide who to share your data with – whether you want to share your DNA with researchers for further analysis or whether you want to share it with the pharmaceutical companies. As the data is encrypted on the chain, it won't be possible for hackers to decrypt. Evidently, people in 2044 will put more value in these type of *data rights* than personal belongings.

A Peek into the Near-Future

Blockchain will thrive as thousands are devoted towards building the technology. In the meantime, cryptocurrencies are likely to recover gradually. Financial markets are astonishingly dynamic, as trillions of worth assets are being transferred and moved around almost every day. The volume has been growing ever since. Investors and traders aim to make the highest return when the market moves in a positive direction. But in a bearish market, they adopt a defensive stance and try their best to protect gains at any cost. A more logical way to protect profits is to move from one asset class to another. That's why, when the recession hits the market, investors protect their gains by using other asset classes such as commodities like gold, or cash equivalent.[45] In such scenario, the traders forecast the best performing asset class based on their own calculations. As cryptocurrency fetched a notable pool of corporate investors and professional traders over the past two years, they have discovered a new type, which in fact is reportedly deemed as the best performing asset class among all listed in the global financial market.[46] Therefore, it is a possibility that during a recession, investors would take advantage of using bitcoin and other cryptocurrencies as a store of value. Due to the design mechanism of cryptocurrencies and limited supply, it is probable that demand would go exponential, as more and more traders flood the market. As a result, the value of these cryptocurrencies are likely to increase drastically.

Lastly, we need banks and centralised authorities to exist. But blockchain will assist in reducing our dependency on using banks to transfer money globally. Blockchain will not radically disrupt the global financial markets; it will neither reform banking operations nor transform the complexities of the energy market overnight. Nevertheless, it has rocked the financial sector, and it is moulding the foundations by gradually improving these sectors. The blockchain technology is not going to end world poverty. It will not alleviate global banking problems by using the power of decentralisation. It may not even be able to alter the process of the present political system in the short-term. Realistically speaking, it would take a tremendous amount of effort for the governments around the world to conduct and track voting system impartially using blockchain technology, especially in third world countries. Furthermore, it will take years of preparation for passing a bill that would decentralise a political system of an entire country using blockchain. The technology will, however, supersede and expand, not exponentially, but steadily, despite the circumstances of the market. Once the scalability issues are resolved, the adoption rate will go exponential. Prospects of bitcoin futures and ETFs under review by the SEC will attract a significant number of corporate investors.[47] Coinbase and larger exchanges are working towards the integration of *over-the-trade* counter and dedicated services for corporate clients. These services are attracting numerous investors, even in the incredibly bearish market. The increasing volume of trading is the proof, with 24-hour volume has reportedly been over the USD 10 billion during the last quarter of 2018.[48] Furthermore, with an aim towards mass adoption, Samsung recently launched *Blockchain KeyStore* with the ability to use and store ether using its phones, starting from S10.[49] It isn't a casual decision to make - any major feature addition requires significant alterations to their product design. The company have thought this through and willing to gain the early-mover advantage.

Over the next few years, destined to be five or ten, a blockchain-led transformation will affect our daily lives. Current leaders in blockchain technology may also be swept away by a new generation of blockchain networks. Remember what happened to Nokia? The "Apple" or "Google" of blockchain will be here within the next ten to twelve years. Cryptocurrencies are likely to become mainstream as investors flood the market with their domination. Although it is a very confident and brave statement to make, nonetheless, based on the development happening underneath all the noise, it is likely to happen. Although decentralisation goes against the ethos of the current banking system, it will not be abolished. Similar to how the investors turned their heads towards blockchain, the global financial system would be disrupted by the empowerment of decentralisation. Banks aren't going anywhere. The financial giants will take over some of the most profitable businesses in the field of the blockchain. It's not surprising that the process has already started as mentioned earlier. It is a form of diversification – more like a wealth management strategy. The financial markets will be enforced to adopt this technology to make global transactions faster and more affordable than ever before. In the next ten-year period, sending and receiving money from third world countries are likely to become easier than current restricted methods. Government institutions are to be expected to adopt blockchain and utilise cryptocurrencies in order to gain momentum and stay relevant – for instance, paying council or vehicle taxes with cryptocurrencies. More importantly, governments will start trialling storage of confidential ID, such as passports on blockchain. With more and more hybrid startups, such as blockchain-AI technologies emerging in the space of the internet, traditional business models will be intimidated by a low-cost easy-to-adopt financial model.[50] With scalability issues settled, blockchain can gain much faster momentum and therefore create a better business, economic, financial and technological models.

The question isn't whether the blockchain technology, cryptocurrencies and DLT would thrive or be destroyed. The ultimate questions are – when are you going to start using blockchain and cryptocurrencies? How is it going to affect your personal life? Are you going to start using the technology for your business, or are you going to use it for day to day lives? Are you going to start tapping into blockchain now, or ten years down the line? Only time will tell.

#BUIDL

The term BUIDL is the misspelt version of the word "Build". Similar to HODL, BUIDL emphasises on building on the decentralised economy instead of just merely holding the tokens. The terms isn't omnipresent, but developers working in the industry widely uses it.

NOTES & BIBLIOGRAPHY

BLOCK 1

1. Professor Juma's book is an excellent read to understand the source of society's response to innovation. This book has been an inspiration to write the first chapter. License has been obtained from OUP to use the excerpt.
Juma, C. (2016) *Innovation and Its Enemies: Why People Resist New Technologies.* New York: Oxford University Press.
2. Delaney, B. (2018) *Digital killed the CD. Will anyone mourn it?* Available: https://bit.ly/2KB4oU2. Last accessed 1 November 2018.
3. McKinney, K. (2015) *Don't just ask whether Tidal will survive. Worry about Spotify, too.* Available: https://www.vox.com/2015/4/23/8484165/tidal-flop-music-streaming. Last accessed 2 November 2018.
4. Kane, C. (2015) *10 inventors who apologized for their inventions.* Available: https://bit.ly/2KAL8FW. Last accessed 3 November 2018.
5. The Telegraph. (2016) *Worst tech predictions of all time.* Available: https://bit.ly/2xWraTm. Last accessed 4 November 2018.
6. Schreiber, K. and Hausenblas, H. (2016) *Why Is Change So Hard?* Available: https://bit.ly/2S7fynI. Last accessed 5 November 2018.
7. Parenti, M. (1997) Methods of Media Manipulation. *The Humanist.* 57(4), pp.5–7.
8. Hickey, W. (2012) *EXPOSED: Here Are The Tricks That Fox News Uses To Manipulate Statistics On Its Graphics.* Available: https://bit.ly/2S4754j. Last accessed 6 November 2018.
9. Pous, T. (2011*) Heart and Brain Surgery — Never Gonna Happen.* Available: https://bit.ly/2VWxwu6. Last accessed 7 November 2018.
10. Skarda, E. (2011) *Online Shopping Will Flop.* Available: https://bit.ly/2KxQn9t. Last accessed 8 November 2018.
11. Van der Wel, P. (2018) *Images and quotes about the future.* Available: https://bit.ly/3cNXKpg. Last accessed 9 November 2018.
12. Szczerba, R. (2015) *15 Worst Tech Predictions of All Time.* Available: https://bit.ly/2xWB2wo. Last accessed 10 November 2018.
13. More scholarly articles regarding the effects of money laundering are

available to read online. This online article discusses the top 5 cases, providing the evidence that fiat currency is constantly used to conduct illegal activities.

Whitehead, H. (2016) *Top 5 Money Laundering Cases of the Last 30 Years.* Available: https://bit.ly/2Y3jZU3. Last accessed 17 Oct 2018.

14. Murray-West, R. (2013) *A 300-year history of British banking and the rise of current accounts.* Available: https://bit.ly/2VBf3Ef.html. Last accessed 11 November 2018.

15. Paypal (2018) *PayPal Fees, Straightforward and No Surprises.* Available: https://www.paypal.com/uk/webapps/mpp/paypal-fees. Last accessed 12 November 2018.

16. CB Insights. (2018) *How Blockchain Could Disrupt Banking.* Available: https://www.cbinsights.com/research/blockchain-disrupting-banking/. Last accessed 13 November 2018.

17. Revolvy. (2018) *Nokia 3310.* Available: http]]]]]]]]s://www.revolvy.com/page/Nokia-3310. Last accessed 14 November 2018.

18. Davis, B. (2014) *2030: have email and social destroyed the art of letter writing?.* Available: https://bit.ly/2VXFmDJ. Last accessed 15 November 2018.

19. Petry, S., Toledo, A and Walden, A. (2017) *Welcome To The Age Of Exponential Technology.* Available: https://adobe.ly/2xPbVfe. Last accessed 16 November 2018.

20. Note: This information will be rapidly shifting over the next few years. Smartphone businesses have made Apple take over the last decade's giant Nokia.

Kharpal, A. (2018) *After overtaking Apple in smartphones, Huawei is aiming for No. 1 by 2020.* Available: https://cnb.cx/3clj2oc. Last accessed 17 November 2018.

21. Statista. (2018) *Percentage of households in the United States with a computer at home from 1984 to 2015.* Available: https://bit.ly/2xbE8wk. Last accessed 18 November 2018.

22. Harvard Kennedy School Belfer Center For Science And International Affairs. (2016) *Harvard study: Why important innovations stall; understanding obstacles to change is key to future.* Available: https://www.eurekalert.org/pub_releases/2016-07/tca-hs062716.php. Last accessed 19 November 2018.

23. Goble, G. (2012) *Top 10 bad tech predictions.* Available: https://bit.ly/3bEYz3I.Last accessed 10 Jan 2019.

BLOCK 2

1. Schumpeter, J. (1955*) History of Economic Analysis.* London: Routledge.
2. Popken, B. (2018) *Google sells the future, powered by your personal data.* Available: https://nbcnews.to/3aF2j3K. Last accessed 1 November 2018.
3. BeBusinessed.com. (2018) *The History of Gold.* Available: https://bebusinessed.com/history/the-history-of-gold/. Last accessed 2 August 2018.
4. Marr, B. (2018) *A Very Brief History Of Blockchain Technology Everyone Should Read.* Available: https://bit.ly/2Y76Yc3. Last accessed 3 November 2018.
5. Burn-Callander, R. (2014) *The history of money: from barter to bitcoin.* Available: https://bit.ly/3eTyuQg. Last accessed 4 November 2018.
6. Hayek, F. (1943) A Commodity Reserve Currency. *The Economic Journal.* 53(210/211), 176-184. doi:10.2307/2226314. https://www.jstor.org/stable/2226314.
7. U.S Currency Education Program. (2018) *The History of American Currency.* Available: https://www.uscurrency.gov/history. Last accessed 5 November 2018.
8. Menger, K. (1892) On the Origin of Money. *The Economic Journal,* 2(6), 239-255. doi:10.2307/2956146.
9. Helleiner, E. (2019) A Bretton Woods moment? The 2007–2008 crisis and the future of global finance. *International Affairs*, Volume 86, Issue 3, pp.619–636,doi:10.1111/j.1468-2346.2010.00901.x
10. D. Bordo, M. (1993) T*he Bretton Woods International Monetary System: A Historical Overview. In: D. Bordo, M. and Eichengreen, M. National Bureau of Economic Research.* United States: University of Chicago Press. 3 - 108. https://EconPapers.repec.org/RePEc:nbr:nberwo:4033.
11. Ghizoni, S.K. (1971) *Nixon Ends Convertibility of US Dollars to Gold and Announces Wage/Price Controls.* Available: https://www.federalreservehistory.org/essays/gold_convertibility_ends. Last accessed 6 November 2018.
12. Harrison, M. (2013) *Did the Gold Standard Work? Economics Before*

and After Fiat Money. Available: https://bit.ly/2Y4FEeF. Last accessed 7 November 2018.
13. Amadeo, K. (2018) *Value of the Dollar Today.* Available: https://bit.ly/3bGHO8q. Last accessed 8 November 2018.
14. Rothbard, M. N. (1990) *What Has Government Done to Our Money?* Ludwig von Mises Institute: Alabama.
15. Bitcoin UK. (2018) *Has the 1988 Economist Magazine Prediction come true?* Available: https://bitcoin.co.uk/1988-economist-magazine-prediction-come-true/. Last accessed 9 November 2018.
16. Spiteri, A. (2018) *What do mortgage lenders look for in your credit report?.* Available: https://bit.ly/2KvjsSW. Last accessed 10 November 2018.
17. FSCS. (2018) *Banks & building societies.* Available: https://www.fscs.org.uk/what-we-cover/banks-building-societies/. Last accessed 11 November 2018.
18. Kagen, J. (2018) *Fractional Reserve Banking.* Available: https://www.investopedia.com/terms/f/fractionalreservebanking.asp. Last accessed 12 November 2018.
19. Dr. Partridge, M. (2014) *Is fractional reserve banking dangerous?.* Available: https://bit.ly/2VZ3o1e. Last accessed 29 August 2018.
20. This is a brief explanation from my own understanding. The underlying design of the system is more complicated. More details and a full course named "Banking and the expansion of the money supply" is available on Khan Academy's website. For more information, please visit: khanacademy.org
21. Reinhart, M, and Kenneth S. (2008) Is the 2007 US sub-prime financial crisis so different? An international historical comparison. *American Economic Review.* 98(2) Pp.339-344.
22. FRED, Federal Reserve Bank of St. Louis. (2019) *Board of Governors of the Federal Reserve System (US),* M2 Money Stock [M2] Available at: https://fred.stlouisfed.org/series/M2. Last accessed: 8 January 2019.
23. US Debt clock website projects an estimated amount of the total debt of the United States. US Debt Clock. (2018) *US Debt Clock.* Available: http://www.usdebtclock.org/. Last accessed 14 November 2018.
24. Hülsmann, J.G. (2014) *The Cultural and Political Consequences of Fiat Money.* Available: https://bit.ly/3aHtbA5. Last accessed 15 November 2018.

25. Melvin, D. (2015) *Between rocks, hard place, Greece picks austerity. How did it get into this mess?* Available: https://cnn.it/2Kw8bSo. Last accessed 1 December 2018.
26. Partington, R.J. (2018) *14m bolivars for a chicken: Venezuela hyperinflation explained.* Available: https://bit.ly/2Yh1rjB. Last accessed 4 December 2018.
27. Phillips, T. (2018) *'A slow-motion catastrophe': on the road in Venezuela, 20 years after Chávez's rise.* Available: https://bit.ly/3cLphYA. Last accessed 18 November 2018.
28. Detrixhe, J. (2018) *Weekly Venezuelan bolivar trading volume in bitcoin.* Available: https://www.theatlas.com/charts/BJhNSW_gm. Last accessed 2 December 2018.
29. Rawlins, C. G. (2018) *See how many bills it took to buy a chicken in Venezuela.* Available: https://nbcnews.to/2Yo3nL. Last accessed 2 December 2018.
30. Nakamoto, S. (2009) *Bitcoin: A Peer-to-Peer Electronic Cash System.* Available: https://bitcoin.org/bitcoin.pdf. Last accessed 20 November 2018.
31. Martindale, J. (2017) *Go ahead, pass laws. They can't kill bitcoin, even if they try.* Available: https://bit.ly/356yWq2. Last accessed 21 November 2018.
32. Park, M. (2018) *The Difference Between Bitcoin and Traditional Currencies.* Available: https://bit.ly/3bCLGqJ. Last accessed 22 November 2018.
33. Baker Tilly Nederland. (2017) *Blockchain Technology: The Rise of the Decentralised Economy by Bettina Warburg.* [Online Video]. 31 October 2017. Available from: https://bit.ly/354PtuB. Accessed: 22 November 2018.
34. Tim Draper was the one of the first bitcoin experts to successfully predict in 2013, bitcoin surpassed his prediction in 2017. Draper still stands by his price target of USD 250,000 by 2022.
35. Rooney, K. (2019) *Facebook's cryptocurrency could be a $19 billion revenue opportunity, Barclays says.* Available: https://cnb.cx/2W1WQit. Last accessed 11 March 2019.

BLOCK 3

1. Bano, S., Sonnino, A., Al-Bassam, M., Azouvi, S., McCorry, P., Meiklejohn, S. and Danezis, G. (2017) *SoK: Consensus in the Age of Blockchains*. 2, 1-17. DOI: http://arxiv.org/abs/1711.03936
2. Kadiyala, A. (2018) N*uances between Permissionless and Permissioned Blockchains.* Available: https://bit.ly/2KBma9s. Last accessed 30 August 2018.
3. Nakamoto. S (2008) *Bitcoin: A Peer-to-Peer Electronic Cash System.* (1), 1-9.
4. Blockchain. (2018) *Transaction.* Available: https://bit.ly/2S4qTVd. Last accessed 1 September 2018.
5. Blockgeeks.com is one of the best learning resources available for free. The contents on this website is incredibly detailed and covers almost every aspect for a beginner who is interested to start learning to develop decentralised application. Blockgeeks. (2018) *What is Blockchain Technology? A Step-by-Step Guide for Beginners.* Available: https://blockgeeks.com/guides/what-is-blockchain-technology/. Last accessed 2 September 2018.
6. Ethereum. (n.d.) *Build Unstoppable Applications.* Available: https://www.ethereum.org/. Last accessed 2 September 2018.
7. Sharma, D.K. (2018) *BLOCKCHAIN: VISION OF A WORLD TO COME.* Available: https://bit.ly/3eUQz0G. Last accessed 3 September 2018.
8. Bearman, A. (2018) *As bitcoin's price plunges, skeptics say the cryptocurrency has no value. Here's one argument for why they're wrong.* Available: https://cnb.cx/2KzFxjl. Last accessed 4 September 2018.
9. Millennial Entrepreneur. (2013) *Gold Mining Process / How is Gold Mined?.* Available: https://www.youtube.com/watch?v=EoRenQKnrTY. Last accessed 20 Jan 2019.
10. World Gold Council. (2018) *How gold is mined.* Available: https://www.gold.org/about-gold/gold-supply/how-gold-is-mined. Last accessed 5 September 2018.
11. Murch. (2011) *'What is a Satoshi'?* Available: https://bitcoin.stackexchange.com/questions/114/what-is-a-satoshi. Last accessed 6 September 2018.
12. Blockchain can be primarily categorised into permissioned and

permissionless network. Both types of network can also be public and private. An excellent explanation of various categories are explained in this article on blockchainhub.net.

More information is available via this URL: https://blockchainhub.net/blockchains-and-distributed-ledger-technologies-in-general/

13. Makhdoom, Imran & Abolhasan, Mehran & Abbas, Haider & Ni, Wei. (2019) Blockchain's adoption in IoT: The challenges, and a way forward. *Journal of Network and Computer Applications.* 125. 251-279. 10.1016/j.jnca.2018.10.019.

14. Etherscan. (2018) Block Information. Available: https://etherscan.io/block/6963591. Last accessed 7 September 2018.

15. Nakamoto. S (2008) *Bitcoin: A Peer-to-Peer Electronic Cash System.* (1), 1-9.

16. Hankin, A. (2018) *Here's how much it costs to mine a single bitcoin in your country.* Available: https://on.mktw.net/2zxhCPl. Last accessed 8 September 2018.

17. Ethermine. (2018) *Ethermine.* Available: https://ethermine.org/. Last accessed 9 September 2018.

18. Dhaliwal, E. and Dr. Gurguc, Z. (2018) *Token Ecosystem Creation.* 1-56.

19. Bonneau, J. (2017) *Hostile blockchain takeovers.* (1), 1-8.

20. Mirkovic, J. and Reiher, P. (2004) A taxonomy of DDoS attack and DDoS defense mechanisms. *ACM SIGCOMM Computer Communication Review.* 34 (2), 39-53.

21. CRYPTOMEDICATION. (2018) *The ultimate guide to hard forks for crypto dummies.* Available: https://bit.ly/2yLOmDS. Last accessed 11 September 2018.

22. Buterin, V. (2014) *Ethereum White Paper.* Available: https://bit.ly/2yMBqO1. Last accessed 26 September 2018.

23. Ray. J (2018) *Proof of Stake FAQs.* Available: https://github.com/ethereum/wiki/wiki/Proof-of-Stake-FAQs. Last accessed 7 November 2018.

24. Steiner. J (2018) *What The Heck Is Web 3.0 Anyway?* Available: https://bit.ly/2Y4ZuGL. Last accessed 21 September 2018.

25. Wood. G (2014) *ÐApps: What Web 3.0 Looks Like.* Available: http://gavwood.com/dappsweb3.html. Last accessed 23 September 2018.

26. United States Naval Academy. Data Link Layer. Available:

https://www.usna.edu/CyberDept/sy110/lec/netData/lec.html. Last accessed 23 September 2018.

27. Fall, K.R. and Stevens, W.R (2011) *TCP/IP Illustrated,* Volume 1. 2nd ed. United States: Addison-Wesley. 13-19.

28. Karamitsos, I., Papadaki, Maria & Barghuthi, Nedaa. (2018) Design of the Blockchain Smart Contract: A Use Case for Real Estate. *Journal of Information Security.* 09. 177-190.

29. Varshney. N (2018) This app lets you trade Bitcoin without an internet connection – but there's a catch. Available: https://bit.ly/2Y7L8VR. Last accessed 22 September 2018.

30. Aki. J (2018) *Cryptocurrency That Works without Internet, mCoin Launches In Africa.* Available: https://bit.ly/3bFR0d9. Last accessed 22 September 2018.

31. JUN. (2018) *Strategy vol. 02.* Available: https://blog.omisego.network/strategy-vol-02-89a4d8476eed. Last accessed 23 September 2018.

32. Agrawal, G. (2018) A Beginner's Guide To Building A Relayer With 0x Protocol. Available: https://bit.ly/2xPLtlF. Last accessed 24 September 2018.

33. DDEX. (2018) *Redefining Decentralized Exchanges.* Available: https://ddex.io/. Last accessed 25 September 2018.

34. Ray, S. (2018*) The Difference Between Blockchains & Distributed Ledger Technology.* Available: https://bit.ly/2S60GWk. Last accessed 8 September 2018.

35. NG, A. (2018) *How the Equifax hack happened, and what still needs to be done.* Available: https://cnet.co/2zx0wRB. Last accessed 9 September 2018.

36. Griffin, A. (2018) *DIXONS CARPHONE HACK: MILLIONS OF CUSTOMERS' DETAILS STOLEN IN HUGE CYBER ATTACK.* Available: https://bit.ly/2xPLTIL. Last accessed 10 September 2018.

37. Dexter, S. (2018) *Why PoS was Necessary for Ethereum's Sharding.* Available: https://bit.ly/2YcAHRf. Last accessed 11 September 2018.

38. Schueffel, P. (2017) *Alternative Distributed Ledger Technologies Blockchain vs. Tangle vs. Hashgraph - A High-Level Overview and Comparison.* Available at SSRN: https://ssrn.com/abstract=3144241 or http://dx.doi.org/10.2139/ssrn.3144241

39. IOTA. (2018) *What is IOTA?* Available: https://www.iota.org/get-started/what-is-iota. Last accessed 16 September 2018.

40. Hedera Hashgraph. (2018) *The five consensus algorithms #5: Virtual-voting by Leemon Baird.* [Online Video]. 15 March 2018. Available from: https://www.youtube.com/watch?v=rleAZVVA3kM. [Accessed: 16 September 2018].

41. Schueffel, P. (2017) *Alternative Distributed Ledger Technologies Blockchain vs. Tangle vs. Hashgraph - A High-Level Overview and Comparison.* Available at SSRN: https://ssrn.com/abstract=3144241 or http://dx.doi.org/10.2139/ssrn.3144241

42. Zhao, W. (2017) *What's Blockchain? HSBC Survey Finds 59% of Consumers Don't Know.* Available: https://bit.ly/2VX1rlT. Last accessed 10 August 2018.

43. Konash, M. (2018) *Blockchain Interoperability: a Necessity for Effective Adoption.* Available: https://bit.ly/2S7cmbC. Last accessed 10 November 2018.

44. Haran, N. (2018) *What's keeping cryptocurrencies from mass adoption?* Available: https://tcrn.ch/2S5sL0g. Last accessed 10 November 2018.

45. GOV.UK. (2018) *Cryptoassets for individuals.* Available: https://bit.ly/2Y3X6A0. Last accessed 1 January 2019.

46. eToro. (2019) *New eToro Survey: Nearly Half of Millennials Trust U.S. Stock Market Less Than Crypto.* Available: https://prn.to/3aK9jN6. Last accessed 11 March 2019.

47. Biesiada, J. (2018) *Millennials traveling and spending more than any other age group this summer.* Available: https://bit.ly/3aCBDkq . Last accessed 22 March 2019.

48. GameKyuubi. (2013) *I AM HODLING.* Available: https://bitcointalk.org/index.php?topic=375643.0. Last accessed 10 November 2018.

49. Brown, M. (2017) *What Does 'Hodl' Mean? The Bitcoin Meme Causing a Storm on Reddit.* Available: https://bit.ly/3eQ70LB. Last accessed 10 November 2018.

BLOCK 4

1. Aziz. (2017) *Coins, Tokens & Altcoins: What's the Difference?* Available: https://bit.ly/2KDr4mg. Last accessed 10 October 2018.
2. Grut, O. (2018) *The crypto world is going wild for 'stablecoins' — here's everything you need to know about them.* Available: https://bit.ly/357hKAT. Last accessed 5 October 2018.
3. Dreyfuss, G. (2018) *New York regulator approves Winklevoss, Paxos dollar-linked tokens.* Available: https://reut.rs/3eSZako. Last accessed 6 October 2018.
4. Knight, S. (2018) *Facebook wants to make a stablecoin for WhatsApp users.* Available: https://bit.ly/2y1MBm1. Last accessed 6 October 2018.
5. Sloman, J., Guest, J. and Garratt, D. (2018) *Economics.* 10th ed. London: Pearson.
6. Blockchain. (2018) *Bitcoins in circulation.* Available: https://www.blockchain.com/en/charts/total-bitcoins. Last accessed 27 September 2018.
7. Giaglis, G. and N. Kypriotaki, K. (2014) *Towards an Agenda for Information Systems Research on Digital Currencies and Bitcoin.* Lecture Notes in Business Information Processing. 183. 3-13.
8. Hileman,G & Rauchs,M. (2017) *GLOBAL CRYPTOCURRENCY BENCHMARKING STUDY.* Available: https://bit.ly/2VFFusK. Last accessed 26 September 2018.
9. Buterin. V (2014) *Ethereum White Paper.* Available: https://bit.ly/3eT0mnG. Last accessed 26 September 2018.
10. Sloman, J., Guest, J. and Garratt, D. (2018) *Economics.* 10th ed. London: Pearson.
11. Canellis,D. (2018) *China brags its cryptocurrency ban has practically killed local Bitcoin trading.* Available: https://thenextweb.com/hardfork/2018/07/09/china-crackdown-bitcoin/. Last accessed 27 September 2018.
12. CoinMarketCap. (2018) *Top 100 Cryptocurrency Exchanges by Trade Volume.* Available: https://coinmarketcap.com/rankings/exchanges/. Last accessed 28 September 2018.
13. Huang, C. (2018) *Guide To Exchange Fees For The Top 10 Crypto Exchanges.* Available: https://www.investinblockchain.com/cryptocurrency-exchange-fees/.

Last accessed 29 September 2018.

14. Rooney, K. (2018) *Cryptocurrency start-up Coinbase valued at $8 billion despite bitcoin's plunge.* Available: https://cnb.cx/2xQx5JX. Last accessed 30 September 2018.

15. Hart., O. D. and Kreps., D. M.. (1986) Price Destabilizing Speculation. *Journal of Political Economy.* 94 (5), pp. 927-952.
Experts at the U.S. Commodity Futures Trading Commission (CFTC) believes that speculative trading in the stock market may not be destabilising, providing evidence that it stabilised future trading market. More information is available via this PDF: https://bit.ly/2Sa4KVF

16. Ciaian, P., Rajcaniova, M. and Kancs, D. (2014) *The Economics of BitCoin Price Formation.* Available: https://arxiv.org/ftp/arxiv/papers/1405/1405.4498.pdf. Last accessed 16 October 2018.

17. Rooney, K. (2018) *Wall Street's crypto bull Tom Lee slashes year-end bitcoin price forecast nearly in half.* Available: https://cnb.cx/3bFSCnd. Last accessed 17 October 2018.

18. Web Summit. (2019) *Crypto's roller coaster year.* [Online Video]. Available from: https://www.youtube.com/watch?time_continue=33&v=poMdExcVtvM. Accessed: 16 October 2018

19. Ciaian, P., Rajcaniova, M. and Kancs, D. (2014) *The Economics of BitCoin Price Formation.* Available: https://arxiv.org/ftp/arxiv/papers/1405/1405.4498.pdf. Last accessed 16 October 2018.

20. CryptoUK. (n.d.) *Members.* Available: http://www.cryptocurrenciesuk.info/members/. Last accessed 16 October 2018.

21. Coin Bureau. (2018) *The Howey Test and Cryptocurrency: Which Coins May Apply?* Available: https://www.coinbureau.com/analysis/howey-test-cryptocurrency/. Last accessed 17 October 2018.

22. FCA. (2018) *Cryptocurrency derivatives.* Available: https://www.fca.org.uk/news/statements/cryptocurrency-derivatives. Last accessed 17 October 2018.

23. Hinman, W. (2018) *Digital Asset Transactions: When Howey Met Gary (Plastic)* Available: https://www.sec.gov/news/speech/speech-hinman-061418. Last

accessed 7 October 2018.

24. Liao, S. (2018) *The SEC says Ethereum tokens are not securities.* Available: https://bit.ly/356D8WC. Last accessed 8 October 2018.

25. Shehhi, A. A., Oudah, M. and Aung, Z. (2014) *Investigating factors behind choosing a cryptocurrency.* 2014 IEEE International Conference on Industrial Engineering and Engineering Management, Bandar Sunway, 1443-1447.

26. Svetlana, S., Angelika, K. and Ifigenia, G. (2017) *In Which Distributed Ledger Do We Trust? A Comparative Analysis of Cryptocurrencies.* MCIS 2017 Proceedings. 21.

27. The World Bank. (2018) *Financial Inclusion on the Rise, But Gaps Remain, Global Findex Database Shows.* Available: https://bit.ly/2VBnEa0. Last accessed 9 October 2018.

28. COR Index Inc. (2018) *November 2018 Crypto Exchange Analytics and Research.* Available: https://corindex.com/uploads/Nov_18_CE_Analytics_and_Research.pdf . Last accessed 9 October 2018.

BLOCK 5

1. Szabo, N. (1996) *Smart Contracts: Building Blocks for Digital Markets.* Available: https://bit.ly/2Y7b2JE. Last accessed 22 September 2018.
2. MyEtherWallet. (2018) *MyEtherWallet.com.* Available: https://www.myetherwallet.com/. Last accessed 22 September 2018.
3. Etherscan. (2018) Address 0x7A6c6C55205337bE5F51801c97Fc22BD9Aa8B588. Available: https://bit.ly/3bCyoKU. Last accessed 22 September 2018.
4. Solidity. (2016) Read the Docs. Available: https://solidity.readthedocs.io/en/v0.5.1/. Last accessed 22 September 2018.
5. Ethereum Improvement Proposals. (2016) *ERC.* Available: https://eips.ethereum.org/erc. Last accessed 22 September 2018.
6. Ethereum. (2016) Pythonic Smart Contract Language for the EVM. Available: https://github.com/ethereum/vyper. Last accessed 22 September 2018.
7. Healy, K. (2019) *Ethereum in Depth: Smart Contracts - Part 2: How to Create and Publish a Smart Contract.* [Online Video]. 10 August 2017. Available from: https://www.youtube.com/watch?v=TC-bDQZbXd0&t=1703s. [Accessed: 14 September 2018].
8. React Native (2015) *A framework for building native apps with React.* Available: https://github.com/facebook/react-native. Last accessed 23 September 2018.
9. Clack, C & Bakshi, V. & Braine, L. (2016) *Smart Contract Templates: foundations, design landscape and research directions.* arXiv:1608.00771v3 [cs.CY].
10. Ko, T. (2018) *A guide to developing an Ethereum decentralized voting application.* Available: https://bit.ly/2S8Mpbu. Last accessed 10 November 2018.
11. Kofler, R. (2018) *How to Vote Safely with an ERC20 Token.* Available: https://bit.ly/3axoKYM. Last accessed 25 September 2018.
12. Levenson. N (2017) *NEO versus Ethereum: Why NEO might be 2018's strongest cryptocurrency.* Available: https://bit.ly/2y2B3PB. Last accessed 24 September 2018.

13. Singh. N (2018) *NEO dApps Ecosystem: Complete List of NEO Decentralized Blockchain Applications.* Available: https://101blockchains.com/neo-dapps-ecosystem/. Last accessed 25 September 2018.

14. thecryptopouch. (2018) *The Top Ten Fastest Cryptocurrency Speeds in 2018 – TPS.* Available: https://thecryptopouch.com/fastest-cryptocurrency-speeds-tps-2018/. Last accessed 26 September 2018.

15. Coincentral (n.d.) *What Is Lisk (LSK)? | A Guide to the Sidechain and Dapp Platform.* Available at: https://coincentral.com/what-is-lisk/. Last accessed 21 December 2018.

16. Zainudin, S. (2016) 8 Things You Should Know About The Lisk Ecosystem and Currency. Available: https://bit.ly/3bQgg04. Last accessed 16 December 2018.

17. Blockonomi (2017) Beginner's Guide to Chainlink. Retrieved from: https://blockonomi.com/chainlink-guide/. Last accessed 16 December 2018.

18. Dale, O. (2017) Beginner's Guide to Chainlink. Available: https://blockonomi.com/chainlink-guide/. Last accessed 21 December 2018.

19. Hyperledger. (2015) *The LINUX FOUNDATION projects.* Available: https://www.hyperledger.org/. Last accessed 11 September 2018.

20. IBM. (2015) *IBM Blockchain based on Hyperledger Fabric.* Available: https://www.ibm.com/blockchain/in-en/hyperledger.html. Last accessed 11 September 2018.

21. Zyskind. G, Nathan. O, Pentland. A.S (2015) *Decentralizing Privacy: Using Blockchain to Protect Personal Data.* 2015 IEEE Security and Privacy Workshops.

22. Ethereum wiki. (2018) *Awesome Ethereum Virtual Machine.* Available: https://bit.ly/3eQYBHA. Last accessed 12 September 2018.

23. Cheng, E and Tausche, K. (2017) *Jamie Dimon says if you're 'stupid' enough to buy bitcoin, you'll pay the price one day.* Available: https://cnb.cx/3eOyKQB. Last accessed 12 September 2018.

24. JP Morgan (2018) *Quorum™.* Available: https://www.jpmorgan.com/global/Quorum. Last accessed 12 September 2018.

25. JP Morgan (2018) *A permissioned implementation of Ethereum supporting data privacy.* Available: https://github.com/jpmorganchase/quorum. Last accessed 12

September 2018.

26. This article is a great source to learn about the details of Quorum. Vasa. (2018) *Quorum 101: Getting started with Quorum.* Available: https://hackernoon.com/quorum-101-getting-started-with-quorum-9906294ea45b. Last accessed 12 September 2018.

27. Hackett. R (2018) *How JPMorgan Chase Learned to Love the Blockchain.* Available: http://fortune.com/longform/jpmorgan-chase-tech-blockchain/. Last accessed 10 September 2018.

28. Business Wire. (2018) *J.P. Morgan Interbank Information Network^{SM} Expands to More Than 75 Banks.* Available: https://bwnews.pr/2KC0Fp0. Last accessed 13 September 2018.

29. Nielsen. P.M (2018) *Hidden in Plain Sight.* Available: https://patrickmn.com/security/hidden-in-plain-sight/. Last accessed 11 September 2018.

30. Volvo Cars. (2019). *Volvo Cars to implement blockchain traceability of cobalt used in electric car batteries.* Available: https://bit.ly/3bFTKXZ. Last accessed 20 April 2020.

31. Hulliet, M. (2018) *Mastercard Awarded Patent for Partitioned, Multi-Currency Blockchain.* Available: https://bit.ly/2yG497s. Last accessed 18 Oct 2018.

32. MasterCard. (n.d.) *MasterCard Blockchain.* Available: https://developer.mastercard.com/product/mastercard-blockchain. Last accessed 20 Jan 2019.

33. Carey, S. (2018) *What is SAP Leonardo? Everything you need to know about SAP's Leonardo platform.* Available: https://bit.ly/2yGnfKy. Last accessed 20 Jan 2019.

34. SAP Leonardo. (n.d.) *Unlock the Intelligent Enterprise with SAP Leonardo.* Available: https://www.sap.com/uk/products/leonardo.html. Last accessed 20 Jan 2019.

35. Dreyfuss, G. (2018) *European investment firm buys digital exchange Bitstamp in all cash deal.*
Available at: https://bit.ly/2ylOeFq. Last Accessed: 18 Oct 2018)

36. Neville, S. & Allaire, J. (2018) *Circle Acquires Poloniex.* Available: https://blog.circle.com/2018/02/26/circle-acquires-poloniex/. Last accessed 10 Oct 2018.

BLOCK 6

1. STAR BIT. (2018) *Introduction of Ethereum Request for Comment | (ERC20/ERC721)* Available: https://bit.ly/3aDxlJt. Last accessed 20 September 2018.
101 Blockchain is another great source to learn about various ERC standards: https://101blockchains.com/erc-standards/
2. Carter, A. (2018) *What is the Ethereum Improvement Proposal (EPI)?* Available: https://bit.ly/2Y57nvR. Last accessed 20 September 2018.
3. Wood, G. and Antonopoulos, A.M (2018) *Mastering Ethereum.* United States: O'Reilly Media, Inc.
4. Ethereum Improvement Proposals. (2016) *ERC.* Available: https://eips.ethereum.org/erc. Last accessed 20 September 2018.
5. McDonald, J. (2017) *Understanding ERC-20 token contracts.* Available: https://bit.ly/2VFLIsC. Last accessed 21 September 2018.
6. William, M. (2018) *ERC-20 Tokens, Explained.* Available: https://bit.ly/2S7w4Um. Last accessed 21 September 2018.
7. Young, J. (2017) *CryptoKitties Sales Hit $12 Million, Could be Ethereum's Killer App After All.* Available: https://bit.ly/3eQBcpH. Last accessed 21 September 2018.
8. Radomski, W. (2018) *ERC-1155: The Crypto Item Standard.* Available: https://bit.ly/35cA2k3. Last accessed 21 September 2018.
9. The Daily Crypto. (2018) *New ERC-1155: Single Contract.* Available: https://bit.ly/3eNQfRj. Last accessed 21 September 2018.
10. Rosic, A. (2017) *Beyond Gaming – Exploring the Utility of ERC-1155 Token Standard!.* Available: https://blockgeeks.com/erc-1155-token/. Last accessed 21 September 2018.
11. Koinbros. (2017) *What are ERC20 and ERC223 tokens?.* Available: https://bit.ly/2S7kmcE. Last accessed 22 September 2018.
12. Delegate call. (2018) *ERC827 vs ERC20.* Available: https://bit.ly/35axCCr. Last accessed 22 September 2018.
13. Trezor. (2018) *ERC20 tokens.* Available: https://bit.ly/2Y7HoEa. Last accessed 23 September 2018.
14. Wood. G (2014) *ÐApps: What Web 3.0 Looks Like.* Available: http://gavwood.com/dappsweb3.html. Last accessed 23 Sep 2018.
15. Raval. S (2016) *What Is a Decentralized Application?* United States: O'Reilly Media, Inc.

16. Azuremarketplace. (2017) *Quorum.* Available: https://bit.ly/2VXv8TU. Last accessed 21 September 2018.
17. Wong, J. I. (2018) *Coinbase bought a "decentralized" crypto exchange. How does that work?.* Available: https://bit.ly/2VVTNIo. Last accessed 12 Jan 2019.
18. Nectar.community. (2018) *Welcome to Nectar.community.* Available: https://nectar.community/#/. Last accessed 20 September 2018.
19. Goldman Sach. (2017) *Blockchain.*
Available: https://bit.ly/3eNQWKp. Last accessed 29 November 2018.
20. Karamitsos, I., Papadaki, M., & Barghuthi, N. (2018) Design of the Blockchain Smart Contract: A Use Case for Real Estate. *Journal of Information Security.* 09. 177-190.
21. Chapman, C. (2018) Front End, Back End, Full Stack—What Does it All Mean? Available: https://skillcrush.com/2017/02/27/-
front-end-back-end-full-stack/. Last accessed 20 September 2018.
22. Bray. T (2017) Request for Comments: 8259. Available: https://tools.ietf.org/html/rfc8259. Last accessed 20 September 2018
23. Ethereum. (2018) *Ethereum Homestead Documentation.* Available: http://www.ethdocs.org/en/latest/. Last accessed 20 September 2018.
24. Casey, M. (2016) *The Blockchain: Decentralized trust to unlock a decentralized future.* Available: https://bit.ly/2Kw7vfU. Last accessed 20 September 2018.

BLOCK 7

1. Moreau, E. (2018) *Kickstarter vs. Indiegogo: Which One Should You Choose?* Available: https://www.lifewire.com/kickstarter-vs-indiegogo-3485780. Last accessed 22 September 2018.
2. eToro. (2018) *Trade with confidence on the world's leading social trading platform.* Available: https://www.etoro.com/. Last accessed 22 September 2018.
3. Crowdcube. (2018) *HyperSciences.* Available: https://www.crowdcube.com/companies/hypersciences/pitches/qDBnyZ. Last accessed 22 September 2018.
4. Eyk, V. (2014) *Ethereum Launches Own 'Ether' Coin, With Millions Already Sold.* Available: https://bit.ly/3bEvoxJ. Last accessed 23 September 2018.
5. Tanzarian, A. (n.d.) *Ethereum Raises 3,700 BTC in First 12 Hours of Ether Presale.* Available: https://bit.ly/2S9hig6. Last accessed 23 September 2018.
6. Wood. G (2014) *ĐApps: What Web 3.0 Looks Like.* Available: http://gavwood.com/dappsweb3.html. Last accessed 23 September 2018.
7. Wall, J. (2018) *Security Token Offerings (STOs) – The Future Of Fundraising In The Blockchain Industry.* Available: https://www.investinblockchain.com/security-token-offerings/. Last accessed 23 September 2018.
8. Tokenget. (n.d.) *ICO & STO TURNKEY PLATFORM.* Available: https://tokenget.com/. Last accessed 23 September 2018.
9. Icodata. (2016) *Funds raised in 2016.* Available: https://www.icodata.io/stats/2016. Last accessed 22 September 2018.
10. Falkon, S. (2017) *The Story of the DAO — Its History and Consequences.* Available: https://bit.ly/2x9Hm3j. Last accessed 23 September 2018.
11. Evans, B.D. (2018) *Status ICO Raised More Than $100 Million for Ethereum-Powered DApps on iOS and Android.* Available: https://bit.ly/3cZsQuv. Last accessed 24 September 2018.
12. Icostats. (n.d.) *RECENT PERFORMERS.* Available: https://icostats.com/. Last accessed 24 September 2018.
13. Yakubowski, M. (2018) *Study: ICO Market Doubled Since Last Year,*

Shows Increased Institutional Investment. Available: https://bit.ly/2VBu3SA. Last accessed 24 September 2018.

14. Macheel, T. (2018) Exclusive: Coinbase Launches Trading Desk For Institutional Investors. Available: https://bit.ly/3aH0aVg. Last accessed 24 September 2018.

15. Athcoinindex. (2018) *Ethereum (ETH)* Available: https://athcoinindex.com/coin/ethereum. Last accessed 24 September 2018.

16. Bitstamp Ltd. (2018) *Bitstamp Acquired.* Available: https://www.bitstamp.net/article/bitstamp-acquired%20-nxmh/. Last accessed 25 September 2018.

17. Doswell, G. (2018) *Wirex earns FCA e-money licence.* Available: https://wirexapp.com/what-the-fca/. Last accessed 26 September 2018.

18. Kharpal, A. (2018) *Revolut becomes latest fintech unicorn after $250 million funding gives it a $1.7 billion valuation.* Available: https://cnb.cx/2yLWSmk. Last accessed 26 September 2018.

19. Aru, I. (2018) *The $257 Million Cryptocurrency that Wants to Upend Cloud Data Storage is Almost Ready to Go Live.* Available: https://bit.ly/3ePHXrW. Last accessed 26 September 2018.

20. Coindesk. (2018) *With Nearly $200 Million on the Line, EOS Is Building A Voting System.* Available: https://yhoo.it/3aCWoME. Last accessed 26 September 2018.

21. ALTCOIN NEWS. (2017) *Successful $33 Million CIVIC ICO Token Sale Concludes Early.* Available: https://bit.ly/2Y7PeNU. Last accessed 27 September 2018.

22. Coin Telegraph. (2017) *The NAGA Token Sale Has Ended with a Huge Success.* Available: https://bit.ly/2KCf2tD. Last accessed 27 September 2018.

23. BAT ICO sales reached its limit in 1 minutes as most the deals were signed prior to the ICO. Source: Keane, J. (2017) *$35 Million in 30 Seconds: Token Sale for Internet Browser Brave Sells Out.* Available: https://bit.ly/2y2COvY. Last accessed 27 September 2018.

24. Cox. L (2017*) At a Glance – Tokenomics.* Available: https://disruptionhub.com/at-a-glance-tokenomics/. Last accessed 2 October 2018.

25. Kagel. J.H. (1972) Token Economies and Experimental Economics. *Journal of Political Economy,* 80, no. 4. 779-785.

26. Sainsburys. (n.d.) *Spending Nectar points.* Available: https://bit.ly/2y2CJZc. Last accessed 2 October 2018.

27. Reese, F. (2017) *The Importance of Liquidity and Volume in Trading Bitcoin.* Available: https://bit.ly/2VEnwXo. Last accessed 1 Oct 2018.
28. Chang, W. (2018) *Market Design with Tokens.* Available: https://bit.ly/2yJOvYy. Last accessed 2 October 2018.
29. Chang, W. (2018) *Market Design with Tokens.* Available: https://bit.ly/2xXrq4w. Last accessed 2 October 2018.
30. Sharpe. W. F (1992) Asset Allocation: Management Style And Performance Measurement. *Journal of Portfolio Management.* 7-19.
31. Lumsden. G (2012) *The 5 asset classes funds invest in.* Available: https://bit.ly/2W1awKe. Last accessed 3 October 2018.
32. IG. (n.d.) *Securities definition.* Available: https://bit.ly/3cShacR. Last accessed 12 October 2018.
33. In the United States, SEC regulates any security issued by blockchain companies, deemded as a security token. SEC has a dedicated section for ICOs: https://www.sec.gov/ICO. More information on the term "Security" can be found here on investopedia: https://bit.ly/2yN2Zak.
34. Kalionova, A. (2018) *Security tokens in the US: regulations and exemptions under the SEC laws.* Available: https://bit.ly/3bEvK7x. Last accessed 12 October 2018.
35. Babin. B. J, Darden. W.R, & Griffin. M. (1994) Work and/or Fun: Measuring Hedonic and Utilitarian Shopping Value, *Journal of Consumer Research*, 20(4), pp.644–656.
36. Polymath. (n.d.) The Future of Securities.Wall Street.Finance.Tokens. Available: https://polymath.network/. Last accessed 12 October 2018.
37. Etherscan. (2018) *Stablecoin in Etherscan.* Available: https://bit.ly/2KwSjiw. Last accessed 13 October 2018.
38. Price. M (2018) *U.S. judge sides with CFTC on virtual currency oversight.* Available: https://reut.rs/3bGkJCv. Last accessed 4 October 2018.
39. ICOscoring. (2018) *Types of tokens. The four mistakes beginner crypto-investors make.* Available: https://bit.ly/2W2xAlE. Last accessed 14 October 2018.
40. Dhaliwal, E. and Dr. Gurguc, Z. (2018) *Token Ecosystem Creation.* Available: https://bit.ly/2xcxtly. Last accessed 14 October 2018.
41. MAC. (n.d.) *What are Outstanding Shares?.* Available: https://bit.ly/2y2H92r. Last accessed 17 Oct 2018.
42. Kenton, W. (2018) *Capital Stock.* Available: https://bit.ly/2KCfzM9. Last accessed 1 Oct 2018.
43. CoinMarketCap. (2018) *Ethereum (ETH)*

Available: https://bit.ly/2zx962L. Last accessed 26 September 2018.
44. Buterin. V (2014) *Ethereum White Paper.* Available: https://bit.ly/2zr5S0x. Last accessed 26 September 2018.
45. The Bank of England. (n.d) *What is quantitative easing?.* Available: https://bit.ly/3bEKdAp. Last accessed 18 Oct 2018.
46. Crypto Compare. (2015) *What is a premine?.* Available: https://www.cryptocompare.com/coins/guides/what-is-a-premine/. Last accessed 14 October 2018.
47. Putnam, B. (2018) *An In-Depth Look At The Economics Of Bitcoin.* Available: https://bit.ly/2xYXm8N. Last accessed 14 October 2018.
48. CoinMarketCap. (2018) *Crypto.com (MCO)* Available: https://coinmarketcap.com/currencies/crypto-com/. Last accessed 14 October 2018.
49. u/idaebaker. (2018) *A skeptic's concern: unlimited supply.* [Reddit] Available: https://bit.ly/2Y2iLbT. Last accessed 14 October 2018.
50. Crowdcube. (n.d.) *Popular Pitches.* Available: https://www.crowdcube.com/. Last accessed 15 October 2018.
51. Ten startups that successfully conducted an ICO on Ethereum network were: Civic, Status, Bancor Protocol, Dovu, Tron, EOS, EthLend, UTrust, WePower, and Monaco.
52. Polymath. (2018) *The POLY Airdrop is officially complete!.* Available: https://bit.ly/3aBo4RZ. Last accessed 18 October 2018.
53. Weiczner. J (2018) *The Night $1 Million in Crypto Began Raining From the Sky.* Available: https://bit.ly/2S7L04V. Last accessed 18 October 2018
54. Applicature. (2018) *Bounty: Yes or No?.* Available: https://medium.com/applicature/bounty-yes-or-no-3249b08c83ec. Last accessed 18 October 2018.
55. Butcher. M (2018) *The Blockchain wallet plans a $125M airdrop of Stellar crypto to drive mainstream adoption.* Available: https://tcrn.ch/3eQDR2F. Last accessed 20 October 2018.
56. Roberts. J. J (2018) *Blockchain Announces $125 Million 'Airdrop' of Stellar Cryptocurrency.* Available: http://fortune.com/2018/11/06/blockchain-stellar/. Last accessed 19 October 2018.

BLOCK 8

1. Blank. S (2009) *Vertical vs. Horizontal Markets.* Available: https://ecorner.stanford.edu/in-brief/vertical-vs-horizontal-markets/. Last accessed 12 October 2018.
2. Coin Payments. (n.d.) *Ether Tokens (Wallet + Payments)* Available: https://www.coinpayments.net/supported-coins-eth-tokens-payments. Last accessed 17 November 2018.
3. Origintrail. (2014) *ORIGINTRAIL Website.* Available: https://origintrail.io/. Last accessed 15 November 2018.
4. Vechain. (2018) *VECHAIN.* Available: https://www.vechain.com/#/. Last accessed 16 November 2018.
5. noahsayres. (2018) *What Is Civic? Blockchain for Digital Identities.* Available: https://hacked.com/what-is-civic-blockchain-for-digital-identities/. Last accessed 16 November 2018.
6. Bitcoin Exchange Guide News Team. (2018) *Medicalchain's Blockchain-Built MyClinic App Facilitates First Medical Service Via Video In The UK, Paid In Crypt.* Available: https://bit.ly/2x8F7gG. Last accessed 16 November 2018.
7. Zhang M, Ji Y. (2018) *Blockchain for healthcare records: A data perspective.* PeerJ Preprints 6:e26942v1. https://doi.org/10.7287/peerj.preprints.26942v1.
8. AXA. (2017) *AXA goes blockchain with fizzy.* Available: https://bit.ly/2yLXWXm. Last accessed 11 November 2018. Note: Other insurance companies are also trialling insurance on blockchain. International consultant firm EY published a paper on how blockchain can affect insurance. The file is available here: https://www.ey.com/Publication/vwLUAssets/EY-blockhain-in-insurance/$FILE/EY-blockhain-in-insurance.pdf
9. Pearson, T. (n.d.) *Will Smart Contracts Eat the World?.* Available: https://taylorpearson.me/smart-contract-applications/. Last accessed 16 November 2018.
10. Burton, C. (2018) *In 2019, a new blockchain will fix how we buy and sell green energy.* Available: https://www.wired.co.uk/article/energy-web-foundation-blockchain. Last accessed 17 November 2018.

11. Chandran, R. (2018) *In a posh Bangkok neighborhood, residents trade energy with blockchain.* Available: https://reut.rs/2ztSJnv. Last accessed 17 November 2018.

12. Grid plus. (2017) *About GRID+.* Available: https://gridplus.io/. Last accessed 17 November 2018.

13. Andoni, M., Robu, V., Flynn, D., Abram, S., Geach, D., Jenkins, D., McCallum, P., Peacock, A. (2019) Blockchain technology in the energy sector: A systematic review of challenges and opportunities. *Renewable and Sustainable Energy Reviews.* 100, pp.143-174. doi: 10.1016/j.rser.2018.10.014.

14. Carson, B. (2018) *Blockchain beyond the hype: What is the strategic business value?.* Available: https://mck.co/2VGqmvb. Last accessed 18 November 2018.

15. Turk, Z., Klinc, R. (2017) Potentials of Blockchain Technology for Construction Management. *Procedia Engineering.* 196 (1), pp. 638-645.

16. Woetzel, J., Sridhar, M., & Mischke, J. (2018) *Opinion: The construction industry has a productivity problem — and here's how to solve it.* Available: https://on.mktw.net/3cPmldy. Last accessed 15 Oct 2018.

17. Zhao, W. (2018) *Alibaba, IBM Top Global Blockchain Patent Rankings, Says New Research.* Available: https://bit.ly/2S6y8MH (Last accessed 16 Oct 2018)

18. Kaplan, A. (2018) *How Alibaba is championing the application of blockchain technology in China and beyond.* Available: https://bit.ly/2Y6tPVt. Last accessed 17 October 2018.

19. Accenture. (2018) *DHL and Accenture Unlock the Power of Blockchain in Logistics.* Available: https://accntu.re/356L5Ly. Last accessed 17 October 2018.

20. Booth, R. (2018) *Grenfell Tower: fire-resistant cladding plan was dropped.* Available: https://bit.ly/353KPNu. Last accessed 18 Oct 2018.

21. Bodnar. K (2010) *7 Reasons Social Media Is Bad for Marketing.* Available: https://bit.ly/2Y6sOMQ. Last accessed 17 November 2018

22. Sweney. M (2018) *Mail Online ad revenues overtake print for first time.* Available: https://bit.ly/357jsCa. Last accessed 18 November 2018.

23. Nation, J. (2017) *Pfizer and Genentech Turn To Ethereum Blockchain.* Available: https://bit.ly/356BCnr. Last accessed 13 October 2018.

24. Hurst, S. (2018) *Origin Protocol Secures $28.5 Million Through Strategic Round.* Available: https://bit.ly/3cSipJ3. Last accessed 18 November 2018.

25. Name Bazaar. (n.d.) *A peer-to-peer marketplace for the exchange of names registered via the Ethereum Name Service.* Available: https://namebazaar.io/. Last accessed 19 November 2018.
26. Known Origin. (n.d.) *Start your rare digital art collection.* Available: https://knownorigin.io/. Last accessed 19 November 2018.
27. Addaquay. (2018) *A Beginner's Guide to IPFS.* Available: https://hackernoon.com/a-beginners-guide-to-ipfs-20673fedd3f. Last accessed 18 November 2018.
28. App Co. (2019) *Popular Decentralised Apps.* Available: https://app.co/. Last accessed 2 Jan 2019.
29. Stox (n.d.) Stox Website. Available: https://www.stox.com/. Last accessed 18 November 2018.
30. Buterin, V. (2018) *Tweets posted by Vitalik Buterin.* [Twitter] Available: https://twitter.com/VitalikButerin/status/1072158957999771648. Last accessed 19 November 2018.
31. Kortendick, B. (2018) *Enjin to Give Away Limited-Edition Korea-Themed ERC-1155 Collectibles at BIC 2018.* Available: https://bit.ly/3bFKIds. Last accessed 20 November 2018.
32. OpenSea. (n.d.) *OpenSea Developer Tutorial.* Available: https://docs.opensea.io/docs/getting-started. Last accessed 21 November 2018.
33. Karamitsos, I., Papadaki, M. & Barghuthi, N. (2018) Design of the Blockchain Smart Contract: A Use Case for Real Estate. *Journal of Information Security.* 09. 177-190.
34. Molteni, M. (2018) *These Dna Startups Want To Put All Of You On The Blockchain.* Available: https://bit.ly/3584CeQ. Last accessed 22 November 2018.
35. Tangermann, V. (2018) *This Blockchain Startup Wants To Pay You For Your Dna Data.* Available: https://futurism.com/the-byte/blockchain-startup-pay-dna-data. Last accessed 22 November 2018.
36. Daniel, A. (2018) Salt vs. ETHLend: A Comparative Study. Available: https://unblock.net/salt-vs-ethlend/. Last accessed 22 November 2018.
37. Karppinen, U. (2018) *BBVA signs world-first blockchain-based syndicated loan arrangement with Red Eléctrica Corporación.* Available: https://bbva.info/3cU0KRj. Last accessed 22 November 2018.
38. JUN_Omise. (2017) Tweet posted by Jun. [Twitter] Available at: https://twitter.com/JUN_Omise/status/919595778632323074. Last accessed: 12 December 2018.

BLOCK 9

1. Buterin, V. (2015) *On Slow and Fast Block Times.* Available: https://blog.ethereum.org/2015/09/14/on-slow-and-fast-block-times/. Last accessed 2 Jan 2019.
2. Bano. S, Sonnino. A, Al-Bassam. M, Azouvi. S, McCorry. P, Meiklejohn. S, Danezis. G (2017) *Consensus in the Age of Blockchains.* 2, pp.1-17. doi: http://arxiv.org/abs/1711.03936
3. Subscribe Coin. (2017) *Goldman Sachs Lou Kerner thinks Bitcoin is a better store of value than Gold - CNBC.* [Online Video]. 28 November 2017. Available from: https://www.youtube.com/watch?v=wtFimdlrde0. [Accessed: 2 November 2018].
4. Doxley, W. (2020) *'95% Confidence': Ethereum Developers Pencil In July 2020 for Eth 2.0 Launch.* Available: https://bit.ly/2zxsUmH. Last accessed 6 February 2020..
5. O'Leary. R. R (2017) *Ethereum Executes Byzantium Blockchain Software Upgrade.* Available: https://bit.ly/2Y47XKg. Last accessed 2 November 2018.
6. Ray. J (2018) *Sharding introduction R&D compendium.* Available: https://bit.ly/2KAn1Hv. Last accessed 10 November 2018.
7. Mearian, L. (2018) *What Vitalik Buterin's tweetstorm means for the future Ethereum blockchain.* Available: https://bit.ly/2xYZMnR. Last accessed 12 November 2018.
8. Adya. A, Myers. D, Howell. J, Elson. J, Meek. C, Khemani. V, Fulger. S, Gu. P, Bhuvanagiri. L, Hunter. J, Peon. R, Kai. L, Shraer. A, and Merchant. A (2018) *Slicer: Auto-Sharding for Datacenter Applications.* Available: https://bit.ly/35hgqvn. Last accessed 12 November 2018.
9. Dexter. S (2018) *Blockchain vs DLT (Distributed Ledger Technology)* Available: https://bit.ly/2S7MDzz. Last accessed 12 November 2018.
10. Kumar. A (2018) *Provisioning Sharding for Smart Contracts: A Design for Zilliqa.* Available: https://bit.ly/2Y5usOV. Last accessed 12 November 2018.
11. ZCash. (n.d.) What are zk-SNARKs?. Available: https://z.cash/technology/zksnarks/. Last accessed 5 Jan 2019.
12. Kilian, J. (1992) A note on efficient zero-knowledge proofs and arguments (extended abstract) *In Proceedings of the twenty-fourth annual ACM symposium on Theory of computing (STOC '92)* ACM. 723-732.

DOI: http://dx.doi.org/10.1145/129712.129782

13. Reitwiessner, C. (2016) *zkSNARKs in a nutshell.* Available: https://bit.ly/3aFtz2j. Last accessed 18 Oct 2018.

14. Luciano. A (2018) *zk-SNARKs—A Realistic Zero-Knowledge Example and Deep Dive.* Available: https://bit.ly/3cOQz02. Last accessed 21 November 2018.

15. O'Leary. R. R (2018) *'500 Transactions a Second': Vitalik Says Zk-Snarks Could Scale Ethereum.* Available: https://bit.ly/2S99LxF. Last accessed 21 November 2018.

16. Poon. J. and OmiseGO Team. (2017) *OmiseGO: Decentralized Exchange and Payments Platform.* Available: https://bit.ly/3bEy3HJ. Last accessed 22 November 2018.

17. Down, M. (2018) *Solving Blockchain Scalability Problems With Layer 2 Solutions.* Available: https://bit.ly/3aBBb5W. Last accessed 22 September 2018.

18. u/ pwolf88. (2018) *How OmiseGO will bring Plasma in everyone's daily life.* Available: https://bit.ly/2x99u6N. Last accessed 23 November 2018.

19. Buterin, V. (2018) *On-chain scaling to potentially ~500 tx/sec through mass tx validation.* Available: https://bit.ly/3ayQwEc. Last accessed 12 November 2018.

20. Etherscan. (2018) *Ethereum Transaction Chart.* Available: https://etherscan.io/chart/tx. Last accessed 12 November 2018.

21. Paradigm. (2018) *0x protocol: Detailed review on the project.* Available: https://bit.ly/2Y4R8Pf. Last accessed 12 November 2018.

22. To date, this is deemed as one of the most controversial cyber attacks in the world of cryptocurrencies. McMillian, R. (2014*) THE INSIDE STORY OF MT. GOX, BITCOIN'S $460 MILLION DISASTER.* Available: https://www.wired.com/2014/03/bitcoin-exchange/. Last accessed 13 November 2018.

23. Zuckerman, M.J. (2018) *Ethereum Proposal To "Resurrect" Disabled $360 Mln Parity Contract Shut Down.* Available: https://bit.ly/2Y2kjCJ. Last accessed 13 November 2018.

24. One of many exchange hacks in Asia. Hankin, A. (2018) *Japanese exchange hack results in 6,000 bitcoin stolen.*
Available: https://on.mktw.net/3eTaRY8. Last accessed 13 November 2018.

25. Excellent resource for building on 0x Protocol. 0x. (2017) *0x protocol monorepo.* Available: https://github.com/0xProject/0x-monorepo. Last accessed 13 November 2018.

26. Warren. W (2018) *The 0x Mission and Values.* Available: https://bit.ly/2x8nOwc. Last accessed 12 November 2018.

27. Griffin, A. (2018) *DIXONS CARPHONE HACK: MILLIONS OF CUSTOMERS' DETAILS STOLEN IN HUGE CYBER ATTACK.* Available: https://bit.ly/3bF9vym. Last accessed 10 September 2018.

28. CNBC Crypto Trader. (2018) *EXCLUSIVE: Taiwan Blockchain week! Including CZ Interview!.* [Online Video]. 10 July 2018. Available from: https://www.youtube.com/watch?v=FNQh2hDGMpU&t=868s. Last accessed 24 November 2018.

29. Binance. (2018) *Binance DEX Preview 2.* [Online Video]. 4 December 2018. Available from: https://bit.ly/3bFdjzt. Last accessed 23 November 2018.

30. Zhechev, L. (2018) *What is 0x (ZRX)? Protocol for Building Decentralized Exchanges.* Available: https://bit.ly/2VWkc9a Last accessed 18 Oct 2018.

31. Paradigm. (2018) *0x protocol: Detailed review on the project.* Available: https://bit.ly/2KDBAtK. Last accessed 14 November 2018.

32. US Patent Office. (2018) *Secure Digital Data Operations.* Available: https://bit.ly/2VF3z2J. Last accessed 25 November 2018.

33. De, N. (2018) *Mastercard Patent Hints at Plan for Multi-Currency Blockchains.* Available: https://bit.ly/2VBRNWM. Last accessed 25 November 2018.

34. Hulliet, M. (2018) *Alibaba, IBM Ranked Top Globally for Number of Blockchain Patent Filed.* Available: https://bit.ly/3eU3ek6. Last accessed 2 Jan 2019.

35. Levy. A (2018) *There's a lot of blockchain hype, but money-transfer start-up Veem is using it today.* Available: https://cnb.cx/3aBpPyz. Last accessed 27 November 2018.

36. Kodrič. N (2018) *BITSTAMP ACQUIRED BY NXMH.* Available: https://bit.ly/2VBRUBG. Last accessed 26 November 2018.

37. Dragonchain. (2018) *A New Era of Blockchain Technology.* Available: https://dragonchain.com/. Last accessed 27 November 2018.

38. Lardinois. F (2018) *AWS launches a managed blockchain service.* Available: https://tcrn.ch/2VEqB9U. Last accessed 29 November 2018.

39. Amazon Web Services, Inc. (2017) *Amazon Managed Blockchain.* Available: https://aws.amazon.com/managed-blockchain/. Last accessed 29 November 2018.

40. Brave Software. (2018) *basic attention token.* Available: https://bit.ly/3cHMQkW. Last accessed 30 November 2018.

41. Panetta, K. (2018) *5 Trends Emerge in the Gartner Hype Cycle for Emerging Technologies, 2018.* Available: https://gtnr.it/3eU3i3k. Last accessed 30 November 2018.
Learn more about Hype Cycle here: https://gtnr.it/2Y7eDHG
42. Charts 9.8 was obtained from tradingview.com on 22 April 2020. Appropriate accreditation has been provided. The charts are available at: https://tradingview.com. The data has been fetched from one of the largest cryptocurrency exchanges Coinbase..
43. Trading View. (2020) *DOW JONES INDUSTRIAL AVERAGE INDEX TVC:DJI.* Available: https://uk.tradingview.com/symbols/TVC-DJI/. Last accessed 22 April 2020.

BLOCK 10

1. IG UK. (2018) *Is bitcoin setting up for a fall to $3000?*. [Online Video]. 16 March 2018. Available from: https://www.youtube.com/watch?v=M3J7COuQe90. Accessed: 30 October 2018.
2. CoinMarketCap. (2018) *Bitcoin Prices.* Available: https://coinmarketcap.com/currencies/bitcoin/. Last accessed 30 October 2018.
Note: The figures in the last section of the previous chapter indicates the correlating prices and bull rides in various years. The data on coinmarketcap goes back until 2013, however, other sources such as:Buybitcoinworldwide.com (link: https://www.buybitcoinworldwide.com/price/) have price information of bitcoin before 2013. Additionally, 99 bitcoins have a full list of relevant events up to 2019. The data is available here: https://99bitcoins.com/price-chart-history/.
3. Note: The founding board and cofounders of the startup Envion clashed with each other and filed court case after they successfully raised USD 100 million. The token is still traded in exchanges, although many early supporters created groups to issue refunds for their investment.
Bulkeley, A. and Iwersen, S. (2018) *Envion: The chronology of a cryptocurrency catastrophe.* Available: https://bit.ly/2zxcpab. Last accessed 31 October 2018.
4. DW Documentary. (2019) *Philippines: Bitcoin, blockchain and the dream of new money - Founders Valley (3/5) | DW Documentary.* [Online Video]. Available: 14 December 2018. Available from: https://www.youtube.com/watch?v=-Jn41vwZd94. Last accessed: 1 November 2018.
5. Buterin, V. (2017) *So total cryptocoin market cap just hit $0.5T today. But have we *earned* it?* Available: https://twitter.com/vitalikbuterin/status/940744724431982594?lang=en . Last accessed 1 November 2018.
6. Barker, C. (2018) *BLOCKCHAIN TECHNOLOGY: CHINA LEADS THE PATENT RACE.* Available: https://bit.ly/2W4Ddq2. Last accessed 2 November 2018.

7. Shilov, K. (2018) *Top 10 Jurisdictions for a Worry-Free ICO in the Current Regulatory Climate.* Available: https://bit.ly/3cLtATJ. Last accessed 2 November 2018.

8. Fintechnews Switzerland. (2018) *Schneider-Ammann: Switzerland Needs More Blockchain Experts.* Available: https://bit.ly/2KwW1IY. Last accessed 3 November 2018.

9. Archer, J. (2019) *Bitcoin was a 'gateway drug' to hook millennials into market trading, says Freetrade founder.* Available: https://bit.ly/3eUGaSn. Last accessed 3 November 2018.

10. Khatri, Y. (2018) *Blockchain Developer Role Tops LinkedIn's 2018 Emerging Jobs List.* Available: https://bit.ly/2x85O55 Last accessed 4 November 2018.

11. The salaries vary from country to country. US and EU countries are more likely to pay a higher salary due to incredible demand for experienced blockchain developers in this region. Mearian, L. (2018) *Blockchain developer salaries now command as much as $175K.* Available: https://bit.ly/2xcBcQ4.html. Last accessed 4 November 2018.

12. Rodriguez, S. (2018) *Salaries for blockchain engineers are skyrocketing, now on par with AI experts.* Available: https://cnb.cx/2VXW31P. Last accessed 4 November 2018.

13. Palmer, D. (2018*) VC Investment in Blockchain Startups Is Up 280% So Far This Year.* Available: https://bit.ly/2VThalW. Last accessed 5 November 2018.

14. Dakwale, N. (2018) *Why Students Should Study Blockchain.* Available: https://bit.ly/2S6dL1S. Last accessed 6 November 2018.

15. Avila, J. (2018) *Introduction to Blockchain and Bitcoin.* Available: https://bit.ly/2SbFpea. Last accessed 7 November 2018.

16. Imperial College London. (n.d.) C*entre for Cryptocurrency Research and Engineering.* Available: https://www.imperial.ac.uk/cryptocurrency. Last accessed 7 November 2018.

17. University of Nicosia. *Professional Certification Programs.* Available: https://digitalcurrency.unic.ac.cy/professional-certification-programs/. Last accessed 7 November 2018.

18. WORLD ECONOMIC FORUM. (2015) *Deep Shift Technology Tipping Points and Societal Impact.* Available: https://bit.ly/2Kwzlst. Last accessed 8 November 2018.

19. Statista (2019) *Growth of the global gross domestic product (GDP) from 2012 to 2022 (compared to the previous year)* Available: https://bit.ly/3eUGzUT. Last accessed 8 January 2019.

20. Marvin, R. (2019) What Tech Will Look Like in 2039. Available: https://uk.pcmag.com/guide/118965/what-tech-will-look-like-in-2039. Last accessed 3 January 2019.

21. Arnold, A. (2018) Blockchain Is Not A Threat To Accounting, It's An Opportunity. Available: https://bit.ly/2zzkviJ. Last accessed 3 January 2019.

22. Yermack, D. (2017) Corporate Governance and Blockchains, Review of Finance, Volume 21, Issue 1, 1 Pages 7–31, https://doi.org/10.1093/rof/rfw074.

23. Wharton University of Pennsylvania. (2018) How the Blockchain Can Transform Government. Available: https://whr.tn/357uwPR. Last accessed 14 November 2018.

24. Bohn, D. (2019) *Amazon Says 100 Million Alexa Devices Have Been Sold — What's Next?* Available: https://bit.ly/3f1sPIe. Last accessed 14 November 2018.

25. Tangermann, V. (2018) *Everyone Is Flipping Out About Google's AI Assistant That Just Booked A Haircut On The Phone.* Available: https://futurism.com/google-assistant-booked-haircut-duplex. Last accessed 14 November 2018.

26. Blichert, F. (2018) *The best smart home hubs.* Available: https://www.androidauthority.com/best-smart-home-hubs-878933/. Last accessed 15 November 2018.

27. Atlam, H. & Alenezi, A. & Alassafi, M. & Wills, G. (2018) Blockchain with Internet of Things: Benefits, Challenges and Future Directions. *International Journal of Intelligent Systems and Applications.* 10. DOI: 10.5815/ijisa.2018.06.05.

28. Sawh, M. (2018) *The best smart clothing: From biometric shirts to contactless payment jackets.* Available: https://www.wareable.com/smart-clothing/best-smart-clothing. Last accessed 15 November 2018.

29. Weaver, D. (2017) *You can poke a hole in this jacket and it'll repair itself.* Available: https://bit.ly/2Y6wHBq. Last accessed 16 November 2018.

30. Bhatnagar, R. (2018) *Machine Learning and Big Data Processing: A Technological Perspective and Review.* doi:10.1007/978-3-319-74690-6_46.

31. Allen, T. (2018) *Almost half of UK businesses are vulnerable to IoT hacking.* Available: https://bit.ly/356EZe5. Last accessed 17 November 2018.

32. Direct Marketing Association. (2018) *Data privacy: What the consumer really thinks.* Available: https://bit.ly/2yLvcxU. Last accessed 17 November 2018.

33. Geggel,L. (2018) *23andMe Is Sharing Its 5 Million Clients' Genetic Data with Drug Giant GlaxoSmithKline.* Available: https://bit.ly/2VCfs9t. Last accessed 18 November 2018.

34. Cong, L., Ran, F. A., Cox, D., Lin, S., Barretto, R., Habib, N., Hsu, P. D., Wu, X., Jiang, W., Marraffini, L. A., Zhang, F. (2013) *Multiplex genome engineering using CRISPR/Cas systems.* 339(6121), 819-23.doi: 10.1126/science.1231143.

35. Cyranoski, D. (2018) *First CRISPR babies: six questions that remain.* Available: https://www.nature.com/articles/d41586-018-07607-3. Last accessed 18 November 2018.

36. Clayton EW, Halverson CM, Sathe NA, Malin BA (2018) *A systematic literature review of individuals' perspectives on privacy and genetic information in the United States.*
PLOS ONE 13(10): e0204417.
https://doi.org/10.1371/journal.pone.0204417
Quote shared under the CC Attribution 4.0 International (CC BY 4.0)

37. CBS News. (2018) *Behind at-home DNA testing companies sharing genetic data with third parties.* Available: https://cbsn.ws/2yM235K. Last accessed 21 November 2018.

38. Chen, A. (2018) *Why a DNA data breach is much worse than a credit card leak.* Available: https://bit.ly/3cLuvDF. Last accessed 22 November 2018.

39. Extance, A. (2016) *How DNA could store all the world's data.* Available: https://go.nature.com/2ztXaPb. Last accessed 23 November 2018.

40. Cox, J. P. (2001) Long-term data storage in DNA. *Trends in Biotechnology.* Volume 19, Issue 7,Pages 247-250, ISSN 0167-7799. https://doi.org/10.1016/S0167-7799(01)01671-7.

41. Federico Tavella, Alberto Giaretta, Triona Marie Dooley-Cullinane, Mauro Conti, Lee Coffey, and Sasitharan Balasubramaniam (2018) *DNA Molecular Storage System: Transferring Digitally Encoded Information through Bacterial Nanonetworks.* 1(1), 21 pages.

42. Netflix. *Travelers.* Available: https://www.netflix.com/title/80105699. Last accessed 25 November 2018.

43. Metacrone. (2019) *Travelers Season 3 Episode 9: David Recap.* Available: https://bit.ly/2S6CfID. Last accessed 8 January 2019.

44. Dickson, B. (2017) *How blockchain solves the complicated*

data-ownership problem. Available: https://bit.ly/2Y2mZ3f. Last accessed 26 November 2018.

45. Bloomberg Markets and Finance. (2018) *Will Bitcoin Rebound in 2019? The Bull vs. Bear Case.* [Online Video]. 17 December 2018. Available from: https://www.youtube.com/watch?v=ik83dXsbAls. Accessed: 19 January 2019.

46. Wall. J (2018) *Anthony Pompliano Calls Bitcoin "Best Performing Asset Of The Decade".* Available: https://bit.ly/3aFwEzo. Last accessed 3 December 2018.

Note: i) UK's Financial Coduct Authority has published their opinion regarding ICOs:
https://www.fca.org.uk/news/statements/initial-coin-offerings
ii) FINMA, the Swiss regulatory authority has their guidelines on ICOs, available via this hyperlink:
https://www.finma.ch/en/news/2018/02/20180216-mm-ico-wegleitung/

47. Aleman, E.A. (2018) *Securities Exchange Act.* Available: https://www.sec.gov/rules/sro/cboebzx/2018/34-84731.pdf. Last accessed 3 December 2018.

48. CoinMarketCap. (2018) *Global Charts.* Available: https://coinmarketcap.com/charts/. Last accessed 3 December 2018.

49. Pelegrin, W. (2019) *Samsung might launch its own blockchain wallet alongside the Galaxy S10.* Available: https://bit.ly/3bFcerA. Last accessed 24 January 2019.

50. Moghe, S. (2018) *Using Blockchain to build payment applications for mass adoption, free from volatility.* Available: https://bit.ly/2KFz46h. Last accessed 4 December 2018.

PHOTO ATTRIBUTIONS

2.3. Web Summit. (2012) *Tim Draper, DFJ, at Venture Summit Content/Photo by Diarmuid Greene/Web Summit via Sportsfile.* Available: https://www.flickr.com/photos/websummit/38161080176. Licensed under CC by 2.0: https://creativecommons.org/licenses/by/2.0/.
3.1: Etherscan. (2019) *Transaction Details.* Available: https://bit.ly/2S89JGs. Last accessed 11 March 2019.
3.3: Popov, S. (2018) *Português: Gargalo de produção da blockchain e da tangle. Source: wikimedia commons.* Available: https://bit.ly/2SowdTV. Last accessed 10 Jan 2019. Licensed under Attribution-ShareAlike 4.0 International (CC BY-SA 4.0): https://creativecommons.org/licenses/by-sa/4.0/deed.en.
4.6: Ethereum DevCon. (2018) *DevCon Photos.* Available: https://bit.ly/2VW0dHu. Last accessed 2 Jan 2019.
4.7: Larnos, J. (2018) *HD Wallets.* Available: https://www.flickr.com/photos/jlarnos/25531229827. Last accessed 10 Jan 2019. Licensed under CC by 2.0: https://creativecommons.org/licenses/by/2.0/.
5.1: Web Summit. (2018) *6 November 2018; David Gorman, Blockchain Engagement, IBM, during IBM startup workshops.* Available: https://bit.ly/2W2J8vL. Last accessed 1 Jan 2019.
6.1: The cryptokitty that I personally own. Source of the image retrieved via etherscan: https://bit.ly/357nIBE
6.2: 1983 via Wikimedia Commons (n.d) *Centralised-decentralised-distributed.* Available: https://bit.ly/2VAI6b4. Last accessed 11 Jan 2019. Licensed under Attribution-ShareAlike 3.0 Unported (CC BY-SA 3.0): https://bit.ly/3aEGRw3.
7.1: TechCrunch. (2015) *DECEMBER 08: Founder of Ethereum Vitalik Buterin.* Available: https://www.flickr.com/photos/techcrunch/23320293410. Last accessed 2 Jan 2019. Licensed under CC by 2.0: https://creativecommons.org/licenses/by/2.0/.
7.2: Web Summit. (2017) *7 November 2017; Nikolay Storonsky, Founder & CEO, Revolut, on MoneyConf Stage.* Available: https://bit.ly/2VEaucA. Last accessed 18 Oct 2018. Licensed under CC by 2.0: https://bit.ly/3cOBhZe

8.3: TechCrunch. (2017) *SAN FRANCISCO, CA - SEPTEMBER 18: OmiseGO Founder and CEO Jun Hasegawa (L) and Bancor Protocol Co-Founder and Head of Product Eyal Hertzog.* Available: https://www.flickr.com/photos/52522100@N07/37185870751. Last accessed 10 Jan 2019. Licensed under CC by 2.0: https://creativecommons.org/licenses/by/2.0/.
9.4: Etherscan. (n.d.) *Ethereum Transaction Chart.* Available: https://etherscan.io/chart/tx. Last accessed 10 Jan 2019.
Social Icons: Designed by alicia_mb.

INDEX

0x Ecosystem, 51,128
Accelerated adoption, 16
Airdrops, 132-133
Alibaba, 144
Amazon Chain, 171
Apple, 194
Artificial Intelligence, 190
Asset class, 62,126-128
Automatable, 39-40
AXA insurance, 139
AWS, 108,171
Azure, 108
Binance, 74,170
Biosynthetic material, 190
Biosynthetic technology, 190
Bitcoin price charts, 173-175
Blockchain academic degree, 186
Blockchain storage, 147
Blockchain jobs, 185
Blockchain frauds, 182
Blockchain without internet, 49
Bounty, 133
Bubble formation, 70
Bullish formation, 182
Buidl, 195
Brave browser, 172
Brexit, 70
Buterin, Vitalik, 117
Bytes, 49
Byzantium Hard Fork, 157
Cash equivalent, 32
CBOE, 119
Coinbase, 69,108,194
Coinpayments, 137
Collaterals, 150

Commodity Future Trading Commission, 128
Confidential data storage, 150
Constantinople Hard Fork, 157
Contract for Difference, 116
Crowdfunding, 116
Cryptographic puzzle, 39
Cryptokitties, 104,148
CRISPR/Cas9, 191-192
DAO, 118
DDoS, 47
Destabilising effect, 70
Destructive competition, 145
DEX, 111,168-169
Direct Acyclic Graph, 52
Disintermediation, 43
Distributed architecture, 107
DHL 144
DNA, 190-192
Domino effect, 62
Dow Jones Industrial, 176
DragonChain, 171
Draper, Tim, 33
Economies of scale, 48
Emirates rewards point, 125
Ethereum blockchain 1.0, 155-157
Ethereum Milestones, 156-157
Ethereum Request for Comments, 101-106
Etoro, 56,115
Exponential technology, 16
Facebook, 12
Facebook's cryptocurrency, 33
Federal reserve, 28
FIAT, 25
Financial Conduct Authority, 72
Fixed supply, 130
GitHub, 117,184

Gold-silver trading era, 40
Goods market, 63
Google, 11,12,158
Gorman, David, 93
Grenfell Tower, 145
Hardware wallet, 75
Hard Fork, 47,50,156
Hasegawa, Jun, 151
Hashgraph, 54
Hodl, 57
Howey test, 72
Hyperledger burrow, 94
Hyperledger Fabric, 92
Hypervolatility, Hyperinflation, 25
IBM, 92-93,170
Imperial College London, 187
Inelastic supply, 64
Initial Coin Offering, 116-123
Intelligent prediction market, 148
IOTA, 52-53,140
IPFS, 147
JavaScript object notion, 109
JPMorgan, 94,119
Juma, Calestos, 11
Landlines, 15
Layer 2 scalability, 50,162
Like-for-like products, 24
Lisk, 91
Marketplace protocols, 147
Market capitalisation, 129
Market vertical, 80,137
Market hype, 69
Mastercard, 95,170
McKinsey & Co Insights, 141-143
MedicalChain, 139
MetaMask, 88,172
Metcalfe, Robert, 18
Millennials, 56

Miners, 47
Molecular nanonetworks, 191
Monetary inflation, 28
Nakamoto, Satoshi, 37
Nasdaq composite, 17
Nebula Genomics, 150
Nectar points, 125
NEO, 90
Network Consensus Algorithm, 156
Network difficulty of bitcoin, 46
Nicosia University, 187
Niche startups, 137
Non-binding arbitration, 89
Non-fungible tokens, 103
OmiseGo, 162-163
Orderbook, 68
OriginTrail, 138
Outstanding Shares, 128-129
Over-the-trade counter, 193
Parallel market, 137
PayPal, 14
Permissionless blockchain, 89
Pfizer, 146
Plasma, 164
Plasma cash, 168
Power Ledger, 140
Pragma solidity, 84
Quorum, 94,108
Remote Procedure Call, 109
Remix Solidity, 88
Reserve currency, 24
Revolut, 120
Sainsburys, 125
Samsung blockchain keystore, 194
Satoshi, 43
SDK, 91
Security, 136

Security Tokens, 127
Securities and Exchange Commission, 72,128,193
Serenity, 157
Sharding, 158,162
Small Medium Entperprises, 145
SMS-based network, 49
Speculation, 70
Spotify, 11
Stablcoins, 128
Stellar, 133
STO, 117
Stratis, 91
Supply vs demand of bitcoin, 66
Taxation, 55
The futurists, 13
Token economics, 124
Tokenised ecosystem, 111
Torrent, 107
Transaction hash, 37,44-45,80
Travelers, 191
Unikrn, 148
USDT, 62
Validators, 55,159
Venezuela, 30
Wirex, 119
Wood, Gavin, 107
World GDP, 188-189
Yahoo, 15
Zcash, 95
ZkSnarks, 159
ZkSnarks use case, 161

Total number of references: 381.
Number of pages: 238.

Font: Source Sans Pro/Variable 14/10.45pt
Cover Design: Farabi Shayor.

If you've found this book useful,
please consider leaving a review on Amazon.

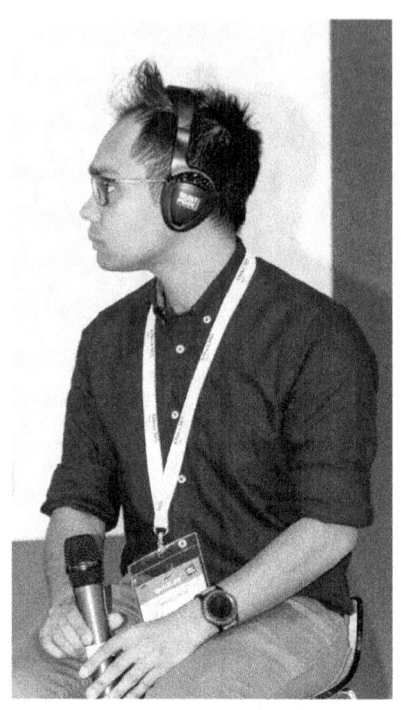

ABOUT THE AUTHOR

Farabi Shayor *BSc MSc MIScT*

Farabi's experience lies in business R&D, developing marketing deliverable, brand identities and working in research-based projects involving applied computational intelligence. He has been conducting research on emerging technologies since 2015, including blockchain and virtual reality. He founded a number of companies including a blockchain startup in 2017. Coming from a mix of finance (BSc) and marketing/research (MSc) background, Farabi has developed vital skills to become an entrepreneur and a researcher, and has gained experience of working with over a hundred companies. He has spoken at a number of international conferences and was mentioned several times on Forbes, The Next Web and Inc Magazine. Currently he is the Head of Research at IntelXSys, and working as one of the Research Leads for "CRI Module" at the School of Medicine, Imperial College London, one of the top 10 universities in the world.

intelXSys

blockchain.intelxsys.com

intelxsys.com

intelXSys

deep tech

Virtual Reality   Blockchain   Genetic Engineering   Virtual Reality   Blockchain
Augmented Reality   Cryptocurrencies   Artificial Intelligence   Augmented Reality   Cryptocurrencies
Genetic Engineering   Virtual Reality   Blockchain   Genetic Engineering   Virtual Reality
Artificial Intelligence   Augmented Reality   Cryptocurrencies   Artificial Intelligence   Augmented Reality
Genetic Engineering   Virtual Reality   Blockchain   Genetic Engineering   Virtual Reality
Artificial Intelligence   Augmented Reality   Cryptocurrencies   Artificial Intelligence   Augmented Reality
Blockchain   Genetic Engineering   Virtual Reality   Blockchain   Genetic Engineering
Cryptocurrencies   Artificial Intelligence   Augmented Reality   Cryptocurrencies   Artificial Intelligence